Stars at Dawn

FORGOTTEN STORIES *of*
WOMEN *in the* BUDDHA'S LIFE

*S*tars
at
Dawn

WENDY GARLING

Shambhala
Boulder
2016

Shambhala Publications, Inc.
4720 Walnut Street
Boulder, Colorado 80301
www.shambhala.com

Excerpts from the *Therigatha*: Reprinted by permission of the publisher from
Therigatha: Poems of the First Buddhist Women, translated by Charles Hallisey,
Murty Classical Library of India Volume 3, pp. 55, 111, 113. Cambridge, MA: Harvard
University Press, © 2015 by the President and Fellows of Harvard College.

Excerpts from the *Lalitavistara*: Reprinted from *The Play in Full*, © Dharmachakra
Translation Committee and used with permission of 84000: Translating the Words
of the Buddha (84000.co). The views and statements in *Stars at Dawn* regarding the
Lalitavistara are entirely the present author's and are not necessarily endorsed by
84000 or the Dharmachakra Translation Committee.

9 8 7 6 5 4 3 2 1

First Edition
Printed in the United States of America

∞ This edition is printed on acid-free paper that meets the American
National Standards Institute Z39.48 Standard.
♻ This book is printed on 30% postconsumer recycled paper.
For more information please visit www.shambhala.com.

Distributed in the United States by Penguin Random House LLC and in Canada by
Random House of Canada Ltd

Designed by Greta D. Sibley

Library of Congress Cataloging-in-Publication Data
Names: Garling, Wendy, author.
Title: Stars at dawn: forgotten stories of women in the Buddha's life / Wendy Garling.
Description: Boulder: Shambhala, 2016.
Identifiers: LCCN 2015042736 | ISBN 9781611802658 (pbk.: alk. paper)
Subjects: LCSH: Gautama Buddha—Family. | Gautama Buddha—Friends and associates.
   | Women in Buddhism.
Classification: LCC BQ933 .G37 2016 | DDC 294.3092/52—dc23 LC record available at
   http://lccn.loc.gov/2015042736

To our Earth

And the reemergence of the sacred feminine

CONTENTS

ACKNOWLEDGMENTS

INTERDEPENDENCE, INDEED. This book could not have been written without the kind assistance and support of many wonderful scholars, mentors, friends, and loved ones. To all of them and to those who remain unseen or unknown I am grateful.

I want to thank the scholars who generously made themselves available both by e-mail and in person to answer my myriad questions in recent years: John Peacock, Rita Gross, Leigh Brasington, Andrew Olendski, and Elinor Gadon. To those who further took the time to read all or portions of my manuscript and offer critical feedback I am especially grateful: Nancy Tingley, Vanessa Sasson, Allie Aitkin, Daniel Aitkin, Vicki Noble, Carol Weingarten, and Julia Aditi Jean. A special thanks goes to John S. Strong at Bates College who was generous in helping me get started and whose own book, *The Buddha: A Short Biography*, was an original inspiration for its methodology of weaving together Sanskrit and Pali sources. Special thanks too to Deepak Anand, archaeologist on the ground in Bihar, India, whose work it is to bring ancient Magadha to life by uncovering those pathways and places where the Buddha walked and taught. I am humbled and grateful to count Bhikkhu Bodhi among the scholars who generously assisted me, patiently offering detailed insights and criticism, even when he did not agree with where I was headed. Finally, I must acknowledge my long-ago mentors in graduate school in the Department of South and Southeast Asian Studies at the University of California, Berkeley: Padmanabh Jaini, the late Barend A. van Nooten, and the late George F. Dales, all of whom helped fuel my fascination with the material that eventually gave rise to this volume.

With special fondness I want to thank two journalists, Betty Rogers and Caleb Garling, for their sharp editorial eyes and keen sense of what makes a story. I also want to acknowledge the women in my book club and Lam Rim study group, whose support and affection have been gently holding me through the travails of writing a book. I continue to draw inspiration from the ten years I spent at the Women's Well in Concord, Massachusetts. The wisdom of the sacred feminine as it emerged in sacred circle there changed my life in many ways, and no doubt helped midwife the idea for this book.

Many dear friends have been supportive of my work and offered a kind, listening ear through its progress: Connie Hershey, Caroline Palden Alioto, Zuleikha, Tamam and Shabda Kahn, Tally Forbes, Olivia Hoblizelle, Lisa Prajna Hallstrom, Meesha Lawson, Tsultrim Allione, Rebecca von Bachelle, Lara Loveman, Richard Snyder, John Whitehead, Maggie Perrin, Todd Lapidus, Aideen and Peter Jenkins, Michael Last, Carol Hamilton and David Khon. A special thanks to Edie Mas and Lora Zorian who opened the door in the very beginning of this project. I also want to thank Nikko Odiseos who readily saw potential in my early, unformed ideas. To the exceptional team at Shambhala Publications I owe tremendous thanks, especially to my talented editor, Liz Shaw.

With palms together, I offer the deepest gratitude to my dharma teachers and guides of whom there have been many, beginning with my refuge lama, His Holiness the Sixteenth Karmapa, who blessed me with the dharma name Karma Dhonden Lhamo. My kind root lama, the late Geshe Acharya Thubten Loden, nourished my spiritual growth unconditionally and continues to point the way despite my many distractions and perceived obstacles. There are no words for the limitless blessings I have received from His Holiness the Dalai Lama, who has been a lamp on the path for me since our first meeting in 1979.

Finally, my life has been blessed with the container of a loving family. To my parents, siblings, nieces, and nephews, I love and thank you all. To my three sons, Whit, Brett, and Caleb, you are the lights in my life and, as you already know, carry with you always my abiding, unconditional love.

INTRODUCTION

FORTY-NINE DAYS after the Buddha attained enlightenment, he got up from his deep meditation beneath the *bodhi* tree to find that he was very hungry. As much as his mind had achieved freedom from worldly ties, his body was in distress and needed food. In Sanskrit accounts of this episode, two merchants passing along the road kindly offered him a meal of gruel sweetened with honey, which the Buddha gladly accepted. In return, he initiated them as his first disciples. But now the story takes a dire turn. The Buddha became violently ill with colic and drew close to death. The evil demon Mara, always trying to thwart the Enlightened One's success, appeared to him and called out for the Buddha to die. However, the Buddha responded that dying was not an option. He had just attained the supreme state of enlightenment and had much work to do in the world. Not only did he rebuff Mara's cruel counsel, but in that moment he made a vow and laid out a blueprint for his ministry: all believers in his faith— women and men, lay and ordained, would become wise and accomplished through his teachings. Within these four groups, some would also achieve sufficient knowledge and insight to teach the sacred dharma to others, and so the dharma would flourish into future generations. Not until that took place would he leave this world. With this statement, the Buddha declared the four assemblies—laywomen, laymen, nuns, and monks—he would be establishing over the next forty-five years. Taken together, they comprised the focus of his life's work, his purpose in becoming an enlightened Buddha.

This little-known story, variants of which appear in both Sanskrit and Pali sources,* is of tremendous significance to contemporary Buddhist women. In the simplest terms, it cuts through millennia of Buddhism's ingrained

---

*While missing from the Pali canon, it is alluded to in the *Mahaparinibbanasutta*

androcentrism and points to the Buddha's original intention: to serve women and men equally. By so saying, the implication is also that women and men are equally up to the task of grasping his profound dharma, realizing its fruits, and teaching it to others. Not that Buddhist women (and many Buddhist men) wouldn't already be confident of this, but words of inclusion spoken by the Buddha himself should be taken as a source of validation and empowerment for women, especially in today's Buddhist world, widely plagued by sexism and patriarchy. Of course, we cannot know for sure what the Buddha did and did not say and, one might argue, this is just a story. But stories, wherever they appear in the earliest Buddhist literature—whether they are recounted in the Pali canon or in equally original, authentic sources recorded in Pali, Sanskrit, and related dialects—are all we have. They provide real-time windows into Buddhism's origins in ancient India and the world of perceptions, memories, and values in which the Buddha lived and taught.

One further detail in the preceding story is of particular relevance here, namely that the Buddha assigned laywomen equal status with laymen and monastics of both sexes in formulating his vision of a fourfold community of disciples. In Buddhism today, there is a focus on nuns as a dynamic cohort carving a new identity within a contemporary Buddhist framework, but very little has been noted about laywomen in similar terms. In recent decades, Buddhist nuns worldwide have stepped up to the challenges of overcoming demeaning inequity within male-dominated monastic traditions, with the goal of establishing themselves as respected, equal participants in both monastic and global contexts. Their efforts have rightfully garnered considerable attention, becoming the subject of numerous books, articles, and global conferences. They have also earned the support of their Holinesses the Dalai Lama and the Seventeenth Karmapa of the Tibetan Buddhist tradition, as well as a small handful of distinguished male leaders and scholars from other Buddhist schools. However, laywomen have established no such clear path or unified identity, perhaps because there is less common ground around which to rally or simply because conditions have not yet arisen for this to take place.

Stories of the nuns in early Buddhist literature, particularly in the *Therigatha*

---

shortly before the Buddha's death when Mara reminds him of their earlier conversation.

of the Pali canon and related commentaries, shine with role models for nuns on the spiritual path, yet there are no such guides for laywomen. One might ask, what, if anything, does the early literature have to offer Buddhist women who have chosen *not* to follow a solitary path of celibacy and renunciation? Are there stories of wives and mothers, single mothers, and unmarried women in everyday life? What did their lives and culture look like at the time of the Buddha? More to the point, are there early stories that provide role models, inspiration or symbols relevant to lay Buddhist women today? These are the questions that gave rise to this book.

As it turns out, quite remarkably, there are many such stories and, even more remarkably, there are many not only translated to English, but an increasing number have been scanned from scholarly archives and are now available in digital format. No longer abiding simply as rare books in academic libraries, they can now be read online or printed out. Some of these early translations turn what we think we know about early Buddhism, especially the Buddha's biography, on its ear. With diligent investigation, we find a trove of "forgotten" stories about laywomen who participated in unique ways in the Buddha's life and spiritual journey. They reveal that laywomen (some goddesses, too) were not just very present, but also instrumental to varying degrees in the emergence of the Buddhist faith. It's long overdue that these forgotten stories be reclaimed by Buddhist women and reintroduced into mainstream Buddhism. Woven together, they form the narrative of this book.

But where did these stories come from? Most of those presented here have been hiding in plain sight among little-known translations of the earliest biographies of the Buddha that originally appeared in the ancient Indian languages. First related via the oral traditions of Buddhism's heartland in northeast India from the time of the great saint's life (circa 480–400 B.C.E.*), the stories that are retold in this book were eventually written down in Sanskrit, Pali, and related dialects beginning about four hundred years later, or at the turn of the Christian era. Almost none of them appear in the Pali canon, although they could be said to date from a similar time period, some even earlier. It's exceedingly refreshing and validating to find that in recounting the Buddha's life story, early bards and chroniclers included many stories about women. Indeed, taken together, these stories provide a more holistic portrayal of the Buddha's life, where women,

---

* The exact dates are uncertain.

goddesses, and symbols of the feminine are integrated at virtually every step along his spiritual journey from birth to enlightenment, through his forty-year ministry, and *parinirvana* or death.

By weaving together these forgotten women's stories, we find an entirely new biography of the Buddha emerges, one that demonstrates not just his influence on women, but also their influences and the power of the feminine in the course of his life. The importance of bringing these stories to light cannot be overemphasized. They not only enhance our understanding of the Buddha as an exceptional historical religious figure whose spiritual realization gave rise to a new religion and spawned an abundance of profound philosophical teachings that continue to benefit humankind, but they provide a direct window into the origins of Buddhism where widespread participation of women was not only noted but often clearly valued.

Of particular significance to Buddhists today, especially Buddhist women, is that these forgotten stories invite a paradigm shift away from the woefully imbalanced, androcentric ownership of the traditional Buddha biography (not to mention the Buddhist faith) that has endured until the present era. Hidden for millennia to all but specialist scholars, these forgotten women's stories are ripe to reemerge and be retold as they were in the oral traditions of ancient India. They have much to add to topical conversations in today's Buddhism as well as to the flow of a relevant Buddhism into the future. Further, these women's stories rightfully belong in a revised understanding of the Buddha's life story and from there in a refreshed view of his ministry, including his original intention of bringing dharma to a world where women and men, lay and ordained, were equal in his eyes. There are many ways to read, contemplate, and interpret these forgotten stories. In this book, they frame a new biography of the Buddha and introduce a wealth of new ideas surrounding the origins of the Buddhist faith.

The Buddha's Biography

What do we know about the Buddha's life? The earliest literary accounts provide biographical fragments but no one complete or connected life story.* Only the Buddha himself could have provided one, and as far as we

---

* The first complete biography was the *Buddhacarita,* in Sanskrit poetic verse, datable to about 200 C.E. Only fourteen chapters survive in the original Sanskrit,

know, he never did. After his death, his monk disciples were much more concerned with preserving details of his teachings than with his personal life. This may account for the virtual absence of personal biographical elements in the Pali canon, particularly concerning his family before he left home to pursue a spiritual path. Still, an assortment of more inclusive biographical stories, many quite colorful and detailed, flowed from the Buddha era through village and monastic oral traditions and were later preserved in the Pali and Sanskrit literature of other Buddhist schools and cultures. Despite a great deal of diversity in these accounts, they offer a far more complete composite of the Buddha's life story than we have seen to date. As such, and not surprisingly, they include many stories about women. These primary sources largely supply the stories that fill the pages of this book.*

All the early biographies explored here share key elements, namely the Buddha's birth as a prince and heir to the throne, renunciation of kingdom and family, enlightenment, and teaching career taking place over a life span of about eighty years. The traditional version comes down to us today in reduced form as a simple parable of a solitary hero engaged in a spiritual quest for truth. Repeated ubiquitously over the millennia in Buddhist literature and art, first in the East and now in the West, this traditional biographical account has become largely fixed over time, a religious artifact that serves as a narrative explanation of how and why Buddhism arose. While it contains Buddhist lessons that may be construed as inspiring, as a story, it offers little if anything that is relatable or empowering for women. Further, the traditional biography clearly sets Buddhism's origins in an androcentric, if not misogynist, framework. Just as Christianity's origin myth negatively defines the female gender through the character of Eve, so the traditional Buddha parable typically casts women as detriments on his path to enlightenment.

The parable generally goes like this: The Buddha was born in Lumbini in present-day Nepal. His mother, Maya, died within days of his birth. The court brahmans predicted that the child, called Siddhartha, would turn out to be either a great king or a great holy man. His father, king of the Shakyas, was determined that his son would be his successor, thus he surrounded

---

while the complete biography in twenty-eight chapters survives in Chinese and Tibetan.

* See the annotated bibliography of primary sources at the back of this book.

the prince with every possible luxury as the boy grew up. When Siddhartha came of age, he married Yashodhara, and they had a son, Rahula. But the prince was restless. Family life was a fetter that bound him to worldly concerns. His charioteer took him on tours outside the palace, where he witnessed the sufferings of old age, sickness, and death. After seeing too the serenity of a holy man, Siddhartha set his heart on pursuing a life of spiritual awakening. The last straw came when he became disgusted by the women of his harem, whose contorted, naked bodies reminded him that worldly pleasure imprisons all beings in the cycle of suffering. Stealing away from his family and kingdom in the dark of night, Siddhartha spent the next six years as a recluse practicing austerities. Finally, while meditating under the *bodhi* tree, he engaged in a battle with the evil demon Mara who, as a last resort, sent his three daughters as seductresses to break the saint's concentration.* However, by the supreme powers of his mind, Siddhartha prevailed and attained his goal of complete enlightenment. In that moment, he shed his past as a prince and became the Buddha. For the remaining years of his life, he traveled throughout the northeast region of India as a religious figure, teaching others what he had learned himself, a body of wisdom known as the dharma, which forms the belief system of Buddhism.

This biographical account survived not because it is "accurate," but because it perpetuated selected values and attitudes of an earlier Buddhist population. Relevant here is that today it persists as the Buddha's biography without undergoing the critical scrutiny that is vigorously applied in so many other areas of Buddhist scholarship. More than just an anachronism, it continues to silently validate androcentrism and misogyny still found at Buddhism's core. But times are finally changing. Buddhism's origin story has outlived its shelf life and deserves another look. We can't change the androcentric past, but we can definitely move to shape a gender-balanced, androgynous future. There is no better way to start than by returning to early Sanskrit and Pali sources to look for forgotten and redacted stories about women in the Buddha's life, their personal relationships with him, and their reported experiences as participants in the emerging religion.

The traditional biographies generally relate the Buddha's life story in three distinct periods: (1) his birth and youth through age twenty-nine,

---

* In some accounts, the daughters attempted to seduce him *after* he attained buddhahood.

when he left his home and family (often called his renunciation, Great Departure, or "going forth"); (2) his six-year term of meditative practice and severe physical austerities that culminated in his enlightenment; and (3) his teaching career, comprising the remaining forty-five or so years of his life. Each stage is a metamorphosis. The texts refer to him by an abundance of different names and epithets during these periods, which can be confusing. To simplify things and to reflect his spiritual maturation, this narrative adopts a different name that is commonly used for each period. Thus, Siddhartha ("He Who Accomplishes His Aim") is our key figure in the first segment, beginning with his birth and continuing through his Great Departure; Gautama*, the Buddha's clan name, is the moniker for his austerities period; and of course, the Buddha ("the Awakened One") is his name from the time of his enlightenment through the end of his life.† Bodhisattva ("Buddha-to-be") is used in some contexts up until the time of his enlightenment.‡ (Please note that Sanskrit rather than Pali spelling is generally used throughout this volume, and quotations are reproduced retaining original transliterations, spelling, and punctuation [including errors] except where clarification may be needed.)

A few comments are in order regarding women's names as well. The Buddha's principal wife is named Yashodhara in almost all Pali and Sanskrit sources.§ However, in some Pali literature, Rahulamata ("Mother of Rahula") often appears instead. This moniker serves to marginalize her important role in the Buddha's biography. Yashodhara's voice, as well as her name, returns forcefully in these stories. Mahaprajapati is similarly marginalized in her role as the mother who raised young Siddhartha after his birth mother— her sister, Maya—died. Again we find distancing language when the stories persist in calling her "aunt" or "foster mother," both technically accurate. As the only mother the Buddha ever knew, Mahaprajapati will also be referred to as his mother here, except where it is necessary to differentiate her from Maya. Clear evidence in many stories demonstrates that she deeply loved

---

* Pali: Gotama

† *Buddha* is an epithet deriving from the Sanskrit past participle of the verb "to awaken."

‡ In this volume, *Bodhisattva* is lowercased to *bodhisattva* and *Buddha* to *buddha* when not specifically referring to Gautama Buddha of this era.

§ In the *Lalitavistara,* she is called Gopa.

Siddhartha, later the Buddha, as her own son. To date, primarily only the stories of her life as a nun are known. Here we'll learn much more about her role as his mother and the importance of their familial relationship.

Before going further, it is important to note that the portrayal of the Buddha is complex and varies widely within Buddhism's many different traditions. While no one today credibly disputes that he was a historical figure, over time stories surrounding his life have naturally spun into religious legend and hagiography. As with any great or beloved hero, humanizing details have often been lost or shrouded in the mists of good storytelling. At his birth, for example, some accounts tell us the infant Buddha speaks and takes seven steps; later in life, he is known to fly through the air. Typical of religious lore, devotion may overwhelm the narrative, as seen for example in portions of the *Lalitavistara (The Play in Full),* with its lengthy passages of exuberant exaltation lauding the many perfect virtues of the Enlightened One. Other characters, too, may be idealized in the stories, no one more so than the Buddha's birth mother, Maya.

Variants also appear that reflect specific doctrinal beliefs that may seem supernatural to non-Buddhists or even Buddhists of a different tradition. For example, the Buddha as *Bodhisattva* (found in both Sanskrit and Pali texts) has special powers of seeing past and present lives and intentionally taking rebirth wherever and however he chooses in order to benefit others. The Bodhisattva's previous lives figure prominently in these narratives because his arrival on earth is attributable to past life conduct and the inevitability of karma. Relationships with his family members and others are often framed as a continuum tracing back to past life interactions, both good and bad. Struggles with his wife, Yashodhara, for example, can be traced to fractious marriages in earlier lifetimes. Similarly, the young mother, Sujata, who nurtured him with rice milk on the morning of his enlightenment had done so for previous buddhas over her countless lifetimes.* Sometimes delightful or magical, many times bizarre, these past life tales, known as *Jatakas,* are often inserted into the biographical narratives as backgrounders to explain outcomes and behaviors. In investigating the Buddha's life, these tales are worth a peek to see where details of past lives, however fanciful, may corroborate or amplify those found in his this-life legend, as the ancient storytellers were in no way beholden to making those distinctions.

---

* The *Buddhavamsa* says there have been twenty-eight previous buddhas.

In contrast, it is also true that very relatable human elements appear in the Buddha's biographical material, varying from story to story, tradition to tradition. Alongside the miraculous, there is often affirmation that the Buddha was an ordinary human being. We saw this in the opening story where, despite just being enlightened, he was hungry and then deathly ill from the food he had eaten. In another example, we hear again from his wicked nemesis Mara, who is frustrated that the Buddha, a human, has outdone him, a god:

> Alas, that Gotama the Recluse who is a mere human should overcome me who am a deva. The body of Gotama the Recluse was born of a mother and a father, it depends on his belly, is a heap of boiled rice and sour milk and is subject to rubbing, massaging, sleep, dissolution, disintegration and destruction . . . alas, that Gotama the Recluse should overcome me.[1]

Some stories also highlight the natural sexuality of the young prince Siddhartha, who (spoiler alert) courted and married more than one wife, and later, like his father, presided over a vast harem. Rather than detract from his persona as a quintessential spiritual role model, his portrayal as a normal, virile young man humanizes him and gives credence to the youthful inner turmoil that drove him to depart for the religious life. As the Buddha, he did not claim to be a god, but a seer.

We also see believable human qualities in other characters in the narratives—for example, his mother, Mahaprajapati, is grief stricken when Siddhartha leaves home. Elsewhere (another spoiler alert), the Shakya citizens are outraged when Yashodhara's ill-timed pregnancy makes it impossible for Siddhartha to be the father of her child. Raw human details such as these pull us in closer, engage us emotionally, and perhaps—by their very ordinariness—point to a more historical record of events. Traditions and individuals hold their own truths, but here it is held that the Buddha's humanity is the entire point of Buddhism. He fully realized the potential of the human mind and spent forty-five years of his life teaching others how to achieve the same thing.*

---

* In Buddhism, the word "mind" includes the heart.

Gender Bias in the Stories

More needs to be said about gender bias in the early texts. It's well known to many, especially Buddhist women, that some—but by no means all—areas of early Buddhist literature are suffused with sexism and sometimes misogyny. The stories that will be brought to light in the following pages are not always exceptions, although overall, positive views of women and the feminine far outweigh the negative. There's no knowing how the first Buddha legends were related in the oral traditions or how the culture held them or viewed women during that time. But when the stories were eventually written down, it was by literate Buddhist chroniclers, who translated, edited, and in some cases amplified them. This was an exceedingly important, pivotal time for early Buddhism, as these chroniclers-cum-editors wielded great power by setting ink to palm leaf. Their work has essentially left us with the textual evidence we have today.

While the Sanskrit and Pali traditions draw from the same or similar early sources, we know almost nothing about the early Sanskrit tradition. In the Pali tradition, the chroniclers were male monastics who, in the words of the Pali scholar I. B. Horner, "had little historical sense and little sympathy with the doings of women."[2] In her discussion, which focuses on early Buddhist literature in general, she suggests that the monks were responsible for, among other things, gender bias in the early Pali texts. In her words,

> It is sometimes impossible to disentangle the original matter from later accretions; and in many places it appears as if much of what Gotama thought, said and did has become lost or distorted. If the monk factor be kept in mind, some of the distortions may be accounted for, and in part rectified. It partially explains the views, more favorable to monkdom than to lay-life, more favourable to men than to women, which are usually ascribed to Gotama. It also partially explains the absence of a connected account of some of the important events of his lifetime.[3]

It is Horner's view, shared by this author and presupposed in the following pages, that bias against women in early Buddhism and early Buddhist literature arose mostly from within the male monastic community and did not originate with the Buddha himself. One area of conspicuous gender discrimination, for example, appears in the monastic code for the ordination of Buddhist nuns.* Ultimately the monks controlled canonical material as well as women's stories, which could readily have been altered or redacted according to monastic, androcentric predilections. It is also reasonable to consider further that, hand in hand with redacting women's stories, the monks would have been inclined to redact references to Siddhartha's sexuality. Indeed, in the more androcentric sources, he is generally quite monkish as a young man, his libido in check, while an entirely different view can be taken from the less redacted sources, mostly found in the Sanskrit literature that dispersed through Tibet and China.

Gender bias in Buddhism is a critical topic that continues to be addressed in contemporary Buddhist writing.† It is also a vast topic that will not be addressed further here except to say that, while arguable to some, the Buddha's deeply rooted egalitarianism shines through in the early literature, where numerous examples demonstrate his tireless commitment to teaching the dharma to any and all who would assemble—women and men, poor and rich, lay and ordained—without regard for gender, caste, or status.‡ He further considered religious women equally competent and held them to the same standards as men. Apparent exceptions to his nonbias in the literature would indicate a casualty, deliberate or otherwise, at the hands of editors.

It is incompatible to simultaneously hold views that the Buddha was both biased and enlightened, since by definition bias cannot exist within the enlightened mind. This alone should be a source of validation to contemporary Buddhist women in their struggles against narrow, antiquated, androcentric polemics. The default position should no longer be that women petition their rightful place in a gender-equal faith, but that those who would disagree provide and justify proof on their own time and to their own cohort. In other words, it's time to move on. To the extent that the intention of the Buddha's teachings has become obscured or confused

---

* This will be discussed further in chapter 7.

† See listings for Gross, Paul, Murcott, Collette, Walters, and Mohr and Tsedroen in the general bibliography.

‡ While the Buddha was available to teach anyone, he calibrated his teachings to the capacity of his audience. See Pali canon, *Samyutta Nikaya* 42:7 ("The Simile of the Field").

over time is more than unfortunate, as it not only limits the benefit that Buddhist teachings naturally generate, but it continues to create pain and distraction over gender inequity, when gender should be a nonissue. Vindication can be found within the stories themselves. For example, in the *Lalitavistara* (which displays its share of sexism, especially in prenativity passages), the Buddha references gender in a teaching on emptiness—Buddhism's highest truth:

> There is no eye, no man, no women, and no self;
> There is no ear, no nose, no tongue, and no body.
> No one created these phenomena and no one experiences them;
> They arise in dependency and are empty both from within and
>   from without.[4]*

The Sacred Feminine

Besides more women's stories appearing in the little-known biographies studied here, we'll find a frequent presence of what is deemed here, "the sacred feminine," referring to goddesses who appear at pivotal moments in the narrative, together with symbolic expressions of feminine wisdom and nurturance. The Buddha lived at a time when an indigenous, tribal, matriarchal culture proliferated in village life. This ancient culture was just beginning to encounter and mingle with the developing, androcentric Vedic/brahmanical religion[†] of northeastern India. We find conspicuous evidence of both cultures in the biographical stories, framed within a Buddhist context.[‡] For example, in one story, the goddess Abhaya—as the Shakya clan tutelary deity—receives the infant Buddha shortly after his birth. Quite unexpectedly, she bows down to him instead of the other way around, signaling her recognition of his superior destiny. In a variant of this story, the child is brought before brahmanical gods (all male), who similarly turn tables and pay homage to him.

The term *goddess* in these contexts generally refers to *yakshis,* or feminine

---

* Sounding similar to the famous Heart Sutra.

† The antecedents of what was later to be called Hinduism.

‡ More narrative elements from the indigenous culture survive in Sanskrit than in Pali sources.

guardian spirits that inhabit the natural world according to this ancient, earth-based people.* *Yakshis* were most closely associated with trees and forests, although they may appear in any number of settings, including rivers, lakes, mountains, cremation grounds, shrines, or human dwellings.⁵ A guardian *yakshi* was said to inhabit the women's quarters of Prince Siddhartha's palace, for example, and another presided as the protectress of his hometown, Kapilavastu. The latter goddess's role came into play when she expressed the collective sorrow of the Shakya people by mournfully calling out to the prince the night of his escape. But most goddesses in these stories are associated with sylvan settings. Pivotal events in the Buddha's life typically took place under trees where an indwelling goddess often made herself known, usually by manifesting in woman goddess form but sometimes through intelligent animation of the tree. Vimala, the goddess of the sacred garden outside Kapilavastu's royal palace, for example, appeared in the sky before the Shakya people to chide them for their foolishness in ornamenting the infant prince with jewels when his immeasurable merit was far more brilliant. Much later, a tree along the Nairanjana River became animated and lowered her branches to assist Siddhartha, who, starving from years of austerities, lacked the strength to climb up the banks himself. Themes of protection and nurturance are further supported by symbols of the feminine such as cows, milk, and rice milk that appear in relation to women and the Buddha in scenes prior to his enlightenment.

Where Did These Stories Come From?

The stories that emerged from India, Buddhism's heartland, flowed across Asia with the spread of Buddhism itself. To the northeast, one tradition traveled through Nepal, across the Himalayas to Tibet, while another spread to China, and farther east to Korea and Japan. To the south, a second tradition established itself firmly in Sri Lanka and also made its way east to Burma, Thailand, and elsewhere in Southeast Asia. Generally speaking, the Buddhist literature that migrated to the north was initially recorded in Sanskrit, while that to the south was recorded in Pali. With these migrations, the Buddha's biographical stories, as well as his dharma teachings, were translated over time into regional languages, where they became more or less

---

* There are also male *yakshas* who appear much less frequently.

fixed verbatim from the original Indian languages or, as mentioned earlier, in some cases altered, redacted, and/or amplified. The relevance of these two traditions, often distinguished as northern and southern, or Sanskrit and Pali, will become clear in the following chapters, as they often recount significantly different versions of the same stories.

In more recent times, Buddhism's migration has continued to the West. In the nineteenth and early twentieth centuries, with the spread of Queen Victoria's vast empire, European scholars "discovered" Buddhism and Buddhist literature within the cultures of South and Southeast Asia. A new field of study began, as translations appeared for the first time in Western languages, especially English. There was an early focus on the Buddha's biography, perhaps because scholars wanted to understand the figure behind this surprising new religion (some early scholars deduced that the Buddha was a mythological god, not a historical figure), but also because the Buddhist teachings themselves (dharma) must have been difficult to understand and even more difficult to translate at that time. Thus, a variety of biographical accounts originally in Sanskrit and Pali were brought to Western audiences from Tibet, China, Burma, Thailand, Sri Lanka, Nepal, and, of course, India. These translations to English, of which there are about ten, constitute the primary sources used in this book.

Several of these translations are more than one hundred years old, yet they are still the most current texts available of important biographical accounts. Furthermore, many of these translations are incomplete since the translators, faced with an enormously vast literature, chose to create anthologies of selected stories and biographical details. Since more and more authoritative translation projects are springing up across the Buddhist world today, one would hope that new biographical accounts are already in the works. No doubt more stories about women in early Buddhism will be collected over time from primary sources. However, this author is impatient and feels that the forgotten stories now available (including little-known variants of more familiar stories) of the women and feminine influences in the Buddha's life cannot wait and deserve to be presented to a general audience as they are now. Clearly there is much more work to be done, but here we have an enticing taste of what may reside in a much larger, still hidden archive.

Of the sources researched here, the Sanskrit and Pali traditions are equally represented. This is important because the geographical divergence that took place as the stories left India led to some stories or story fragments surviving in one tradition but not the other. Both traditions yield surprising new details that can be treated as puzzle pieces in shaping a greater understanding of the Buddha's life and the cultural context in which he lived. Looking across these translations now allows for some of the puzzle pieces to be put back together. Where there have been gaps in the traditional biography, some of these stories add fresh detail or introduce intriguing variants that may point to entirely new storylines.

Scholars of early Indian Buddhism reading thus far may be chafing that issues of dating within the Sanskrit and Pali traditions have not been addressed. Nor will they be. This is foremost a book of stories. Dating is largely irrelevant to this author's methodology. It is also an arena that is highly problematic and should be treated separately, if at all. For example, the *Mahavastu* is an unedited, thousand-page compilation of early prose and verse material thought to have been collected over at least six hundred years.[6] Mixing hybrid Sanskrit and dialects similar to Pali, the styles and voices range greatly, demonstrating that dating just within *one text* would be a daunting task. Similarly, the *Lalitavistara,* considered a Mahayana text, is a compilation with no single author. It contains both late themes and verses from the earliest literary strata, as old or even older than corresponding Pali accounts.[7] Another important source, the *Buddhacarita,* was composed in ornate classical Sanskrit verse (considered late), yet its author, Ashvaghosa, draws in part from very early, even pre-Buddhist material and himself is believed to have belonged to an early (*Nikaya*) school.[8]

Discussions on textual dating too often devolve into sectarian debates over "authentic" versus "inauthentic" material (the argument being that earlier material equates with "authentic")—distinctions that, even if valid, are irrelevant in the investigation of stories. Two hundred years of Western Buddhist scholarship have demonstrated that dating early Buddhist texts remains highly subjective and largely unknowable. That's unlikely to change, since uncertainty stems also from the period in which the literature was held in the oral traditions. Just because content was written down sooner, does not mean it is more accurate or "authentic" than similar content recorded later. In fact it could be argued the other way around—the longer material was held in the oral traditions, the less apt it was to get altered or deleted by overzealous editors (of course, there could have been overzealous storytellers too).

Simply stated, the methodology adopted here embraces available stories that originated in India, were eventually recorded in Sanskrit or Pali (in some cases, further translated into other Asian languages), and relatively recently translated to English. The author has consulted many secondary sources but has relied almost entirely on primary sources to produce this work.

Women's Stories

Stories are tools of empowerment, and stories about women in traditional Buddhism have been sorely lacking. Those that appear in the following pages fill many gaps in the Buddha legend and affirm that women and feminine influences played a significant role in the Buddha's life, as well as in the hearts and minds of the diverse peoples touched by the new faith. These stories also provide an abundance of original material that invites further exploration and a reimagining of the Buddha legend in new and usable ways. It is hoped that the stories presented here will empower present-day Buddhist women in their own lives and practices and in their efforts to assert equal footing with men in both lay and monastic Buddhist communities. These stories from Buddhism's past also belong to a growing global archive of women's stories that are currently being reported in other world religions and traditions, where to date women's stories have similarly been forgotten, redacted, and suppressed.

In a final note, it must be remembered that this book does not intend or attempt to approach the textual sources critically from a literary, religious, or historical standpoint. Commentary where it does arise focuses mostly on women's issues relevant to a contemporary audience. Overall the intention is simply to weave a new biography of the Buddha based on women's stories from his life and era. There is no one way to understand or retell them, and just as the Buddha legend was originally a living narrative, so it should continue here. While there is much to be gained and learned from this fresh account, further gaps, ambiguities, and questions inevitably arise. We cannot ask more of these stories than they are able to give us. Add in our own insight and imagination, however—now that's another story.

I

Maya, Mother of the Buddha

$\mathcal{M}$aya is remembered as a beautiful young queen who gave birth to the Buddha in the lush woodland of Lumbini's grove surrounded by women, including her sister, Mahaprajapati, and clanswomen from her village who arrived to assist with the birth. Maya had always intended to deliver in Lumbini's grove, taking leave of her husband to travel there in the full bloom of pregnancy accompanied by her female attendants, as this was a sacred place of protection for women in childbirth. On arrival, as the pangs of labor overcame her, she sought refuge under a magnificent *shala* tree,* whose indwelling goddess lowered her boughs in recognition that the time of the birth had come. Grasping a branch with her raised right hand, Maya, who was standing with her sister gently supporting her, delivered her only child, a son whose destiny was to cast a brilliant light into the darkness of human suffering. As the infant Buddha's life began in this sublime setting, delivered into the hands of women, so Maya's life sadly ended. The stories are consistent that she died soon after childbirth.

However, the Buddha's birth story usually isn't told this way. In the traditional account, his mother gave birth surrounded by brahmanical gods (all male) anxiously awaiting the delivery of the exalted child, with no mention at all of women or a goddess being present. It was entirely random that Maya gave birth in Lumbini, as the grove was just a stopping point along the route she was traveling at the behest of her husband to reach her father's home for her confinement. Rather than insinuate details of

---

* *Shorea robusta,* native to the Indian subcontinent.

midwifery or natural birth, the traditional account relates that the infant was delivered miraculously and immaculately from Maya's right side into a golden net held by the god Brahma. Although uninjured by this method, she died inexplicably seven days later.

All of the preceding details appear in the Buddha's early biographical accounts. Yet the second version of the birth story has thrived over the millennia, while the first is reconstructed here from fragments found in forgotten stories scattered among the earliest texts. As we see, the traditional account has been stripped of any feminizing detail—a feat of androcentric imagination seeing as how it is a birth story. It's worth pausing here to consider the far-reaching significance of this. Not subtly, Buddhism at its (literally) most seminal moment is characterized as having an all-male cast. The fact of the founder's mother being present as he entered the world effectively appears as an unavoidable, if inconvenient, detail. More than just marginalized, her early demise notwithstanding, Maya as a woman and mother is scarcely even mentioned in the traditional records. In the vast Pali canon, for example, her name appears only once*—and not in the birth sequence—where the authors focus on her womb and assure us of her suitability as a proper birth vessel. There, as in other sources, we're told that at the moment of conception, she became "intrinsically pure" in body and mind, and at the time of birth, the infant Buddha emerged from her body "clean and unsullied" by "blood or any sort of impurity."[1] Thus was Maya not just defeminized but dehumanized, reduced to an iconic figure that fulfilled the expectations of those who would deify the Buddha and the means and methods of his birth.†

This version of the nativity story more or less persists today, without allowing for the fact that Maya must have been a historical woman since her son was indeed a historical man. The value of myth and symbol, which in many contexts immensely enriches the Buddha's biography as well as the Buddhist faith, is not at issue here; rather, it is the underlying androcentrism if not misogyny embedded in the nativity account. And that's just the beginning, since the trend of marginalizing women and their roles in

---

* With the exception of the *Khuddhaka Nikaya*, where her name appears at least twice in sections thought to have been written by women. See chapter 7.

† In contrast to ancient Buddhist art, which typically depicts Maya as exquisitely sensuous and feminine.

Buddhism was not confined to traditional stories but flourished in real life and became de rigueur to varying degrees across all Buddhist traditions over the centuries. There would be many reasons for this, but it seems fair to say that Buddhism got off on the wrong foot when it came to acknowledging and including the participation of women.

Returning to Maya, we find that forgotten stories in both Sanskrit and Pali literature have much more to tell us about her and her short life. Some tales even relate that after her death in Lumbini's grove, she lived on as a goddess persona who never stopped watching over her son from the heavenly realms, appearing to him at critical moments throughout his life as a concerned, loving mother. These stories suggest early traditions that esteemed mothers generally and Maya's role specifically in her son's extraordinary life. They add richness to the overall Buddha legend as well as to her personal story. There are pieces of Maya's story we will obviously never know, but what follows are fresh glimpses of her, not just as the Buddha's mother, but also as a woman, daughter, sister, and wife. We begin with stories of her as a simple girl married at the age of sixteen, the daughter of a noble family in a tribal region of southern Nepal approximately twenty-five hundred years ago.

A Shakya Girl

Maya grew up in a family that hailed from the Shakya clan, an ancient tribal group that traced its origins to the mythical King Ikshvaku whose progeny spawned what was known as the Solar Dynasty. Descendants in Maya's line used the patronym Gautama, a name commonly found in the Buddha's biography that refers not just to the great teacher, but also to other male relatives. The feminine version, Gautami, appears too, and, especially later in the biography, becomes a common moniker for Maya's sister, Mahaprajapati. The meaning of the name Shakya is described variously in the legends, but in Sanskrit, it means to be strong, powerful, able, or competent. The Shakyas were of the *kshatriya,* or warrior, caste and by reputation a very proud and insular people. At the time Maya lived, they inhabited the fringes of the brahmanical region of northeast India in southern Nepal, where they retained many of their own indigenous beliefs and customs. We find evidence of these two cultures—the tribal and the emerging brahmanical—layering and mingling throughout the biographical accounts, set within a Buddhist framework by the storytellers. Many of the stories' variations can be characterized as deriving largely from one cultural context or the other.

Although the stories often refer to the Shakya region as a "kingdom" and the Buddha's father (and grandfather) as the "king" (*raja*), other textual evidence suggests that Shakyas were historically more of a feudal agrarian society governed by local aristocrats within the larger kingdom of Kosala.[2] There is some speculation that King Suddhodana (the Buddha's father), was not a hereditary monarch at all, but an elected official, although this is not borne out in the biographies where a consistent theme is his preoccupation with securing his son as the heir to the throne. One detail that points to a more democratic forum, however, is the recurrent mention of the Shakya council of elders to whom the king is answerable on important issues. He turns to them for counsel, for example, at Maya's death when he needs to provide a wet nurse for his newborn son and again much later when he anxiously confers with them on strategies to prevent the prince from abandoning the kingdom. Quite refreshingly, this council of elders is consistently portrayed as made up equally of women and men, suggesting an indigenous, nonbrahmanical society.

Colorful legends relate the founding of the Shakya lineage and homeland by Maya's ancestors. In style and content, the stories have been compared to the *Ramayana* and brahmanical Puranic tales that emerged around the same time in northern India.[3] The far-flung Asian Buddhist traditions hold diverse and separately embellished variations of the Shakya genealogy, but the following summary provides a bird's-eye view.

Due to a jealous junior queen, four princes were banished from their ancestral home in the region of Benares (India) and made their way north, with a loyal retinue, to the foothills of the Himalayas. After arriving at the hermitage of a *rishi* named Kapila, they decided to settle and establish their rule. An ancient storyteller captures the wondrous beauty of this place:

> They arrived at a valley on the southern slopes of the mountains, broad and level, without any precipices or hillocks; the land fertile, with no brambles or weeds, and very free from stone and grit. Nothing but the most beautiful forest trees grew there—the Sala tree ... and others; all intertwining their branches, and so making an agreeable shade. Moreover there was a great variety of flowers

there ... [some] just opening and some falling—some in the bud and some burst from the bud; again there was every variety of fruit tree. ... Besides this there were great numbers of wild animals there ... the Stag, the water Buffalo, the white Elephant, the Lion .... Again there were many birds—such as the Parrot, the Peacock, the mountain Pheasant, the white Pheasant .... Again there was every variety of pleasant lake, with flowers floating thereon [such as lotuses] ... and on the banks of the lakes every kind of flower overhanging ... the water perfectly pure and bright, neither deep nor shallow ... among the trees that surround the lakes [were found] every kind of amphibious animal—Turtles, Tortoises, ... and every kind of aquatic bird, Ducks, Geese ...[4]

Kapila showed the brothers where to build their town and generously marked it out with golden sand mixed with water. Because he gave them the soil (*vastu*) of the place, they called it Kapilavastu.[5] Their new domain grew rapidly:

And the city of Kapilavastu became prosperous, rich, peaceful, well-supplied with food and densely populated with happy citizens with a wide area of populous country around. It was known far and wide, and had many festivals and fairs; it was a favorite resort of merchants and the centre of a busy trade.[6]

Over time, the population of Kapilavastu burgeoned, and a *deva* (god) showed the brothers a new spot across the river on which to build a second town. This one was named Devadaha, or "shown by a deva." It was here that between a handful and fifty thousand or so generations later (depending on the version of the story), the Buddha's grandparents were born.[7] A variation of the story in the *Mahavastu* adds that thirty-two sons of a sage named Kola and his Shakya wife gave rise to another branch of the Shakya clan known as the Koliyans.[8] Maya is sometimes said to be from the Koliyan side of the family.

At the time of Maya's birth, her father, Suprabuddha, ruled as king in Devadaha. Across the river, the Buddha's paternal grandfather, Simhahanu, was king in Kapilavastu. During this time, the stories say there was peace and prosperity throughout the land. Both kings had many siblings, and consistent with the Shakya fiat to marry only within the clan, marriages occurred commonly between the two families. Maya's mother may have been Simhahanu's sister, Amrita, elsewhere called Yashodhara.* Her name appears in the Thai variant as Queen Sunantha, and here we hear her voice. Prescient that her future grandson will be a buddha and mournful that she will never know him, Sunantha makes offerings of candles, incense, rice, and flowers, followed by a prayer:

> In that I am old and shall not live to see the child that this my daughter will bring forth to be the holy Teacher, may I after death be reborn in the heavens of the Brahmas, and thence come to listen to the Wheel of the Law that I may escape further evils in the circle of existence.[9]

Of particular interest is that Maya's mother's name also appears as Lumbini. We learn that the beautiful grove where the Buddha was born was named after her because it was a gift from his grandfather to his grandmother and was originally called "Lumbini's grove."† The Kangyur story is recounted as follows:

> [King Suprabuddha] married a woman, by the name of Lumbini, who was exceedingly fair; and in her company he was in the habit of visiting a beautiful grove near the city, which belonged to a wealthy citizen. The queen took such a fancy to the place that she begged the king to give it to her. He told her he was not able to do so; but had her one made more beautiful still, and it was called Lumbini's grove.[10]

In other descriptions of Maya, her father was a wealthy merchant, not a king, so it is possible that the two male figures mentioned here became conflated over time. In any case, the significance of Lumbini's grove to the Buddha's story cannot be overstated. While today's legends typically refer to his birthplace as Lumbini or the Lumbini grove, discovering the variant, Lumbini's grove,‡ and learning that this place may have held significance

---

*Not to be confused with the Buddha's principal wife.

† The same possessive form appears in the *Mahavastu*.

‡ Which works equally well as a translation from the Sanskrit "Lumbinivana."

for Maya's mother adds heartwarming detail to Maya's story and the story of the Buddha's birth. This narrative will thus reclaim the name Lumbini's grove to remember the Buddha's grandmother and secure her place in his and Maya's story.

As mentioned earlier, Maya had a sister, Mahaprajapati. Their names may appear differently and even get reversed, for example in the Kangyur, Maya is named Mahamaya and her sister is named Maya. The stories do not agree on which sister was older, although both became wives of the Buddha's father, Suddhodana of Kapilavastu, son of King Simhahanu. Maya's name is given various meanings in the stories: often as "illusion," referring metaphysically to the cause of material creation,[11] although the Sanskrit could also mean "wisdom" or "extraordinary power."[12] It has been suggested that her name was originally Mata (mother), but the legends yield no evidence to support this intriguing theory.[13] One scholar steps away from speculation altogether and says simply that Maya was her name "because she was so-called."[14]

In some stories, Maya was one of seven sisters, and Suddhodana requested her in marriage because of a prophecy that she would bear a great monarch. Looking out for all his daughters, Suprabuddha refused, saying that the older sisters had to be married off first. Not a problem in a culture of harems and cowives; Suddhodana took all of them, keeping Maya and Mahaprajapati for himself and offering the remaining sisters to his brothers.[15] Another version says that Mahaprajapati was the king's first choice as queen, not Maya.[16] The following passage from the Sinhalese legend is rare because it describes Maya and Mahaprajapati together. Here they are acclaimed as equally virtuous, in words that suggest the values of the time:

> These princesses were beautiful as [celestial] queens; no intoxicating liquor ever touched their lips; even in play they never told an untruth; they would not take life, even to destroy insects; and they observed all the precepts.[17]

Polygamy was practiced not just by the Shakyas, but by other castes and societal groups, especially kings and nobles, during the Buddha's era. It was not a brahmanical tradition, although it was tolerated within early brahmanical society. As we shall see, the stories have much more to say about harems and cowives, not just where Maya is concerned, but also in tales of her famous son.

Maya's Wedding

Little is known about Maya before her marriage, but a lovely account of her as a girl of sixteen appears in the Burmese legend, translated from an early Pali account: Maya is amusing herself in a garden outside the city with other young girls. A delegation from King Simhahanu is out searching for a royal princess suitable for marriage to the eighteen-year-old Prince Suddhodana and finds her there. So overcome is the chief minister by Maya's beauty that he faints three times in succession while trying to speak to her. Each time the girls run over and douse him with pitchers of water. Finally coming to his senses, he states the purpose of the visit and entreats Maya to accept jewels and rare gifts from the prince. She demurs sweetly, saying that she is under the care and protection of her beloved parents, whose will she would never resist. She asks that the matter be referred to her father and mother and, for her own part, promises to abide by their wishes. So the delegation makes its way to the palace, where her father graciously accepts the gifts and agrees to the marriage. Through the following beautiful passage, we are invited to witness the wedding of the Buddha's parents:

> [Simhahanu] and his son set out with a countless retinue for the city of [Devadaha]. In a grove of mango-trees an immense building was erected, out of the city, for their reception and accommodation; and in the middle of that building a spacious hall was arranged with infinite art for the marriage ceremony. When all the preparations were completed, the bridegroom attended by his father, King [Simhahanu] and the chief of Brahmas, went out to meet the bride who was coming from the garden accompanied by her mother, the wife of the great [Shakya]. Both advanced towards the centre of the hall, near a stand raised for the occasion. [Suddhodana] first stretched forth his hand and laid it over that place. [Maya] gracefully did the same. They then took each other's hands, in token of the mutual consent. At that auspicious moment all the musical instruments resounded, and proclaimed in gladdening airs the happy event. The [priests], holding the sacred shell in their hands, poured the blessed water over their heads, uttering all sorts of blessings. The parents and relatives joined in invoking upon the young couple the choicest benedictions. The king, princes, priests

and nobles vied with each other in making them presents, and wishing them all sorts of happiness.[18]

The simplicity of this story is striking, if not exquisite, as if coming to us fresh from an ancient village tradition, unspoiled by religious overlay and androcentric redesign. We're shown a touching custom where the bride and groom are given in marriage by their same-gender parents—Maya by her mother, Suddhodana by his father. This glimpse into Shakya clan tradition suggests that equal value was assigned to matrilineal and patrilineal sides of the family. It's hard to imagine an occasion more significant than marriage where this might be demonstrated.

A Thai version of this tale appears to flow from the same core story yet adopts some androcentric narrative detail. Here Maya's story begins in a previous lifetime where as a young princess she made an offering to the Buddha Vipassi (a predecessor of the Buddha of our era), with the supplication that in a future life she might be the mother of a buddha. After countless additional lifetimes accumulating merit, she is born as the princess Maya of our current story, where she is distinguished by her generosity and healing powers:

> One day when distributing rice to the poor, her bowl supplied the wants of a vast number of people, and yet remained full . . . all sick persons who touched her hand were cured of their diseases. . . . Whenever she saw poor men or hermits, her desire was to help them, and the gifts she desired to present to them came miraculously to her hands.[19]

In the garden scene with her friends, Maya is occupied with collecting flowers and weaving garlands, which she offers in prayer to previous buddhas with the fervent wish that she become the mother of a buddha. Meanwhile, in Kapilavastu, King Simhahanu has had a prophetic dream that appears to portray Maya side by side with her future son. A magnificent jeweled palace and throne rise up to the heavens and illuminate the vastness of space with radiance. Seated on the throne are a "lion-like man beside a beautiful lady." A gentle rain falls over the entire world as the man teaches virtue and bestows happiness on all beings. A vast sea appears, and the man makes a ship so that all who so desire can cross it. Together the man and woman preside over the realm of living beings. The next morning Simhahanu's soothsayers tell him his dream portends that a suitable princess has been found for his son, Suddhodana, and that her child will someday become an enlightened buddha.

Soon wedding preparations are under way, and a procession led by the groom's father proceeds from Kapilavastu to Devadaha. Additional details emerge that enhance the marriage story:

> Then King [Simhahanu] assembled the Sakyas (the princes of his family), and made a broad road from his own country to Dewadaha. Beside it were planted sugar canes and bananas, and it was adorned with royal standards and other insignia. In the adjoining fields were halls for music, and all kinds of festivities. Over the road was spread an awning of white cloth, hung with bunches of flowers, filling the air in all directions with their rich fragrance. And all being prepared, King [Simhahanu] and Prince Suddhodana, mounted on royal elephants, with gorgeous trappings, and surrounded by a large escort, with ten thousand horsemen, and a great train of chieftains and ladies marched towards Dewadaha.[20]

This story goes on to describe an intimate moment between the Buddha's two grandfathers when they and their retinues meet midway in a bucolic grove along the route. They clasp hands and sit close together in conversation as Maya's father discloses that he would normally escort his guest to his city, but that due to an epidemic, it would be best if they remained where they were on the outskirts. For this reason, the wedding ceremony is arranged there on that spot. We learn about the preparations of the bride and groom:

> The King of Dewadaha caused his royal daughter to be bathed with sixteen bowls of scented waters, and to adorn herself with rich garments, like an angel of the Tushita heavens. And King [Simhahanu] caused his son to bathe, so that not a spot of impurity might remain on his body, then to anoint himself with scented waters, and put on the vestments of king, with the five insignia* requisite at the coronation of sovereigns.[21]

---

* The white umbrella, the sword, the royal fan, the golden slippers, and the jeweled crown.

Maya's mother, described as "the noblest lady of the harem," gives her daughter in marriage. We learn that both bride and groom are sixteen years old and that a host of heavenly beings—including "angels of the earth . . . angels of the trees . . . and angels of the air"—arrive as wedding guests, led by the Vedic god Indra, joyously singing praises. Their jubilation is not due to the marriage per se, but to the covenant that marks Maya's impending motherhood. Apparently privy to his daughter's destiny, her father is overcome with pride:

> Wonderful is the merit of my daughter, and worthy of all praise; the very skies are radiant with the glory of the heavenly host which comes to praise her.[22]

The wedding ceremony brings about miracles across the lands. Shortly afterward, Simhahanu dies, and Suddhodana becomes sovereign of the Shakyas with Maya as his queen. During this time, Mahaprajapati becomes a junior wife or consort, although there is no mention of her wedding ceremony in any of the legends.

A Queen in Kapilavastu

With her marriage to Suddhodana, Maya's story resumes in Kapilavastu, where the spotlight turns to her life as chief queen and mother-to-be. Most of the legends introduce her at this point in the narrative, after she has become Suddhodana's wife. That the couple was beloved by their people is universally expressed in the literature. A touching example is found in the opening verses of the *Buddhacarita*, which compares the royal pair to Sakra (Indra), chief of the Vedic gods, and his queen:

> The unconquerable king of the Sakyas, the progeny of Iksvaku, was endowed with virtue and pure riches, and so his name was Suddhodana.

> Living beings happily looked up to him, as to the moon which had just risen. The king was like Sakra, ruler of the gods, and his wife was like Saci.

Her steadfastness was as solid as the earth and her thoughts were as pure as a lotus flower. By way of comparison she was called Maya, but she was beyond compare.[23]

While largely silent about Maya's life so far, the literature now erupts with accounts of the forthcoming infant Buddha and his mother's participation as the sacred vessel bringing about his earthly appearance. It is here that the Buddha's karmic genealogy conspicuously intertwines with the Shakya legend. Early religious and folk traditions merge at this point, nowhere more obviously than in the stories of the Buddha's conception, gestation, and birth. It is neither possible nor desirable to separate these two narrative strands, and commentaries and retellings of the legend, past and present, don't try. From the religious side, we find that many stories of Maya's pregnancy and motherhood flow from androcentric imaginations that would distance her from the realities of human birth and transform her into an iconic goddess figure. While this is the lot of mothers of saints in devotional religious systems and has its place in Buddhism, it is not a complete or satisfactory record of Maya, whom we know to have been a historical woman and not a mythical being. The following discussion takes a more contemporary approach to the material.

We return to our storyline where we find that producing a royal heir is not just Maya and Suddhodana's concern. Residing as a bodhisattva in the Tushita celestial realm, the Buddha has been planning his next rebirth. His karmic pledge is to be born among humans in order to alleviate their suffering, something he has done countless times over previous eons. Once again, the conditions in the world are such that the time has come for him to take rebirth. He makes his intention clear, saying,

For the last time I take up my abode in a woman's womb for the sake of devas and men.[24]

By this he means that his cycle of reappearing as a bodhisattva will come to an end with this next incarnation because he will achieve full enlightenment or buddhahood, after which his teachings will endure but not his form. From his heavenly perch, the Bodhisattva peers throughout the universe to assess the karmically optimal rebirth scenario. It turns out a bodhisattva has many factors to consider in this decision-making process. In the *Abhinish-*

kramanasutra, the Buddha as Bodhisattva accepts counsel from companion celestial beings and debates at length the pros and cons of their various suggestions.[25]

It turns out that karmic guidelines are very specific about rebirth matters and stipulate five areas a bodhisattva must investigate: caste, family, country, timing, and mother. Caste is straightforward because the choice is between brahman (priest) or *kshatriya,* whichever dominates at the time of the birth.[26] In this case, *kshatriya* won out.* When it comes to family, there are no fewer than sixty requirements, which the Shakyas, to the exclusion of all other clans, successfully fulfilled point by point:

> Looking through all of Jambudvipa,†
> All the major royal families and royal lines
> Were found to be flawed. Considering this,
> The Sakya clan alone was seen to be free of faults.[27]

The criteria, which vary slightly in different texts, point to an overall emphasis on the purity of ancestral bloodlines and uninterrupted generations of noble conduct in both parental lines. It is noteworthy that the key word *family* is meant literally here and does not just refer to the patriarchs. The following are highlights of the list:

> This family ... must have excellent marital unions, ... must have many men and women, ... should be steadfast in its friendships and safeguard the lives of all beings throughout the animal kingdom ... [It must be] benevolent and industrious ... inspired to give, be generous, and remember the kindness of others ... they must respect their fathers, mothers, mendicants, and priests.[28]

While there is invariably sexism in the descriptions of women ("women of the family must be famed for their beauty"[29]), qualities for men are similarly idealized. The bodhisattva's family requirements, surprisingly for the literature, are generally gender balanced.

---

* In Hinduism, the brahman caste is considered superior to the *kshatriya* (warrior) caste, but in early Indian Buddhism this ranking is reversed.
† The realm of human beings. The word is also sometimes used to mean India.

Kapilavastu, the seat of the Shakyas, also proves to be a suitable locale for the birth of the Bodhisattva, thanks to its beauty as well as the might of its people. It is noteworthy that while the clan had perfected the arts of war, harming others appears to be proscribed:

> The city is filled with gardens, groves and palaces;
> The beautiful city of Kapilavastu is the most suitable birthplace.
> All its inhabitants are mighty and powerful,
> With the strength of two or even three elephants.
> They have perfected their training in archery and weapons
> And do not harm others, even to protect their own lives.[30]

The appropriate timing for the Bodhisattva to descend to the human realm is discussed at length in the Burmese legend. It is argued that in epochs when humans live excessively long lives (as in thousands of years), there is no value in introducing a buddha's profound teachings on matters concerning the miseries of birth, life, death, and so forth, since there would be insufficient interest:

> Vain and fruitless would have been the efforts to disentangle [these humans] from the ties of passions.[31]

The optimal era for a buddha's teachings is said to be when the human life span is about one hundred years, another good fit for our story. In the *Mahavastu,* the Bodhisattva bluntly explains his timing this way:

> Now at this moment, is it time for me to depart hence. For men are sunk in gross darkness, are blinded, and of dimmed vision. Attaining me, they will be delivered.[32]

A consistent proviso in the legends is that descent into the mother's womb can take place only during the full moon. There are also astrological signs that signal the proper time.

The Bodhisattva's final consideration for taking rebirth is his choice of mother. In the *Mahavastu,* he asks,

> Who can bear me for ten months? Who has merit to win such honour?
> Who, now, shall be my mother? Whose womb shall I now enter?[33]

The single most-repeated criterion for candidacy is that she must be karmically predestined to die ten (lunar) months and seven days from conception, in other words, a week after childbirth.* Some legends tell us the Bodhisattva enumerated thirty-two additional requirements that his mother must have. Specific criteria for fathers are not addressed and seem to flow from clan. Unfortunately, it is here that we bump into cringeworthy sexism. Called "signs of female excellency" in the *Lalitavistara,* the portrait of the mother worthy of a bodhisattva is one who has an attractive body ("excellent figure ... excellent proportions") and unblemished behavior ("not coarse, easily distracted or prone to gossip") and who is obedient to her husband (with "excellent discipline, ... a devoted wife"). Item 30 is a catchall: "She should be free from the faults of womankind." In fairness, the list also includes "fearless, learned, wise, honest." And finally, "She must not have given birth previously." [34]

Whether or not Maya met any or all of these criteria, we'll never know. We can be sure, however, that at the time she conceived her son, there was no such list. More than likely, it emerged long after the fact from within the Buddhist monastic literary tradition, which conjured its own misogynist views of Maya and motherhood. It is especially egregious when sexist passages such as these are attributed to the Buddha (in this case, the Bodhisattva) himself. This type of gender bias—so embedded in Buddhist literature— sadly continues to give rise to confusion and division within the Buddhist world today. That it surely flowed from the ignorance of male chroniclers and editors rather than the Buddha is a distinction that continuously needs to be pointed out.

On Conceiving a Bodhisattva

While the Buddha was preparing for his descent from heaven, Kapilavastu was awash in auspicious omens. The royal palace became bedecked with flowers, and multitudes of songbirds arrived from the Himalayas. Musical instruments burst into song of their own accord; stores of precious provisions such as sesame oil and sugar spontaneously replenished; and

---

* Unlike ordinary humans, bodhisattvas remain in utero ten months rather than nine.

brilliant light filled the sky. It was a time of festivities for the townsfolk too, as they celebrated providential astrological signs with rejoicing, feasting, music, and sports. With some exceptions, the Sanskrit traditions tells us that the rejoicing took place during the full moon in April/May, while in the Pali sources, it was July/August.

Maya, meanwhile, was making preparations of her own at the palace. The legends turn to themes of purification as a necessary prerequisite for her to conceive the Bodhisattva. While spiritual practice would make sense on such an occasion, many of the narratives assume a tedious preoccupation with the purity of Maya's uterus. More salient here is what we can glean from the stories about Maya herself as she embarked on her pregnancy and the resultant birth of her son—the final chapter of her life.

Several legends reveal tender conversations between Maya and her husband in advance of the conception. Intuiting that change is imminent, she approaches him with two fervent requests. The following passages provide an intimate glimpse into their world and relationship:

> Queen Maya bathed and applied perfumes to her body. She ornamented her arms with many bracelets and dressed in the softest and most beautiful garments. Joyful, happy, and rapturous, accompanied and encircled by ten thousand women, she went to where King Suddhodana was seated comfortably in the music hall. She seated herself to his right on the fine, precious throne draped with jeweled latticework. With a smiling and trusting face, free from anger, she spoke to [the] King.[35]

First she requests that he release her from her conjugal obligation, specifically that he no longer ask her for sex:

> Do not then, O king, desire me with thoughts of sensual delight. See to it that you be guiltless of offence against me, for I would observe chastity.[36]

She explains that her choice is to live apart from him and to have no contact whatsoever with men. As if choosing to be a nun, she asserts that she wishes to assume a contemplative life, observing fasting and self-discipline. For her second request, Maya asks that Suddhodana provide separate quarters in the palace for her and her female attendants so that she may immediately commence her religious observances:

> Your Highness, I beseech you, quick, say yes, today!
> Inside the cool pavilion at the top of the palace where the swans roost,
> On a soft and sweetly scented bed scattered with flowers,
> I would like to live happily, always surrounded by my female
>   friends.[37]

Maya does not say just why she is making these requests. The stories imply but do not state that she knows conception is imminent. In one text, she simply says,

> All night long this resolve has been stirring in me.[38]

Significantly, neither does Suddhodana ask any questions. Magnanimously he rises to the occasion, whether understanding the significance of what is unfolding or simply out of love for his wife. His response to the sex matter is especially gallant:

> As your heart desires! act as you wish. I will even give up my kingdom rather than that you should not so act, if you desire it.

The text then switches to the phrasing *sister* and *mother* to denote that he has willingly abandoned his sexual desire for her:

> The [King] beholding the Mother of Bodhisattva
> Respectfully rose from his seat before her,
> Regarding her as his Mother or elder Sister,
> His heart wholly free from any thought of sensual desire.[39]

Elsewhere, it says:

> I shall comply with all your wishes. Be at ease. You have taken up a noble life, and I and my whole realm will obey you.[40]

Now Suddhodana commands his retinue to make the proper arrangements for Maya and her attendants. Enthusiastic and loving, his words are free of kingly arrogance. Despite the implied austerity of his wife's request, he has the apartments exquisitely adorned for her:

> Make the finest preparations in the upper quarters of the palace.
> Decorate them with beautiful flowers and use the best incense and
>   perfume;
> Adorn them with parasols, banners, and rows of palm trees.
>
> Place on guard twenty thousand brave fighting men in armor,
> Brandishing swords, arrows, spears, and lances.
> Let them guard the quarters where the swans call out melodiously;
> Let them guard the queen with loving care so that she is
>   not afraid.[41]

The ladies retire to their new quarters, and from then on Maya and her husband sleep apart. It should be mentioned that although Suddhodana had another wife and a harem, he voluntarily followed Maya's lead in observing spiritual practice and celibacy for the duration of her pregnancy.[42]

From a narrative standpoint, it is obvious that Maya's self-imposed chastity is establishing the miraculous nature of the Buddha's conception. Accounts vary on just how long she spent in seclusion before this took place. The *Lalitavistara* says she was chaste for thirty-two months in preparation for the event. However, in some legends, it appears she conceived the same night she took religious precepts. One way or another, we're to understand that Suddhodana was absent and that Maya slept alone the night she conceived. The Burmese legend says,

> The day before the full moon she rose up at an early hour, bathed in perfumed water, and distributed to the needy four hundred thousand pieces of silver. Attired in her richest dress, she took her meal, and religiously performed all the pious observances usual on such occasions. This being done, she entered into her private apartment, and, lying on her couch, fell asleep.[43]

The Buddha's conception ensues. Most stories concur that Maya conceives during a dream in which the Bodhisattva enters her right side in the form of a brilliant white elephant with six tusks. In more elaborate versions, she is transported by gods to the Himalayas where she is attended by four celestial queens. They bathe her in a sacred lake (thereby cleansing her of human impurities), then dress her in lovely garments, anoint her with divine scents, and scattering flowers, leave her reclining in a cave. Here the young Bodhisattva-as-elephant, roaming outside, finds her:

> On the extremity of his trunk, lifted up like a beautiful string of flowers, [the elephant] carried a white lily. His voice, occasionally resounding through the air, could be heard distinctly ... and indicated his approach. He soon entered the cave, turned three times round the couch whereupon sat the princess, then, standing for a while, he came nearer, opened her right side, and appeared to conceal himself in her womb.[44]

That he enters her body on the right side is consistent with his eventual manner of birth, which is traditionally reported also to have been from the right side. Elsewhere, the scene goes on to liken Maya's experience to the highest states of meditative absorption:

> She had never seen, heard of, or experienced
> Such a rare happiness.
> Feeling this physical and mental bliss,
> She became absorbed in concentration.[45]

Meanwhile the celestial realms are abuzz with celebration and activity. Throngs of gods and goddess maidens surround the young queen to protect her and bear witness to the blessed conception. A humorous detail has a bevy of young goddesses circling the sleeping Maya on her couch. They are curious to see what human woman could possibly be so meritorious as to be the chosen mother of the coming Buddha. Gossiping among themselves they are awestruck by her radiance and sing her praises:

> There can be none like her, even among the consorts of devas.
> Ah! dear friends, observe the loveliness of this woman. How befitting (a Conqueror's mother). As she lies on her bed, she is radiant and alluring, and gleams like a stream of gold.

And to Maya, they say,

> In you whose belly, with its fair streak of downy hair, curves like the palm of the hand, and whose renown is bright, the Exalted One has taken up his abode. . . . You are a worthy woman, supreme of mothers as he, your son, is pre-eminent, he who ends existences, and is blessed. What more can you want, O Queen? [46]

Awaking the next morning, Maya immediately seeks her husband to tell him about the dream with the white elephant and ask his counsel on what it means:

> She . . . arose from her bed and made her way down from the upper floors of the palace, surrounded by her female attendants. She proceeded to the . . . forest, where she felt at ease. Once there, she sent a message to King Suddhodana: "Your Majesty, please come, the queen would like to see you." [47]

Meanwhile, the gods have informed the king that his wife has just conceived a great bodhisattva who will be his son. He hurries to meet her:

> Then, joining his palms and bowing his head,
> The king went into the forest, overwhelmed by reverence and awe.
> Without pride or arrogance, he looked at Queen Maya
> And asked, "What may I do for you? Tell me what to do."

After recounting her dream, Maya asks,

> I wonder if this dream of mine shows happiness or sorrow for our
>   family? [48]

Without delay, Suddhodana calls on priests and soothsayers for their predictions. They tell him that Maya is carrying a son and add that Suddhodana must show reverence to both mother and child. They inform the parents that the boy will bear the thirty-two marks of a great man, which signify a *chakravartin* (universal king) if he stays home to rule the kingdom, or a perfectly enlightened buddha if he renounces the world.

Here, for the first time, we sense a hint of ambivalence in the parents as they digest the news. After all, their intention has been to bring forth an heir, not a buddha. In the *Mahavastu,* Maya insists that the son she bears is a universal king but is gently countered by the *devas,* who assert that he will become a buddha. In some legends, Suddhodana is described as experiencing foreboding mixed with joy during this encounter. While the soothsayers respond to Maya's question with assurances that the birth of her child will bring only joy to the Shakya clan, that in fact does not prove to be the case. Not only is Maya set to die within months, but as we shall see, the choices made by her son when he comes of age will bring untold sorrow to his family and kingdom. The Bodhisattva's birth, while a gift of joyful promise to the world, comes at the cost of much anguish to his loved ones in Kapilavastu.

But why an elephant? The legends provide an array of explanations. In the *Lalitavistara,* we learn that earlier, in Tushita heaven, the Bodhisattva convened a meeting of his celestial colleagues and consulted them as to which form he should take on entering his mother's womb. After considering their suggestions, which included various forms of gods or supernatural beasts, he decided on a white, six-tusked elephant, since it was the correct method according to brahmanical scriptures.[49] In the *Mahavastu,* the god Brahma says,

> The woman who in her dream has seen a white elephant enter her womb will give birth to a being as select as the elephant is among animals. He will be a Buddha.[50]

In the *Lalitavistara,* the glorious attributes of the elephant are assigned equally to Maya and the Bodhisattva, as only a mighty mother could carry such a son.[51] The elephant dream as an auspicious portent of the Bodhisattva's arrival into the earthly realm is one of the most popular images in early Buddhist iconography.

Not all the Buddha legends include Maya's austerities and dream, and several are ambiguous about the nature of the conception. The Kangyur tells us that while Maya and Suddhodana enjoyed sexual relations in their marriage, she "bore him no children," leaving it unclear whether the king participated in the conception on the night of the dream or not.[52] The *Buddhacarita* tells us he did not ("without defilement she received the fruit of the womb"[53]), while the *Abhinishkramanasutra* simply says that the Bodhisattva entered her womb "in a spiritual manner."[54] The Pali canon implies a natural conception, saying only that the Buddha was well born on both his mother's and father's side.[55] The *Mahavastu* states that sex is unnecessary for bodhisattvas to be born in the human realm:

> Bodhisattvas are not born of the intercourse of a father and a mother, but by their own merit independently of parents.[56]

Elsewhere, it says,

> Although the [Buddha's] corporeal existence is not due to the sexual union of parents, yet Buddhas can point to their fathers and mothers. This is mere conformity with the world.[57]

Regardless of one's preferred version of the conception story, it should be noted that while most of the stories describe an "immaculate" conception, nowhere in any legend of the Buddha is there a suggestion that Maya was a virgin mother.[58] The notion of virginity as a desirable or ennobling attribute in women is virtually nonexistent in Buddhist religious literature. The vow of chastity or celibacy, on the other hand, as taken by nuns and monks (and sometimes lay practitioners) in many Buddhist and non-Buddhist religious traditions, is commonly found as a meaningful aspect of religious life. This is the step Maya takes to prepare for her pregnancy and for which she entreats understanding from her husband.

Consistent too, is her wish to shun the company of men and surround herself with women as a prerequisite for undertaking spiritual practice. Sexual abstinence is just one of a handful of self-imposed rules of discipline she observes in preparation for carrying the Bodhisattva. In one story, Maya further decides to relinquish the religious practices of her people during this time (it's pointed out that the teachings of the Buddha were yet unknown) and no longer subordinate herself to priests. Instead, she chooses to "[worship] according to her own thoughts."[59] We are to understand that from the moment the Bodhisattva enters her womb she becomes exempt from impure words or thoughts, illness or suffering. Besides choosing celibacy, she no longer feels carnal desire, and she can no longer inspire it in anyone, including her husband. Sexism unfortunately creeps into the narrative here, too—we're told that once Maya becomes pregnant, she experiences "no female deception, guile, envy or feminine disturbing emotions."[60]

The Bodhisattva in Utero: Maya's Pregnancy

The notion "miracle of birth" is taken to creative new heights in stories of Maya's pregnancy. Rapturous accounts in the literature tell us a lot about the imaginations of the male chroniclers and very little that remotely rings true for a mortal mother-to-be. Here, more than anywhere else in Maya's hagiography, she is cast as superhuman, a goddess, a body-as-tabernacle bearing the holy child who awaits entry into the earthly realm. In no way do the facts of female anatomy or reproductive biology get in the way of these good stories. This wouldn't be an issue if both Maya and her son were truly held to be deities. Divine beings can get away with just about anything, and when it comes to procreation, methods run the gamut (think: Athena bursting from Zeus's forehead or Brahma emerging from a lotus in Vishnu's naval).

But this is where Buddhism gets confusing and, to many adherents (especially women), off-putting. Depending on the context or the teaching, we find conflicting notions of both the humanity and the divinity of the Buddha and, by extension, his mother. There is a vast and significant chasm here, mixed up with complicated layers of tradition, belief, story, and history. Fanciful stories can provide powerful symbols and instructive analogies, not to mention humor and entertainment, but they can also be misleading, even destructive, and lose significance if not taken with a grain of salt. The improbable ways the various Buddhist traditions conjure details of Maya's pregnancy tell us less about her as a historical woman and more about the imaginations of the storytellers and their audiences. However we feel about the narrative details as they come down to us in the legends, they are what we have, and all of them are part and parcel of Maya's story.

When we left our story, the Bodhisattva was descending as a white elephant into Maya's womb. Once arrived, however, he appears as a miniature boy, fully formed and aware, about the size of a six-month-old infant. The transformation is not discussed. Of his state of consciousness, we are told,

> [The Bodhisattva] sat in the womb enjoying the full use of his reason, and fully aware of the three circumstances of his existence, namely his conception, his gestation, and his birth, unlike other beings, which have no knowledge of these things.[61]

Intrauterine protocols are discussed at length. Generally we're told that he sits cross-legged on his mother's right side, although one variant says it's also okay to stand in the mother's womb to the back, in her belly, or to the side.[62] Even more specific, another passage tells us that he does not occupy a position that is either too high or too low in utero; he does not lie on his face, back, or left side; and he never squats on his heels.[63] We are to understand that he is fully formed because he is not in any way a fetus dependent on the body of his mother for nourishment and growth:[64]

> The body of a bodhisattva in his last existence is free from the four stages of embryonic development. Instead he appears seated with all his limbs, organs, and characteristics fully formed.[65]

How he survives a ten-month gestation in this way is made clear in the *Lalitavistara,* where we learn that on the night of the conception, the god Brahma gave the Bodhisattva a potent elixir that contained the divine essence of all worldly and celestial realms. In a nod to his status, only a bodhisattva who has arrived at his final birth after countless lifetimes accumulating merit has earned the power to digest such a substance. From this miraculous drop, he gained superknowledges and the vitality to remain robust within Maya's womb for ten months.[66]

At this point, we realize that the term *gestation* is technically a misnomer and have to ask, if the Buddha arrived fully formed and aware, why did he need Maya's body in the first place? We've already seen that he apparently did not need a father, so why a mother, especially if there is never really a physical link between the two of them? The *Lalitavistara* deftly anticipates and addresses this question. The storytellers pull back from mythologizing here and turn to the attributes of the bodhisattva: a human being in the process of full awakening through lifetimes of activity benefiting others. Due to the fact that he was born, they can no longer avoid the truth of his humanness. It is easier to assign miracles to the unseen, such as conception, but now the Bodhisattva is emerging in the flesh into the human realm. The explanation? He is born of a woman as he has always been born in countless previous lifetimes. To do otherwise, even if it were karmically possible, would be inconsistent with his mission to uplift humanity by abiding and behaving in the world as an ordinary—albeit exemplary—human being. In other words, the Bodhisattva is meant to be someone to whom we can relate. As such and with full self-awareness, he acts as a role model for humanity, beginning with the fact that he has a mother.

While being born of a mother may be one concession to his humanity, there are many ways in which Maya's is not an ordinary pregnancy. The fixation on the purity of her uterus is pervasive. In the *Mahavastu,* we're told that the Bodhisattva "is not polluted by bile, phlegm, blood or any other foul matter,"[67] and elsewhere, "the usual secretions are not formed."[68] The *Lalitavistara* goes on about this in great detail. In a glaring misogynist flashback scenario, an assembly of celestial beings mulls over how, if even their own kind are repulsed by human smells, could the supreme Bodhisattva possibly have endured ten months in his mother's body:

> How could the pure Bodhisattva, who is free from bad-smelling odors, superior to the entire world, a jewel among beings, transmigrate from the divine realm . . . and remain for ten months in the foul-smelling human body inside his mother's womb?[69]

This same question is posed to the Buddha by his disciple Ananda, who says he finds it "astonishing" that The Blessed One could have entered the world in such a manner, especially when the Buddha has taught him and his fellow monks that "the female body is inferior and enjoys desire."[70]

Ouch. Time-out for some context. The question of the Buddha's (and Buddhism's) position on women generally and the female body specifically is a topic of contention in both lay and monastic Buddhist communities today. Ananda's remarks reflect revulsion for the female body that appears in early literature, including the Pali canon, although the preponderance of this type of content proliferated more in the later commentaries.[71] As stated earlier, the position held here is that it originated with misogynist editors, not the Buddha himself. Related to this view, however, the Buddha did teach a meditation that had disciples focus on their *own* bodies as a collection of impure constituents, which he taught to both women and men as a method for understanding the impermanence of the human form and uselessness of sensual attachment. Combining the beauty of analogy with a lack of delicacy often found in Buddhist literature, he compares the body to a bag with openings on both ends, filled with all manner of foul body parts and secretions, which are enumerated at length and in graphic detail.[72] This meditation is not genderized, and nowhere in the Pali canon does he instruct the monks to use it to focus on women's bodies.[73]

In the *Therigatha,* the Buddha gives such a teaching to a nun named Sundarinanda* in an effort to counter her vanity. His point is not that her body should be viewed as foul because it is female but because, like all bodies, it is subject to decay and useless as an object of pride or attachment. He urges her to investigate this line of thinking in order to develop her own wisdom:

> Look at this body, Nanda, it's sick, it's dirty, it's foul.

> Use what is unpleasant to cultivate the mind,
> make it focused and attentive.

> Just as this is, so is that, just as that is, so is this:
> stinking, foul, the delight of fools.

> When you look at it this way,
> day and night, always intently,
> someday you will see,
> breaking through with your own wisdom.

Sundarinanda replies,

> This body was seen as it really is, inside and out,
> as I examined it carefully and thoroughly.

> I became tired of the body, inwardly disinterested,
> diligent, released, at peace, free.[74]

---

* His half-sister, the daughter of Mahaprajapati and Suddhodana.

Not only is Sundarinanda not offended by the Buddha's words, she takes them to heart and achieves the desired result of liberation. It's not hard to imagine how misogynist monk-editors, possibly struggling with personal issues of celibacy, might selectively misconstrue a profound dharma teaching such as this by projecting "foulness" onto women's bodies—in this case Maya's—when embellishing their teacher's biographical narrative.

But back to Ananda's question. It turns out that foul smells were not at issue since Maya's was not an ordinary uterus, but a pristine, jeweled sanctum within her body. The *Lalitavistara* describes it as follows:

> The jeweled structure . . . was finely shaped, exquisite and beautiful to behold. It was square in form and had four pillars. At the top was a beautifully adorned upper floor scaled to fit a six-month-old fetus. Inside that upper chamber was a throne with a sitting area that was likewise scaled to fit a six-month-old fetus . . . it gleamed, radiated heat and shone brightly. This multistoried structure was as resplendent as gold that has been smelt twice by an expert goldsmith so that it has become perfectly refined and free from any impurity.[75]

The accolades continue for several paragraphs, where we learn more about this sanctum's extraordinary attributes, which exceeded even those of a celestial temple. In terms of how it got inside Maya's body, it simply manifested prior to the Bodhisattva's arrival. The sculptures in Borobudur, a ninth-century temple in Indonesia, depict a variation of this detail in a scene in which the Bodhisattva is shown descending from heaven, not as an elephant, but as a miniature child within a jeweled box.[76]

The jeweled sanctum arrangement would sound exceedingly onerous for the mother, yet the stories are adamant that Maya was never harmed. Firm and indestructible like a diamond, this vessel was said to be as soft to the touch as the finest Benares silk. Indeed, what's not to covet about a pregnancy that goes like this:

> Queen Maya did not feel any heaviness in her body. On the contrary she felt light, supple, and happy, and did not experience any uncomfortable pains in her belly . . .[77]

Another source says,

> And [Maya] felt no pain, nor had she the troubles of other women in her condition, nor was the elegant contour of her figure enlarged or changed.[78]

And the *Mahavastu* tells us,

> She enjoys a digestive heat that is equable, being neither too cold nor too hot and thus ensuring a regular digestion.[79]

Within the pristine tabernacle, all manner of "sublime and perfect forms, sounds, smells, tastes, and textures" (ambiguously) manifested, and special garments also appeared for the tiny Bodhisattva.[80] Celestial musical instruments played without ceasing day and night, as blossoms and sandalwood-scented incense fell from the sky.[81] Indra and a retinue of more than five hundred celestial beings arrived to guard and protect him, while four goddess maidens attended him, for the duration of his intrauterine stopover.

Miracles beget miracles. Maya's body became transparent and clear, the golden radiance of the Bodhisattva emitting brilliantly from within, "like a great fire burning on a mountaintop during the darkest night."[82] As a result, she could observe the son she was carrying:

> When Queen Maya looked inside her belly, she saw the [Bodhisattva] resting on the right side of her womb. She could see this as clearly as if she was looking at her own face in a spotless mirror. Seeing him in that way, she was satisfied, elated, and delighted. She felt extremely happy, buoyant, and joyful.[83]

While the legends share miraculous details, not all the stories go to the extremes of the *Lalitavistara*. The *Abhinishkramanasutra* implies that Maya experienced no harm because the Buddha was careful not to move to her left side, which would have caused her "pain and anxiety."[84] From the Sinhalese story, it appears that the Bodhisattva grew naturally as a fetus (still within the jeweled sanctum), which Maya experienced with a mother's tenderness:

He grew every succeeding day. The wonder of the queen was excited by these circumstances; and for the better preservation of her infant she moved about with care, like one who carries a vessel full of oil that he is afraid to spill.[85]

Like one doll slipped inside another, son and mother manifested a miraculous display, suffusing the palace and surrounding region with a luminous and sublime aura. The *Lalitavistara* tells us that the tiny Bodhisattva used his time in the womb to launch his earthly mission and grant teachings to visitors. Vast multitudes of celestial beings and bodhisattvas arrived to pay homage and hear him give discourses on the dharma from inside his mother's body. Before departing, they would circumambulate the Bodhisattva and Maya three times. Ordinary people from Kapilavastu also came to pay their respects: women, men, boys, and girls. First the Bodhisattva and then his mother would welcome them. As when she was a little girl, Maya's healing powers manifested during this time:

> Any woman or child afflicted by suffering,
> Possessed by spirits, with troubled mind, naked and covered with
>   dust,
> Recovered their senses upon seeing Queen Maya.
> With intelligence and mindfulness restored, they returned to their
>   homes.
>
> Those afflicted by illness caused by disorders of wind, bile, or
>   phlegm,
> And those with body and mind tormented by diseases of the eyes
>   and ears,
> And all those stricken by many different kinds of ailments,
> Were freed from illness when Queen Maya placed her hand on
>   their heads.
>
> Moreover, gathering herbs from the ground,
> Maya gave them to the sick, who all became cured.
> Happy and healthy, they returned to their homes,
> While the King of Physicians, the remedy itself, dwelt in the womb.[86]

Maya was secluded in the women's quarters for the duration of her pregnancy, adorned in seraphic raiment like her son, and surrounded by the pleasures and enjoyments of earthly and celestial women. One hundred thousand or so goddess maidens attended to rubbing, massaging, and anointing her body by day and fanning her with garlands from the coral tree by night.[87] It is described as a merry place, full of women joined in laughing, music-making, dancing, and singing—not at all the portrait of solemn religious observance we might have imagined following Maya's earlier conversation with her husband. Meanwhile, the people of Kapilavastu similarly celebrated, feasted, and enjoyed all good conditions on the occasion of Maya's pregnancy. Only Suddhodana withdrew into asceticism, setting aside the affairs of his kingdom to fast and practice austerities. The pregnancy chapter in the *Lalitavistara* concludes as he breaks from his penances and greets his wife with the gentle words,

> How blissful your body must be, bearing the Perfect Being![88]

The Journey to Lumbini's Grove

The legends all tell us that Maya delivered her son midst the lush beauty of Lumbini's grove, the dense woodland area of tall trees along the road between Kapilavastu and her family home of Devadaha. Several Pali texts describe it as an enchanting "pleasure grove," where townsfolk from both communities would sport and amuse themselves.[89] Could it also be the gardens where Maya and her friends played as young girls or where she was later married? The Thai legend treats us to a delightful description of the grove:

> Between the cities of Kapila and Dewadaha, there was in those days a forest of the most splendid trees, named [Lumbini's grove]. It was a lovely spot. Interlacing branches, richly covered with foliage, sheltered the traveller as if he were covered with a canopy. The sun's scorching rays could not penetrate to the delicious shade. All over the trees, from their trunks to their very tops, bunches of flowers budded, bloomed, and shed their fragrant leaves, and unceasingly budded and bloomed again. Attracted by their sweet pollen, flights of shining beetles buzzed around them, filling the air with a melodious humming like to

the music of the heavens. There were pools full of lotuses of all colors, whose sweet scent was wafted around by gentle breezes, and whose fruit floated on the waters in all stages of ripeness.[90]

The texts explain the circumstances that gave rise to Lumbini's grove being the Buddha's birthplace in a variety of ways. The traditional version tells us it was the custom for a daughter to return to her father's home to give birth; thus in her tenth month, Maya asked permission of her husband to return to Devadaha, and it was just happenstance that the birth took place before she got there. This very patriarchal slant is not consistent with a more nuanced look at the sources. We know that Maya left Kapilavastu as her time of delivery drew near, but why and how she did this invites a closer look at the legends and a dose of common sense.

We can imagine Maya at full term in her pregnancy, a young woman anticipating the imminent birth of her first child. Her attention would naturally be on a safe delivery and a healthy baby. Both she and Suddhodana are described as anxious during this time. In the *Mahavastu,* we hear Maya's urgency as she implores her husband to make arrangements quickly for her departure, not to Devadaha, but directly to Lumbini's grove:

> My course is clear to me. I have had a notion to go out into the [Lumbini] park, O King, quickly get ready for me a fitting carriage and an escort.[91]

Suddhodana swings into action and directs his attendants,

> Quickly get ready an army of troops . . . and a large host of foot soldiers. . . .
>
> Quickly deliver to me exceedingly well-equipped elephants, armoured and most richly caparisoned . . .
>
> Let women in garlanded raiment take to the queen a splendid horse-chariot fitted with many a tinkling bell and coated in a network of gold.
>
> Quickly make the Lumbini grove like a celestial abode for the queen, clean and pleasant, with the grass, mire, leaves and litter swept away.[92]

It certainly sounds as if labor has started and Lumbini's grove is the chosen birthing site. We find a similar verse passage in the *Lalitavistara*, where Maya again entreats her husband to go immediately to Lumbini's grove—in this case, asking him to accompany her.

A variant in the *Abhinishkramanasutra* foreshadows Maya's death. Here her father Suprabuddha sends messengers to Suddhodana expressing concern that his daughter will not survive childbirth. He asks that she return home under his protection for the duration of her confinement:

> As I am informed my daughter, Maya, the queen of your majesty, is now with child, and already far advanced in pregnancy, and, as I fear that when the child is born, my daughter will be short lived, I have thought it right to ask you to permit my daughter, Maya, to come back to me and rest in my house; and I have prepared for her reception the Lumbini garden, and every proper amusement. Let not the king be displeased at this request, for immediately the confinement is over, I will send my daughter back to her home with you.[93]

We're not told what has prompted Suprabuddha's fears, but we see that he too feels it is best for Maya to spend her parturition in Lumbini's grove. In his mind, there is clearly something special, perhaps protective, about that place for his daughter during childbirth. Suddhodana assents to his father-in-law's request. Ornamented with jewels, flowers, and perfumes, mounted on a white elephant, Maya proceeds forthwith to Devadaha in an elaborate procession, replete with musicians, dancing women, and armed guards:

> She arrived at last at her father's house in the city of Devadaho; and as she approached, surrounded by the vast retinue of warriors, elephants, horses, and chariots provided by Suddhodana Raja, then forth from Devadaho came Supra Buddha and all his ministers and nobles to meet and welcome her approach.[94]

Shortly after her arrival, Suprabuddha himself escorts his daughter to Lumbini's grove, where the narrative proceeds to telling of his grandson's birth. This is the only story among the primary sources studied here where Maya arrives home in Devadaha prior to proceeding to the birthing site.

Thus the Sanskrit traditions hold that the intended destination was always Lumbini's grove, while the Pali sources more ambiguously state that Maya simply wanted to go home to her family. These are not necessarily contradictory accounts, but perhaps illustrate the storytellers' different perceptions of what was going on. We already know that Lumbini's grove is just outside of Devadaha, so the key distinction is more a question of whether Maya always intended to give birth in Lumbini's grove. The Pali sources are much briefer in this area of the Buddha legend. Also, that husband and father participate in the decision for Maya to leave Kapilavastu appears to have more to do with managing the logistics of the journey than granting permission. The dangers of childbirth are not unknown to them. Obviously, both Suddhodana and Suprabuddha are concerned about Maya and trying to do all the right things to ensure her comfort and welfare.

But more questions arise. Recalling Maya's extremely pregnant state, why would she intend to travel at all? Women on the cusp of childbirth don't choose to make long and arduous journeys (especially on the back of an elephant) unless there is a very good reason. An entirely pragmatic answer will be posited here. In most premodern cultures, childbirth was entirely the province of women. We don't know the childbirth customs of the Shakyas, but within the matriarchal traditions of ancient India (and rural India today), there was a practice of daughters returning to their family home to give birth, not so much for sentimental or social reasons, but because their own mothers and the women of their family were best disposed to care for them and the newborn child.[95] Nowhere is Maya's mother mentioned in these sequences (only "parents" or "family"), yet in this context, it makes sense that Maya would seek the succor of her mother on the occasion of giving birth, which would account for her resolve to travel at what was otherwise an extremely imprudent time. In this scenario, it would have been Maya's intention all along to return to her family home to give birth, not a sudden impulse.

Then why do the Sanskrit sources tell us that Lumbini's grove was Maya's intended destination? A second supposition flows from the matriarchal theme already cited, but first we must digress to establish some context. Thanks to an ancient pillar marking the spot, and despite the fact the bounteous forest landscape described in the literature has long since become parched and barren, today we know the precise location of Lumbini's grove, the Buddha's birthplace, which is located along Nepal's southern border with India. Today the village area is known as Rummindei, meaning "Rummin goddess," named for an ancient goddess sacred to mothers and mothers-to-be seeking fertility, healthy children, and protection in childbirth. Scholars have speculated that the name Rummini is an iteration of the ancient Lumbini. It remains a site sacred to village women where practices associated with fertility and the mother goddess tradition are non-Buddhist and more aboriginal in nature, though a well-worn shrine to Maya (where she appears to have merged with the goddess) is still venerated.[96] A spring festival honoring the goddess is held there each year coinciding with the Buddhist celebration of Vesak, which commemorates the Buddha's birth.

Recent archaeological discoveries suggest that this goddess site has been continuously inhabited for thousands of years, at least since the time of the Buddha, with evidence showing human habitation as early as the eighth or seventh century B.C.E.[97] This present-day evidence ties in with what we already know about the early matriarchal, non-Indo-Aryan culture in that region, where the mother goddess was not only venerated but whose domain was located outside the village in a jungle grove or thicket, often sanctioned only for women. Typically these sites were along important roads or at crossroads between villages and were destinations for women seeking to propitiate the goddess for blessings and protection, particularly in matters related to children and childbirth. The sacred shrine within the grove would be a specific tree worshipped as the goddess herself, their mutual fertility and vitality symbolically merging as one. This primal mother goddess brooked no consort and could be as fierce and gruesome as she was protective and beneficent. Portrayed ubiquitously in early Indian art, she is rendered in vibrant and voluptuous female form, often beautifully entwined and merged within a tree's lush ebullience. She is thought to be the prototype for the brahmanical goddess Durga, which places her in the company of early tantric deities.[98]

When we consider some of the local customs and history, Maya's determination to go to Lumbini's grove makes more sense. It would have been the sanctuary of the mother-goddess in that region, a destination where Maya, consistent with the customs of her people, would pay homage to the goddess and under whose protection she would give birth. It would have been an occasion for the village women to gather to assist Maya, share in the birthing rituals, and facilitate the delivery and aftercare of the new mother and baby. Maya's mother no doubt would have been present, perhaps taking charge of this proceeding and, with the other women, bringing forth her wisdom and skill in birthing practices that flowed from her own mother, matrilineal forebears, and village traditions. Indeed, this sacred site would have had special meaning to all the women present, as it was likely where they birthed their own sons and daughters and where they themselves had been born a generation earlier. It is worth imagining that Maya and her sister, Mahaprajapati, may also have been born in Lumbini's grove.

The *Mahavastu* says that a goddess of Lumbini's grove* and the goddess Abhayadevi, or "Protection Goddess"—appears shortly after the birth.[99] While it is impossible to know for sure from the tiny fragments in the stories, it is likely that these two goddesses are one and the same, given their association with the nativity and their mutual tutelary roles. No goddess of either name is known in the Vedic or brahmanical traditions, which further affirms that she is a vestige of the preexisting matriarchal culture. Further, village women in Rummindei today still remember the goddess Abhayadevi by that name, no doubt from a continuing oral tradition.[100] These literary references to a primal mother-goddess in the *Mahavastu* must be very old indeed, predating the Vedic and brahmanical segments of the narrative. It certainly seems doubtful that later male chroniclers would have embellished the Buddha's birth story with feminizing details such as a goddess. Ancient stories that were transmitted orally and are now lost must have had quite a different flavor, one more inclusive of—if not dominated by—themes of women, nature, birth, death, fertility, and the sacred feminine. That vestiges of a mother-goddess presence have survived at all in Buddhist literature is a tribute to her endurance in the face of the tradition's androcentric storytellers and redactors, both brahmanical and monastic, past and present. To refresh the biography of the Buddha in contemporary terms requires reintroducing, if not highlighting, glimpses of the sacred feminine still extant in the ancient literature, as these nuggets of content no doubt once comprised and informed the oral tradition of the legend that flourished long before anything was written down. We'll discuss Abhayadevi and other primal goddesses as they appear later on in the legends.

---

* Lumbinivanadevi.

Now we return to the narrative, where Maya, heavy with child, prepares to leave Kapilavastu for Lumbini's grove. Perhaps her anxiety has abated at the thought that she will soon be under the care of her mother and the protectress Abhayadevi. To ensure her comfort, her husband has had the road leveled and swept clear of debris, sprinkled with scented water, and scattered with flowers. A massive procession of elephants, chariots, dancers, and musicians will be her escort.[101] Suddhodana also ensures that Maya will be accompanied by the women of his court (his harem), over which she presides as queen consort. The *Lalitavistara* describes it this way:

> The sublime lord of men, with a joyous mind,
> Entered the palace and spoke thus to the women:
> "Those of you to whom I am dear and who would like to bring
>   me joy,
> Follow my command and adorn yourselves.
>
> "With colorful clothes, beautiful and soft,
> And fragrant with enchanting perfume,
> Adorn your chests with necklaces of pearls;
> Today everyone should wear all their ornaments!
>
> "Bring hundreds of thousands of delightful instruments:
> Hand drums, flutes, lutes, clay drums, and cymbals.
> Hearing the melodious sound of these instruments, even the gods
>   will be pleased!
> You make the goddesses similarly joyful!"[102]

Women far outnumber men in this procession, which includes sixty thousand each of Shakya maidens and women and eighty-four thousand each of various female divine beings. All are lavishly ornamented, playing musical instruments and singing songs of praise to Maya.[103] With similar exuberance, the *Mahavastu* tells us that multitudes of bedecked celestial maidens descend from the sky to accompany the procession:

> Wearing earrings of crystal gems and resplendent garments, and carrying fragrant garlands they come floating down the pathways of the sky.

Some carry baskets full of flowers of the coral tree; others baskets full of yellow sandalwood flowers. . . .

Deva maidens . . . carrying full eighty-four thousand sunshades of gold and jewels.[104]

That Maya was surrounded almost entirely by women during the final days of her life is noted throughout these legends. In the Burmese account, we find the added detail that she is joined by her sister, Mahaprajapati, as she departs for Lumbini's grove. This is the first time Mahaprajapati appears anywhere in the stories, except for the brief mention noted earlier that she was Suddhodana's cowife. It is touching and also fitting that Mahaprajapati attends her sister here, joining the women of her family in Lumbini's grove to assist in the birth of her nephew:

[Maya], seated on her couch, along with her sister [Mahaprajapati], desired her attendants to have it moved closer to [a *shala*] tree. . . . She then rose gently on her couch; her left hand, clasped round the neck of her sister, supported her in a standing position. With the right hand she tried to reach . . . a small branch.[105]

This literary reference to the sisters together is echoed in early Buddhist art, where Mahaprajapati can be seen tenderly supporting her sister on the left side, holding her by the waist, as Maya gives birth to the Buddha.[106]

Buddha's Birth, Maya's Death

The stories all agree that Maya's labor was rapid, and the Buddha was born shortly after her arrival in Lumbini's grove. The lush surroundings and wildlife became animated, appearing to rejoice as the moment of birth approached:

Five water lilies shot forth spontaneously from the stem and the main branches of each tree, and innumerable birds of all kinds, by their melodious tunes, filled the air with the most ravishing music. Trees, similar in beauty to those growing in the seats of the [gods], apparently sensible of the presence of the incarnated Buddha, seemed to share in the universal joy.[107]

Delighted by the beauty of the place, and surrounded by her company of ladies, Maya playfully dances from one *shala* tree* to another, until she is enticed by the most magnificent of them all. Reaching up, she grasps a branch with her right hand, and in the next moment, the Buddha is born.

Not surprisingly this pivotal scene is nuanced differently in the traditions. While the grove goddess is not named in the preceding episode, the tree becomes animated as Maya approaches and bends its branches toward her that she might seize the one of her choosing. In the *Lalitavistara,* the entire tree bows down in reverential homage to Maya and her Bodhisattva son. Some stories say that a strong wind comes up at this moment, dispersing the entourage to a distance, while Maya's attendants encircle her with a curtain, presumably to preserve her modesty. Elsewhere, Maya faces east, gazes upward into the expanse of sky, and simply stretches her body to birth her child.[108] The *Abhinishkramanasutra* says the Bodhisattva made the decision to be born at that moment:

> At this time, [Bodhisattva] perceiving his mother Maya, standing thus with the branch in her hand, then with conscious mind arose from his seat [in her womb] and was born.[109]

A rainbow of thousands of goddesses appears in the sky, showering Maya with divine flowers, incense, jewels, and garlands. Singing to her in sweet voices, they reassure her that they have come to assist her, serving, it would appear, as her celestial midwives. In the *Mahavastu,* they say,

> Today O Queen, you will give birth to him who crushes old age and rebirth, a tender youth of immortal stock, honored in heaven and on earth, friend and benefactor of men and devas.
>
> Do not give way to anxiety, for we shall render assistance to you. Only tell us what is to be done, and lo! It is all done. Be not anxious.[110]

As much as the birth scene is marked by the miraculous and supernatural, we're reminded again that Maya is a normal woman, not a goddess. She is "anxious"—a natural feeling for a woman in the throes of childbirth. The

---

* In some accounts, the Buddha is born under an *ashoka* tree.

Buddhacarita reminds us that both parents were apprehensive during this time.[111]

The *Abhinishkramanasutra* offers the most complete and informative version of the birth story. In anticipation of the birth, Suddhodana's regiment, led by the chief minister, has been dispatched to Lumbini's grove, where the men stop and linger outside the gate. Awestruck, they ponder the import of numerous miracles taking place around them—an earthquake, an eclipse, trees unseasonably in blossom, flowers falling from the sky. Suddenly from the forest, a woman comes rushing toward the gate:

> Oh! Sakyas! It is wonderfully good news! . . . The queen has borne a son . . . so beautiful and such a lovely child without peer on earth! and the Devas are scattering flowers about him, and there is a heavenly light diffused round his person.[112]

The happy tidings are swiftly relayed to Suddhodana in Kapilavastu, who rides back out with his men to Lumbini's grove. Along the way, he shares with them his foreboding as he reflects on his newborn son's future and the meaning of the miracles. The men stop again at the gate and dispatch a message to the queen within, congratulating her and requesting permission for Suddhodana to enter the grove. Described as "glowing with joy," Maya welcomes her husband. In their final conversation, the new parents discuss the portents that suggest their son will be a great king (not mentioning that he may become a buddha). Suddhodana makes arrangements for the baby to return to Kapilavastu, and there is no further mention of Maya. We have to wonder if he had been summoned to Lumbini's grove because, in fact, she was dying. As husband and father, he would attend to her funeral rites and the care of their son. That the men were barred entry to the garden gives credence to the earlier suggestion that Lumbini's grove was a sacred site sanctioned only for women.

With the exception of the *Buddhacarita,* all traditions agree that Maya gave birth standing up (in the *Buddhacarita,* she reclines on a couch shaded by an awning). Standing may be a narrative modification of the squatting posture common in midwife-assisted births. The popular legend and, indeed, many of the ancient iconographic representations further tell us that the infant Buddha was born miraculously from his mother's right side, thereby avoiding a vaginal birth. The Kangyur and Pali sources are silent on this matter. However, miraculous births are de rigueur for miraculous beings. Storytellers may well have borrowed the right-sided motif from ancient Vedic lore in which Indra, king of the gods, is said to have been born from his mother's right side. In the following passage from the Rig Veda, Indra tells us that all gods are born this way:

> This is the ancient and accepted pathway by which all Gods have
> come into existence.
> Hereby could one be born though waxen mighty. Let him not,
> otherwise, destroy his Mother.
> Not this way go I forth: hard is the passage. Forth from this side
> obliquely will I issue.[113]

It was also a widespread Indian belief that the trauma of passage through the birth canal wipes out all memory of previous births. Since a bodhisattva is said to remember all previous existences, he cannot therefore be born vaginally.[114] On this matter, the *Buddhacarita* says simply, "He did not come into the world through the portal of life."[115]

The right-sided birth motif is also consistent with the purity theme that persists throughout the stories of Maya's pregnancy. The *Lalitavistara* puts it bluntly:

> In this way he was unstained by any impurities of the womb, which
> otherwise are said to stain everyone else.[116]

The *Mahavastu* compares the infant Bodhisattva to a lotus that has emerged from muck:

> His body is untouched by the impurities of the womb, even like the
> exquisite lotus that is born in the mud of pools.[117]

The *Nidanakatha* ventures a detailed, albeit humorous, portrait of the Buddha emerging from his mother's body:

> Now other living things, when they leave their mother's womb,
> leave it smeared with offensive and impure matter. Not so a
> [Bodhisattva]. The future Buddha left his mother's womb like a

preacher descending from a pulpit or a man from a ladder, erect, stretching out his hands and feet, unsoiled by any impurities from contact with his mother's womb, pure and fair, and shining like a gem placed on fine muslin.[118]

And what happened to the jeweled sanctum-cum-uterus so painstakingly reported throughout the pregnancy episodes? Only the *Lalitavistara* mentions it again. Turns out the supreme god Brahma himself carried it off to the celestial realm where it was enshrined in a temple and venerated by the gods.

Just as the infant is not sullied, so the mother is not harmed by the birth. As Indra says earlier, not to "destroy his Mother" is a factor in right-sided god births. Here again we find a tension between the humanity and the divinity of Maya and her son. Try as the legends do to insist that bodhisattvas never harm their mothers (or anyone), Maya in fact dies shortly after the Buddha is born. This is an incontrovertible detail in all the legends, and one of the few held as likely historical truth. While the stories minimize—and in some cases, omit—this sad event, it is one that informs the rest of the Buddha's life. A touching scene in the *Lalitavistara* presages Maya's imminent death during what sounds like a sort of celestial baby shower. Just following the birth, multitudes of divine maidens flock to Maya bringing exotic gifts for her son, including celestial swaddling clothes and baby ornaments. Each time they deliver a gift, they query anxiously, "How was the birth? Are you feeling weary?"[119] To them, she's not a goddess, but a vulnerable woman who has just experienced childbirth.

There is no discussion of the death itself in the narratives. Maya simply vanishes from the storyline shortly after the birth takes place. No lamentations or funeral processions, just deafening silence. It's not hard to imagine how sad the occasion must have been and how conflicted the Shakyas must have felt—on the one hand, joy at the birth of their beautiful prince and heir to the throne, and on the other, abject grief at the death of their beloved queen. At this point, the stories turn squarely to extolling the Bodhisattva's joyous arrival, celebrated throughout the worlds with countless miracles. It's not reported that Maya ever nursed her son, but most sources tell us that she held him. Her final appearance in the Pali sources occurs during the delivery, as Brahma himself catches the baby in a golden net and presents him to his mother with the words,

Give yourself up, O Queen, to joy and rejoicing; here is the precious
and wonderful fruit of your womb.[120]

An interesting variant in the Kangyur has Indra, not Brahma, catching
the baby after assuming the appearance of an old woman, perhaps to avoid
the indelicacy of a male being present at the birth. It could also signal an
awareness of the taboo against males setting foot in a sacred birthing grove.
Having gods present in the birth scene (sometimes four of them) suggests
the brahmanization of an earlier story where only women, and no doubt
Abhayadevi, would have been present.

The literature uses a variety of creative workarounds to explain Maya's
death while absolving the birth event itself of being the cause. For example,
the *Mahavastu* goes to great lengths to assert that Maya's flesh was not torn
by the delivery because the nature of the baby Buddha was not flesh but
consciousness:

Tathagathas are born with a body that is made of mind, and thus the
mother's body is not rent, nor does any pain ensue.[121]

It continues later:

Immediately after the Sugata* was born, the mother of the Bodhisattva
was without hurt or scar. The womb of the Bodhisattva's mother was
unscathed and at ease.[122]

The *Lalitavistara* reminds us that Maya's short life was karmically ordained
(recall that this was one reason she was chosen to be the Bodhisattva's
mother in the first place), and tells us her early death was to spare her the
eventual sorrow of losing her son to his renunciation:

You may think that it was because of the Bodhisattva that Mayadevi
died. But you should not look upon things that way, since she had
reached the maximum extent of her lifespan. . . . Seven days after the
bodhisattvas of the past were born, their mothers also died. And

---

* Epithet for the Buddha.

why is that? Because once a bodhisattva is born and has grown up, it would destroy his mother's heart if he were to renounce his home.[123]

In the *Buddhacarita,* it was joy rather than sorrow that overwhelmed Maya:

> When queen Maya saw the vast power of her son, like that of a divine seer, she was unable to bear the joy it caused her; then she went to Heaven to dwell there.[124]

In the *Nidanakatha,* Maya's death is a necessary consequence of purity:

> But as a womb in which a future Buddha has dwelt, like a sacred relic shrine, can never be occupied by another; the mother of the [Bodhisattva], seven days after his birth, died, and was reborn in the City of Bliss.[125]

But the purity prize goes to the *Mahavastu,* which holds that Maya had to die because it would be unseemly for her ever to have sex again (but if she did, it would be her husband's fault). This explanation is attributed to the Bodhisattva himself:

> "It is not fitting that she who bears a Peerless One like me should afterwards indulge in love."
>
> For if the mothers of a Sugata should indulge in the pleasures of love, the hosts of devas would say that the king was violating his duty.[126]

All the finger-pointing distracts from the elephant in the room. Reading these stories millennia later with a modicum of common sense, it becomes obvious that Maya died from childbirth. Possibly she lingered until the seventh day or so postpartum as the legends insist. Or perhaps the seventh-day detail was invented to distance the death from the birth. Possibly, too, the element of the Bodhisattva's requisite ten-month gestation arose as a rationalization around Maya's actual pregnancy extending unnaturally past a normal due date, which gave rise to fatal complications. In any case, maternal and infant mortality would have been commonplace. "That hour brings as much danger to the body as the clash of armies," says the *Buddhacarita.*[127]

There is no other apparent or logical explanation for Maya's sudden death, and if there were, the storytellers surely would have included those details in the larger tale.

As it is, we see how painstakingly their narratives work to deflect blame away from the infant Bodhisattva. Indeed, it must have been distressing to the people and emerging Buddhist culture of the time to imagine that he— the ambassador of compassion and loving-kindness to the world—could in any way, however innocently, be a source of harm or human suffering, especially concerning his mother. The birth of the Buddha was meant to be remembered as an occasion of inexpressible joy. Reconciling that with the tragedy of Maya's death was the storyteller's challenge. Surely for a woman so beloved by her husband and her people, the death must have come as a shocking blow. Grief and jubilation no doubt flowed in equal measure from that momentous birth in Lumbini's grove. We're not asked to grieve or share anyone else's sadness, as Maya's death is presented as a fait accompli, her karmic destiny, the fruit of her merit and long-held wish to be the mother of a buddha. Through all the rationalizations, the *Abhinishkramanasutra* alone states plainly that Maya died as a result of childbirth:

> The Prince Royal now being seven days old, his mother the Queen Maya, being unable to regain her strength or recover the joy she experienced whilst the child dwelt in her womb, gradually succumbed to her weakness and died.[128]

Scholars have speculated that the detail of the right-sided birth could have been the storytellers' spin on a possible caesarean section performed on Maya. This and other surgical procedures were known in ancient cultures including India, although caesarean sections were only performed on dead or dying women in an effort to save the child.[129]

The literature is mixed on the topic of where Maya died, but it appears likely that she never returned to Kapilavastu. Failing from the birth, it is doubtful she would have survived the trip home. The legends say that upon her death, she was immediately transported to a celestial realm where she enjoyed the reverence of the gods. The Sinhalese story wants us to know that at that time she was fortunate enough to attain the body of a male god who became the guardian deity of Suddhodana's palace (nonetheless named Matru, meaning "mother").[130] Early artistic representations portray a triumphal procession returning from Lumbini's grove to Kapilavastu, although mother and child are often absent.[131] Where there is a woman holding a child, it could be Mahaprajapati or a wet nurse holding the baby Buddha, or simply artistic license.

A touching, final moment between Maya and Suddhodana appears in the *Abhinishkramanasutra*. Newly arrived in heaven, she descends in a vision to comfort him and implore him not to grieve for her. She assures him that she is equally as joyous in heaven as she had been during her marvelous pregnancy. Before departing, Maya praises their precious son:

> Freed from all partialities,
> Persevering without interruption,
> Ever thinking aright
> Without confusion from first to last.
> His appearance pure as gold,
> His faculties perfectly under control,
> My son can declare the Law,
> And is worthy of all honor.[132]

As we shall see, Maya persists as a loving presence in the Buddha's life. In magical, mythic fashion, they meet again at pivotal moments, either through her returning to earth or his visiting her in heaven. Maya's love for her son is unbroken by death and has become iconic within the Buddhist tradition as the perfect, unconditional, mother's love.

Mahaprajapati, Goddesses, and Growing Up in the Harem

$\mathcal{F}$rom all the legends we know that Mahaprajapati became the Buddha's adoptive mother, the only mother he ever knew. We learn that she took him to her breast and nursed him when Maya died and loved him as her own son throughout her life. While the stories persist in referring to her as his "aunt" or "foster mother," they make it clear that in every way Mahaprajapati was no less a loving mother than Maya would have been. According to the *Buddhacarita,*

> The queen's sister, who equaled [Maya] in majesty and did not fall below her in affection and tenderness, brought up the prince, who was like a scion of the gods, as if he were her own son.[1]

There is touching symbolism in the birth scene mentioned earlier, where Mahaprajapati gently holds her sister around the waist as Maya grasps the branch of the *shala* tree in Lumbini's grove. In a prophetic sense, the sisters are sharing the birth experience, simultaneously becoming the mother of the Buddha as he enters the world. This was hinted at in prophecies made at their own births—each sister was predicted to become the mother of a universal king. Who knew this would someday mean sharing the same great son?

Around this time, Mahaprajapati herself birthed a son. His name was Nanda and his father was Suddhodana, making him the Buddha's half-brother. Nanda was probably slightly older, since it is said that Mahaprajapati gave him over to a wet nurse when Maya died so that she could nurse the newborn herself. According to some legends, Mahaprajapati also had a daughter, Sundarinanda ("beautiful Nanda").* These siblings rarely appear in the stories, but we know that much later each was ordained and became a disciple of the Buddha. In terms of Suddhodana, we learn that Mahaprajapati, already a consort wife in his harem, became his principal wife and queen after Maya's death. Unfortunately, the legends have very little to say about her during the Buddha's early years at home. What we know about her from this time comes entirely from the Sanskrit tradition, as recounted in the following stories.

Who Will Be My Mother?

Returning to Kapilavastu with his infant son, Suddhodana finds himself a single father with many new responsibilities. Foremost is providing for the care and nurturance of the baby. According to the customs of his clan, it is not entirely up to him who will be his wife's successor as the mother of the prince. Although Suddhodana is deemed king of the Shakyas, matters of importance fall to his council of clan elders, a democratic body of women and men charged with upholding the best interests of their people. The upbringing of the heir to the throne definitely falls within their purview. Having convened the council, Suddhodana broaches the question,

> Now that this babe has lost his mother, who is there we may select to take her place, and act as a foster mother to the child?[2]

The elders agree that they are looking for someone who is loving, kind, and selfless. The story now takes a humorous turn as scores of recently married young women step forward, insisting,

> I will care for the Prince! Please let me take care of him![3]

In their wisdom, the elders conclude that the young women are too foolish and caught up in the vanity of their youth and beauty to care appropriately for the prince. Collectively they conclude that Mahaprajapati, as the infant's maternal aunt, is best suited for the task. Not only would she raise him well,

---

*Mentioned earlier in the verse from the *Therigatha*.

but she is already a favorite of the king. (It is not mentioned here that she is a wife.) With the elders' encouragement, Mahaprajapati accepts the honor of becoming mother to the prince and formally addresses the king:

> As your Majesty commands, my care over the child shall be most constant.[4]

Suddhodana turns his son over to her and appoints thirty-two attendants to the little prince's nursery: eight as wet nurses and eight each to wash, carry, and play with him. The *Abhinishkramanasutra* describes Mahaprajapati's sweet attentiveness to her son:

> She . . . attended him without intermission . . . as the sun tends on the moon during the first portion of each month, till the moon arrives at its fulness. So the child gradually waxed and increased in strength; as the shoot of the . . . tree gradually increases in size, well-planted in the earth, till itself becomes a great tree, thus did the child day by day increase, and lacked nothing.[5]

There is also a description of their loving bond:

> The child causing his loving mother
> Always to abound in most nutritious milk,
> So that even supposing it were not sufficient (naturally),
> It became more than enough (thro' his influence).[6]

In the Pali legends, we're told only that Suddhodana retained nurses to attend to his son. Their qualifications were quite different (and quite sexist), similar to those for the Bodhisattva's mother when Maya was selected. The Burmese legend states it this way:

> Suddhodana, with the tender solicitude of a vigilant father, procured for his beloved offspring nurses exempt from all corporeal defects, and remarkable for their beautiful and graceful appearance.[7]

In the Sinhalese legend, Suddhodana selects one hundred young Shakya "princesses" based entirely on their physical appearance. They must be free from the following "faults":

She was not to be too tall, or the neck of the infant would be stretched; nor too short, or his body would be bent; nor too large, or his legs would be contracted; nor too weak, or his body would not acquire firmness; nor of too full a habit, or her milk would be hot, and cause his skin to become red; nor of too dark a complexion, or her milk would be cold, and cause his flesh to be in lumps, in some parts hard and in others soft.[8]

Be that as it may, many doting women including Mahaprajapati and the appointed nurses would have nurtured the young prince as he grew up in the women's quarters of his father's palace. It should be mentioned that the king himself, while sometimes conflicted or confused by his son's behavior as he grew older, is almost invariably depicted in these early legends as attentive and loving. Indeed, as a parent, Suddhodana was very present in his son's early life and, in his own fatherly way, as much of a nurturing force as the women.

The Voice of the Goddess

An important task for any new Shakya father, especially the king, is to attend to the proper birth rituals for his newborn child. Soon after the birth, there was a naming ceremony, and the baby Bodhisattva was called Siddhartha, meaning "He Who Accomplishes His Aim," auguring his successful life ahead. Suddhodana chose the name because his son's birth had brought untold blessings to his kingdom, including, significantly, the "conatal" or simultaneous births of thousands of Shakya children and beasts, as well as the occurrence of many natural wonders. The names of specific children born concurrently with Siddhartha vary in the different texts, but three who are always identified are Yashodhara, a princess who would become Siddhartha's principal wife; Chandaka, born of one of Suddhodana's concubines, who would become Siddhartha's servant; and Kalodayin,* a trusted childhood friend and later a devoted disciple of the Buddha. That almost all the legends introduce these three characters at the Buddha's birth

* Also known as Kaludayi or Udayi.

sets up their later significance and invites special scrutiny as key players in his life. They will be discussed at length as we go along.

There was also the matter of paying proper homage to the goddess Abhaya who, as we have already learned, presided over the nativity and without whose protection the healthy baby may not have survived. While she has not yet appeared in goddess form, her presence animated the *shala* tree as Maya delivered her son. According to the *Mahavastu*, Abhaya meets the newborn in the Shakya clan temple immediately following the birth. In this story, Maya has not yet died because Suddhodana orders that both queen and prince be taken forthwith from Lumbini's grove to the holy temple. One can imagine that this trip may have served a dual purpose: on the one hand, to propitiate the goddess in gratitude for the healthy baby and to anoint him as a clan member; on the other, to invoke the goddess's intervention in saving Maya's life, as she was clearly succumbing from childbirth. Failing the latter, dying at the feet of the goddess was surely a blessed way to die. The focus turns to the baby as Suddhodana instructs his ministers,

> Now lead the child, who is the strength of the Sakyas, to the temple to worship at the feet of the goddess Abhaya.[9]

This remark is important because it reveals just who, in Suddhodana's mind, should be bowing to whom. Obviously the little prince should show proper reverence to the clan goddess. However, horror ensues, as not only does the Bodhisattva resist entering the temple, he refuses to bow down to the goddess. Instead, he puts his feet forward, suggesting that she should be bowing down to him. Normally this would be an egregious offense, but in her wisdom, Abhaya perceives the superiority of the child and "joyfully" bows her head. The text says,

> Against his will, the great Saviour of the world, the teacher of kings, entered the shrine. But when they would have him salute the goddess with his head, it was his feet that he put forward.
>
> Then the Goddess Abhaya said, "It is not fitting that he should worship me. If he should make obeisance to anyone, that one's head would surely split in seven."[10]

The latter remark reflects the belief that certain destruction would come to anyone, god or human, to whom the Bodhisattva might bow down. That their head would split in seven pieces vividly demonstrates his superiority. In sparing Abhaya that fate, he is showing her his compassion. As a narrative device, this scene signals that the Bodhisattva's birth marks a sea change in the prevailing religious hierarchy. While the goddess detail survives, the story functions to assert primacy of the new Buddhist faith over the indigenous, earth-based goddess religion. Similarly, here and elsewhere in the Buddha's biographical legends, the all-male brahmanical pantheon is consistently portrayed as subordinate to him. In this story, for example, four brahmanical gods are the palanquin bearers conveying Maya and the infant to the temple, while mighty Indra and Brahma form the escort. It has been noted that pre-Indo-Aryan divinities* play a more prominent role in the *Mahavastu* than in other Buddhist works, a testament to its antiquity.

Although the *Mahavastu* variant of this episode is the most detailed, fragments of parallel stories are found in other Sanskrit sources. In the *Abhinishkramanasutra,* the story is almost identical and Abhaya's name is the same, although her gender appears to be male. Of interest in this story is that a woman, rather than his father, presents the baby to Abhaya. Could this have been Maya? Mahaprajapati? The Tibetan Kangyur notes that it was the custom for all newborn Shakya children to be taken to the temple to propitiate the tutelary clan deity, and here again, the deity bows to the Bodhisattva. One can imagine that the clan temple in these stories held a statue or symbol of the deity—perhaps a stone or living tree.

A later pilgrim to Lumbini's grove is said to have met Abhaya in person. In the *Ashokavadana,* Emperor Ashoka† wishes to hear her account of the Buddha's miraculous birth. The goddess appears before him as she is invoked in front of the tree‡ where the nativity took place:

> Let the divine maiden who resides in this *asoka* tree
> and who witnessed the birth of the Buddha

---

* Referring to the early matriarchal culture.

† Reigned as emperor of the Mauryan dynasty in India about two hundred years after the Buddha.

‡ Here the tree is an *ashoka* not a *shala.*

make herself manifest in her own body
so that King Asoka's faith will grow greater still.[11]

After hearing her account, Ashoka makes an offering of one hundred thousand pieces of gold. In the late 1800s, a German archaeologist working in the Lumbini region of Nepal uncovered what he claimed were the remains of Abhaya's temple.[12]

Anyone who is already familiar with the Buddha's biography will have noticed the similarities between Abhaya and the seer Asita, who figures more commonly in popular versions of the legend and who appears in the Pali canon. In the Sanskrit tradition, he appears as a male *rishi* with varying degrees of supernatural powers such as flying through the air and paying visits to gods in the heavenly realms. Learning from these gods of the birth of the miraculous child, he proceeds quickly from his abode in the Himalayas to Suddhodana's palace to see for himself. In some variants the baby extends his feet rather than bow down, thereby averting the catastrophe of the *rishi's* head splitting into seven pieces. Not only does Asita bow down to the Bodhisattva, but so too does Suddhodana—one of four times the king does so over the course of his son's life. Asita is overjoyed that he has met the excellent child, whose arrival on earth had been heralded by the gods:

> This day is born in the world, in the Northern region, just under the Himalaya Mountains in the city of the Sakyas, called Kapilavastu, of a Father Suddhodana, and a Mother Maya, a very beautiful child, perfect in every respect; endowed with the thirty-two superior signs . . . and destined to become completely illuminated, and to preach the perfect Law. Doubtless this child by his Divine wisdom is acquainted with all events, past and future, and will therefore be able to preach the Law, even for our sakes, and determine how we and all sentient creatures may escape the entanglements of sorrow and pain.[13]

With this statement, Asita proclaims positively that the child will grow up to be an exalted buddha. Brahman soothsayers are also consulted at this time and come up with a mixed message (just as they did after Maya's pregnancy dream), proclaiming that the royal heir was bound for greatness, but whether as a great king or a great sage remained to be seen. Asita's prophecy and Suddhodana's stubborn struggle against his son's destiny become a major theme in the legends from this point on. The king is determined to see his son succeed him as regent of the Shakyas and forbids anyone in his kingdom ever to tell the prince of Asita's prophecy. As Siddhartha grows up, Suddhodana does everything in his power to keep his son at home, benevolently retaining the prince within the palace walls while indulging him in every sort of pleasure.

The Pali variants of this story suggest a bridge back to the goddess as the tutelary clan deity. Here the Asita figure is Kaladevala,[14]* a preeminent holy man who serves as Suddhodana's personal religious advisor and the Shakya clan priest. He was the previous king's chief counselor, but since the beginning of Suddhodana's reign, he has lived in retirement as an elder ascetic in the palace garden. Said not to be a follower of Indra or Brahma, his religion is ambiguous, although he has achieved the supernatural powers that come with meditative attainment. In the Sinhalese story, Suddhodana brings the infant to the garden to pay homage to Kaladevala. A temple is not mentioned, yet the priest is seated on a high throne. Upon seeing the baby, he immediately descends and bows down of his own accord, fully cognizant that the child is his superior. After examining the child and recognizing the thirty-two marks of greatness, he too proclaims that the prince will grow up to be a buddha.[15] While we don't hear Abhaya making a prophecy, it may well have been part of her original story. It seems that Abhaya and Kaladevala's roles as clan hierarchs became conflated in the legends. Her gender may well have been an impetus for the change, as the cultural context—both brahmanical and Buddhist—grew increasingly androcentric over time.

One last variant of this story bears noting, chiefly because it offers a rare glimpse of Mahaprajapati as the infant's mother. In the *Lalitavistara,* the Shakya elders tell Suddhodana that it is time for the prince to pay homage in the temple. The king orders a grand celebration and has Kapilavastu festooned with banners and garlands. Musicians strike up their instruments as citizens gather to watch the magnificent procession make its way from the palace. In preparation for the little Bodhisattva's first public event, Mahaprajapati dresses and ornaments him in his finest princely attire. Fully

---

* Asita and Kala are synonyms for "black."

aware of everything going on, the infant smiles and addresses Mahaprajapati affectionately in the following conversation:

> "Mother, where are you taking me?"
> She replied: "Son, I am taking you to the temple."
> The Prince then smiled, laughed, and spoke these verses to his
>   maternal aunt:
>
> "When I was born, this trichiliocosm trembled.
> [The gods and demigods . . .]
> All bowed their heads to my feet and paid homage to me.
>
> "What other god is there who is superior to me,
> Who my mother takes me to worship today?
> I am superior to all the gods; I am the God of Gods.
> There is no other god like me, so how could anyone be superior?
>
> "Still, mother, I will allow worldly customs;
> When beings see my miraculous displays, they will be pleased.
> It will inspire them with great respect,
> And gods and humans will know that I am the God of Gods." [16]

When he is brought into the temple, numerous statues of brahmanical gods become animated and prostrate to him. After a series of miracles, they return to their pedestals, inert once again. As in the *Mahavastu* variant, this story functions to display Buddhism's primacy over a prevailing religion—in this case, brahmanism. The temple goddess has disappeared entirely and been supplanted by the brahmanical pantheon. We will hear from the goddess Abhaya again later in Siddhartha's life as she counsels the grieving Suddhodana over his son's decision to leave home. As we shall see, other pre-Indo-Aryan goddesses pop up every now and then in the Buddha's biographical legends. They are of particular significance here because their presence speaks to the belief system in the region where he grew up. While we'll never really know, it's worthwhile imagining how a more gynocentric—or at least a more gender-balanced—culture may have influenced the young Buddha in his early years before he left home.

Childhood Stories

Large gaps in the Buddha's biography leave a spotty narrative with little or no sense of chronology or connection between the stories that do exist. Nowhere is this more true than during his childhood years. With so much left unsaid and unknown, there are two remaining stories that bear retelling here. The first concerns the presentation of offerings to the infant prince and is found only in the Sanskrit tradition.

At the proper astrological time, the Shakya people hold an offering ceremony for their new prince. The king commissions priceless ornaments from the finest artisans in the land: bracelets, anklets, crowns, necklaces, earrings, armbands, belts, bangles, diadems, and countless other jewelry, all worthy of the gods. The Shakya families also have precious ornaments made as gifts for Siddhartha. On the day of the presentation, a long procession of chariots loaded with gifts winds through the streets of Kapilavastu, with throngs of spectators, particularly women, on every side:

> Countless women, with every kind of ornament upon their person, occupied the tops of the balconies and towers, the windows and the open vestibules, holding flowers in their hands, desirous to behold the Royal Prince, and to scatter the flowers on his person. Moreover, there were crowds of women on each side of the road accompanying the procession with fans to fan his body, and with brushes to clear the road from impediments.[17]

With the king and his company in the lead, Mahaprajapati rides in the royal chariot with Siddhartha on her lap. They are making their way to a sacred garden where the ritual presentation will take place over seven days, after which the tiny prince will be outfitted with innumerable gleaming ornaments. It is a joyous occasion during which the heir to the throne is duly celebrated by all his people and, in time, utterly covered head to toe with jewels. In the end, however, it is the brilliance of the prince himself, his own luster, that eclipses all the bling. The jewels appear as no more than blackened ashes surrounding pure gold. As if in reprimand, the goddess of the sacred garden, Vimala, reveals her vast body before the Shakyas. Scolding them from her sky perch, she points out the foolishness of

gemstones adorning one who is already brilliantly adorned with the merit
of countless lifetimes:

> He is brimming with hundreds of qualities, adorned by his own
>   magnificence;
> Not beautified by ornaments, his body is perfectly stainless.
> The glows of the sun and moon, the stars, jewels, fire,
> [Indra] and Brahma are no longer bright in front of his intense
>   glory.
>
> His body is adorned with signs, the result of previous virtue,
> So why would he need ordinary ornaments made by someone else?
> Remove the ornaments! Do not disturb the One Who Makes the
>   Foolish Wise—
> He, who brings supreme knowledge, does not wear artificial
>   ornaments![18]

Remove the ornaments indeed! In her wisdom, Vimala calls out that
Chandaka, the concubine's son, should be given all the jewels. By that act
of generosity, rather than false ritual, would the Shakyas reap true merit.
With those parting words, the garden goddess showers the baby prince with
flowers and disappears.[19]

The second story has an agricultural theme and is found in all the
legends, with significant variants. In the Pali tradition, it begins with a
ritual celebration: the Shakyas' annual ploughing festival. As ever on these
occasions, Kapilavastu is festooned with banners and the citizens turn out
in their finest attire. Toting their picnic feasts, they head to the countryside.
This big event marks the sowing of the season's first seeds as thousands of
gaily bedecked ploughs pulled by as many pairs of bullocks crisscross the
farmlands and break up the earth. As king, Suddhodana presides over
the festivities, taking the helm of the most magnificent plough of all. His
entire royal household has similarly journeyed outside the town to join the
picnickers, including five-month-old Siddhartha tended by one hundred
nurses. Captivated by the excitement, the nurses leave the baby on a cushion
asleep under the shade of a rose-apple tree and go off to get a better view of
the spectacle. Unfortunately, they forget about him and don't come back
for hours. Meanwhile, the little Bodhisattva has been sitting up, cross-
legged, blissfully immersed in deep meditation. Despite the movement of

the sun across the sky, the shadow cast over him by the tree has remained miraculously unmoved. The errant nurses finally return in haste and are dumbfounded to see the prince still protected from the hot sun by the tree's shade. When Suddhodana hears news of the miracle, he is reminded of his son's greatness and bows down to him for a second time.[20] The Sinhalese story adds a detail where the king weeps with joy and says to his son,

> Had your royal mother been here, and seen you, she would have made an offering to you of her life; but now that I am left alone, why do you exhibit to me these wonders?[21]

While we cannot know what is intended by his question, it would seem Suddhodana is referring to Maya and not Mahaprajapati. His touching display of emotion suggests that his joy for his son has stirred up grief for his deceased wife.

The Sanskrit tradition spins the ploughing story quite differently. Here the emotional content suggests despair rather than celebration. Siddhartha is much older, perhaps a teenager or young man, when he accompanies his father and a troupe of Shakya princes to the countryside to view the ploughing of the fields. There is no festive attire in this story; the ploughmen are naked from the waist up, laboring strenuously in the hot sun, their filthy bodies running with sweat. Hungry and thirsty, panting with exhaustion, the oxen strain under their heavy burdens, rumps streaming with blood from constant goading. Flies and insects swarm their snot-smeared faces and infest their open, oozing wounds. Birds throng their backs in a feeding frenzy to peck the bugs. Further, all kinds of small creatures are killed and injured as the plough blades stir up the earth. Siddhartha has never seen such a horrific sight and is overcome with sorrow. In the Kangyur, he learns that the ploughmen are the property of the king and forthwith sets them free to "live in joy." He similarly liberates the oxen, invoking them to "eat the sweetest grass and drink the purest water." Deeply moved, he then goes off to meditate under the rose-apple tree.[22]

Other versions take this story further, and here they insert a magical episode. Five *rishis* are flying through the air en route to the Himalayas only to find their flight pattern disturbed by the powerful aura emanating from a grove of rose-apple trees. Inflated with self-importance, they become grumpy and decide to investigate. Who is this child "blazing with glory," mightier than the gods? It is now that the goddess of the grove shows up to explain things. Like Vimala, she understands the significance of the Bodhisattva's presence and frames the larger picture:

> It is the Sakya Prince, descendant of the best of kings, who shines
>   like the dawn;
> This wise, supreme man has a moon-like face with the beauty of a
>   blooming lotus.
> He, whom gods, naga kings, gandharvas, and yaskas revere, is in the
>   park, concentrating;
> His power, gained from merit in millions of lives, is thwarting your
>   miracles.[23]

The *rishis* rejoice at the tidings and pay homage to the child. The goddess-as-tree also bows down to him, suggesting that it was her doing all along that the shadow did not move. Here again, we find a sylvan goddess who represents Siddhartha's best interests and enables his progress as an emerging buddha. Meanwhile, Suddhodana has lost track of his son and frantically dispatches search parties to locate him. In a rare instance where we find Siddhartha's parents in the same story, Mahaprajapati also has been searching and finally, distraught with worry, implores the king to find their son. It is here that Suddhodana comes across Siddhartha peacefully meditating under the shade of the rose-apple tree and once again prostrates to him.[24] That the overall point of the ploughing story is the suffering of sentient creatures is dramatically borne out in the poetry of the *Buddhacarita,* where the scene takes place shortly before the disheartened prince renounces worldly life and begins his search for truth.[25]

The Harem as Family

By all accounts, Siddhartha was raised in the women's quarters of his father's palace. There are no stories that directly relate his experiences there, although many accounts reference harems and harem life in general. This is a window into a distant past and way of life, not a concoction by sexist chroniclers, although their brushstrokes can certainly be felt in the telling of some stories. In contemporary terms, of course, the notion of females in a single household living separately from the men—or much worse, women held as concubines or sexual slaves—is galling and abhorrent, no less so because such injustices persist today. Yet holding such (rightful) feelings can be more of a deterrent than a tool in understanding the lives of women in ancient times. Present-day views may not be a fit with what was happening then. While historians would want to source their evidence more broadly, there is much to be learned about women and their experiences from stories of the harem in early Buddhist literature. We'll stay within those boundaries here, allowing the harem stories to speak for themselves, both about the women who lived in them and about the broader cultural context from which the stories arose.

Harem life by its very nature is hidden. While we don't have a written record about Suddhodana's private household, we can put together clues to get an idea of what it was like. Since the Buddha-to-be grew up in the women's quarters, we can imagine that there must have been influences from that world that carried over into his later life. Of most significance is simply that he grew up in an insular community of women, a detail that may account for the virtual silence in the legends about his childhood years— not because anything was necessarily redacted, but simply because stories were not generated outside the palace walls, and early traditions had no interest in this phase of his life. By the time he grew up and became famous, storytellers would draw from highlights of his life—his birth, renunciation, enlightenment, and *parinirvana*—rather than his childhood to construct his hagiography. From the legends, we know that Siddhartha's family environment was typical of other aristocratic households of the time, a private enclave within a larger "palace" compound, removed from the outside world, and privy only to the family patriarch; in this case, Suddhodana, the king and Siddhartha's father.

While the terms are often used interchangeably in the stories, a distinction will be made here between the harem and the women's quarters. To Western ears, *harem* suggests an exotic sort of brothel, and indeed, high-ranking patriarchs generally had multiple wives and concubines or consorts (according to the exuberance of the storyteller, they often numbered in the thousands, even tens of thousands—exaggeration that no doubt intended to insinuate the patriarch's wealth and virility). The harem in this sense served the sensual/sexual pleasures of the patriarch and, as such, comprised a sector within the larger women's quarters. As used here, the term *women's quarters* generally refers to family quarters where *all* the women lived, including the consorts as well as grannies, wives, unmarried or widowed female relatives, female servants or slaves (some stories mention eunuchs), and young children whose mothers lived there—both girls and boys, the latter until they came of age. An emblem of class and wealth, the women's quarters would constitute the patriarch's personal domain of family and leisure. On the flip side, it provided a safe haven for women in a culture where they were without identity and exceedingly vulnerable if not under the protection of a man. Further, the women's quarters would provide a "village" environment for the patriarch's wives and children, where children of different mothers (the presumed father being the patriarch) would grow up as playmates and where biological lines could easily blur among the women when it came to mothering and looking after the kids.

Beyond mentioning principal wives, the legends normally don't individualize the women in a patriarch's household. We do hear though that they were accomplished musicians; that music flowed continuously in the harem and women's quarters; and there was always dancing, singing, and the cadence of drums. The patriarch's principal wife would preside over this domain as the queen consort. In Suddhodana's court, that would have been Maya until she died. Then, as junior or cowife, Mahaprajapati would have stepped into the role. It was in this milieu among the women and children that the young Siddhartha spent the first fifteen or so years of his life.

It's apropos here to comment further on the two boys, Chandaka and Kalodayin, whose births were said to have taken place simultaneously with Siddhartha's. Conatal births suggest auspiciousness or special status, although it's not always clear why. As we shall see, as Siddhartha's personal servant, Chandaka becomes a beloved and important figure in his life story, especially in the Sanskrit sources. This is probably not random, since a close look at the stories reveals that Chandaka was often referred to as the son of one of Suddhodana's concubines or slaves. Not only would this mean that Siddhartha and Chandaka grew up together in the same household from birth, but that they were likely half-brothers.* No wonder there was always a special bond between them.

Similarly, the figure of Kalodayin bears a second look. He too is touted throughout the legends as particularly trustworthy and beloved, not only

---

* As the king's "natural" child, Chandaka (and others born in similar circumstances) would have no royal status.

to Siddhartha, but also to the king. He is described as being close friends with Chandaka; in later years, they took ordination together with the Buddha. His maternal line is obscure, although the stories often remark that he and Siddhartha grew up together from infancy, even that they made "mud-pies" together as little boys.[26] In later years, every time Suddhodana needed a trusted envoy to take a message to his son, it was always Kalodayin (sometimes with Chandaka) he chose. Similarly, during his ministry, the Buddha entrusted Kalodayin with personal family matters, acknowledging that they shared a lifelong bond. As an adult, Kalodayin freely visited the women's quarters of Siddhartha's household, which would be a huge taboo if he were not considered part of the extended family.[27] Sources say variously that Kalodayin was the son of Suddhodana's minister or his priest. Son of his priest could mean that Kaladevala, mentioned earlier, was his father, which is supported by the similarities in their names. Since the priest was in service to the king, it would make sense that his son would be considered part of the royal household and be raised in the women's quarters of the palace.

There are many different ways to imagine how and why these story fragments arose. In any case, evidence strongly suggests that the deep lifelong friendship between Kalodayin, Chandaka, and Siddhartha was formed during their childhood years growing up together in the women's quarters of Suddhodana's palace.

3

Yashodhara, Mrigi Gautami, and the Harem Wives

*A*sita's prophecy that young Siddhartha's destiny was to become a saint rather than a king rested heavily in Suddhodana's heart as the prince was growing up. On the one hand, Suddhodana loved his son and feared losing him, while on the other, the king had a responsibility to the Shakya clan to provide an heir and ensure the continuity of the noble line. In Suddhodana's mind, his own happiness and that of his people fell squarely on Siddhartha's shoulders. Besides, what could possibly be the allure of a mendicant's life? Every possible luxury and pleasure was at his son's bidding.

After witnessing the miracle under the rose-apple tree and the fearsome power of his son's meditative concentration, the king became even more concerned that Siddhartha would choose the religious life. When the prince was twelve, Suddhodana summoned the brahman soothsayers to ask what would provoke his son to leave home. They named "four sights": old age, sickness, death, and a holy man. Were the prince to witness these things, he would surely renounce the world. Suddhodana vowed this would never happen and cleared Kapilavastu of the dreaded objects for a distance of several kilometers. Posting sentries at every gate, he redoubled his efforts to keep his son at home.[1]

But such drastic measures may not have been needed so soon. An important stage in the prince's life was coming up, and asceticism couldn't have been further from his mind: Siddhartha was becoming interested in girls. Legends concerning this time—his coming of age until his leaving home at twenty-nine—abound with tales of courtship, marriage (more than one), and the prince's harem life. To varying degrees in the different traditions, he is portrayed as a virile and sexually active young man. This may be disturbing to traditionalists who prefer to think of the Buddha as being monkish his entire life. Indeed, that version of events is often found (or understood) in accounts where his life before enlightenment is largely ignored. His youthful, libidinous phase (which ended abruptly when he left home) is treated briefly, if cryptically, in the Pali tradition, where early monk editors were likely uncomfortable with this aspect of the teacher's biography and chose to alter or suppress the details. Siddhartha's sexuality is less hidden in the Sanskrit texts, but there we sometimes find a different sort of prudishness: we are reminded that he was a bodhisattva, so he could display sexual behavior without experiencing actual lust or attachment.

Most useful perhaps is simply remembering that under all the story layers, the Buddha was human. He experienced ordinary feelings and navigated his way through ordinary human struggles. This notion should fuel rather than detract from the power of his life story. From the cultural context of his time and status, we would expect him to wind up with multiple wives and a harem, just like his father. When we are introduced to him as a young man, he is encountering his first feelings of lust and love. The *Lalitavistara* even has him sneaking out with Chandaka to meet some girls. Chandaka says,

> Young Prince, come on!
> Let's go and take a look at the forest.
> What use is staying in the house like a priest?
> Come on, let's go call on some girls.[2]

And off they go, unnoticed and, as the text points out, without Siddhartha asking his parents' permission. Sounds like teenage behavior just about anywhere.

Courtship in Kapilavastu

As Siddhartha came of age,* the king became obsessed with securing his son's patrimony. Like his father, Simhahanu, before him, Suddhodana took

---

*Probably around sixteen.

this responsibility very seriously. Not only the future of his family, but the future of the entire Shakya clan was at stake. As a first step, he had three separate palaces built for his son, one for each season of the year (hot, cold, and rainy). Here the young prince would set up his household, which, according to the aristocratic conventions of the time, meant establishing his own harem and family. No expense was spared. Luxuriously appointed and festooned with flowers, these residences included a train of royal courtiers who attended to the prince's every whim: preparing the purest food; dressing, anointing, and bathing him; perfuming his garments; weaving garlands for his hair. It could not have appeared more idyllic. The Buddha himself described the extravagances of his upbringing to his disciples in later years. Here is a sampling of colorful verses from the *Mahavastu* that describe his childhood:

> I was most delicately brought up, monks. And while I was being thus delicately brought up, my Sakya father provided me with the means of enjoying the five varieties of sensual pleasure, namely dance, song, music, orchestra and women, that I might divert, enjoy and amuse myself.
>
> I was most delicately brought up, monks. And while I was being thus delicately brought up, my Sakya father provided me with various means of conveyance, elephants, horses, boats and palanquins, that I might divert, enjoy and amuse myself. . . .
>
> I was most delicately brought up, monks. And while I was being thus delicately brought up, my Sakya father had a sunshade held over me when I went [outdoors] lest the heat, dust or light torment me, and so that I might divert, enjoy and amuse myself. [3]

It is a recurring theme in the legends that beautiful women were considered the strongest weapon in the arsenal designed to keep Siddhartha contented and at home. Suddhodana reportedly installed tens of thousands of consorts in each palace for the prince's pleasure. This was not just the king's idea; it came also from the Shakya elders, the council of women and men he had consulted earlier concerning a mother for his son. The elders were as mindful as the king of Asita's prediction and were equally intent on lavishing Siddhartha with every possible indulgence in order to keep him home. [4] Losing the king's only heir would be disastrous to the clan.* They instructed the king,

> You ought, O King! To construct another Palace for the Prince, and let there be prepared there every accommodation for voluptuous pleasures, with women and hand-maidens; so the prince will give up the idea of leaving his home and becoming a recluse. [5]

Now we're talking about the harem as the separate, "adults-only" area of the women's quarters, often described as being on the uppermost story of the palace. The following is a rare description of what it was actually like behind the gossamer veils of Siddhartha's harem. It is there that the prince–cum–Buddha-to-be, still caught in the net of worldly desires, indulged in very human pleasures as a young man. The *Abhinishkramanasutra* relates that

> Suddhodana . . . caused a vast hall to be constructed, with a half-subdued light . . . in which matters might be only half observed as it were, and adapted for secret pleasures at any time; . . .
>
> Thus then the Prince passed his time in the midst of a hundred thousand most beautiful and accomplished women, enjoying every species of delight and receiving every service and attention at their hands, whilst they, adorned with every kind of ornament of gold, silver, and precious stones, etc., conspired to amuse and gratify him with music and dancing, even as [Indra] participates in every sort of pleasure at the hands of his attendants, sometimes chatting with one in words of soft dalliance, glancing . . . smiling . . . embracing . . . sighing, ogling . . . indulging in every kind of soft caress. . . . Thus! thus did the Prince pass his time with the beautiful women of his harem, and receive every possible pleasure, without leaving his palace. [6]

Clearly the arts of love were what the harem was all about. From a Buddhist perspective, it serves as a metaphor for the ties to worldly existence that must be cut in order to become free.

---

* Suddhodana and Mahaprajapati's son, Nanda, is not mentioned as a possible heir until much later in the legend.

Next came the task of finding a wife for the young Bodhisattva. Suddhodana called on the Shakya families to put forward their daughters as potential
candidates. The royal tradition was that one maiden would be selected for
marriage, while the remaining contenders would become consorts in the
harem. The bride would become the principal wife and consort, as well
as presumably the mother of the next heir. But Suddhodana's proposition
fell flat. The Shakyas were unimpressed. The young prince, they claimed,
was unfit for marriage. He had spent too much time "among the women"
growing up in the harem, and even now, he squandered his days with the
consorts. As a result, they said, Siddhartha never learned the manly skills
requisite for a proper husband, much less a future king. The Pali tradition
has them stating,

> O, King! Thy son is of proper birth, and his appearance is admirable;
> but so far as we know he has never learned anything, and has no
> knowledge or accomplishments. Therefore we hesitate to offer our
> daughters to him![7]

The Sinhalese account is particularly scathing:

> The prince is very delicate; he is also young; even to this day he has
> not learnt a single science; if hereafter there should be any war, he
> would be unable to contend with the enemy; he has not the means
> of maintaining our daughters; we cannot, therefore, consent to send
> them to one who is so utterly destitute of every endowment that he
> ought to possess.[8]

In the *Lalitavistara,* even the gods complain that the prince spent too much
time with his consorts![9]

These passages come across as quite humorous. Turned down in his
quest for a daughter-in-law, Suddhodana becomes dejected. We can feel
his sense of parental failure, even embarrassment. What to do? Enter the
prince. Siddhartha assures his father that his superiority in all subjects of
learning and athletics is a foregone conclusion. The implication is that
his many lifetimes as a bodhisattva have provided ample training in these
areas.[10] As proof, he calls for a tournament in seven days and challenges all
the Shakya youth from Kapilavastu and surrounding provinces to compete

against him. The young men will vie for excellence in such skills as archery, swordsmanship, wrestling, swimming, running, and combat. Some sources add writing and mathematics.* The big day arrives to great excitement. From near and far, Shakyas take to the grandstands, as the eligible young ladies, hearts aflutter, look on in suspense. Our prince prevails, of course, and wins the beautiful girl. This story with variants appears in all the legends and is our introduction to the young Shakya maiden Yashodhara, Siddhartha's principal wife.

Who Is Yashodhara?

That Siddhartha had a wife is undisputed in the literature. What we know about her, however, varies widely across the traditions. The Pali canon essentially disappears her, just as it does Maya, although it acknowledges that the Buddha had a son with vague references to a wife.† Most sources call her Yashodhara, although there are minor variants. We know that she was Shakya both because the legends make that clear and because the Shakyas were very insular and never married outside their clan. As usual, the genealogy is confusing and contradictory. In Pali sources, she is the Buddha's first cousin, the daughter of Suddhodana's sister, Amita, and her husband, Suprabuddha.‡ In this scenario, her brother is said to be Devadatta, a murderous villain who is obsessed with subverting the Buddha's power and influence. In other traditions, she is the daughter of Mahanaman, Suddhodana's loyal chief minister (who rode out to Lumbini on the occasion of the Buddha's birth). Elsewhere, she is the daughter of Dandapani, a wealthy merchant in Kapilavastu. Her mother never appears in these stories, nor is there any mention of sisters.

What's striking about Yashodhara is that she shows up a lot in the Buddha's biography—not as a passive, stock character dotted through the narrative, but as a fairly believable woman with admirable agency caught in a difficult marriage. Difficult indeed. Imagine marrying a prince who

---

* There is little evidence that the Buddha had a formal education.

† A significant exception appears in a little-known segment of the *Khuddhaka Nikaya*, where we find the hagiography (*apadana*) of Yashodhara as both a nun and the Buddha's wife. See chapter 7.

‡ Suprabuddha and Amita are also sometimes said to be the parents of Maya.

becomes an ascetic who turns out to be the Buddha. When Siddhartha goes off on his spiritual journey, she doesn't disappear from the narrative but spawns her own stories of psychological process and struggle. Clearly she was an evocative character who caught the imaginations of early storytellers. When we first meet her, she appears as a resolute young woman as much in pursuit of the handsome Bodhisattva as he is in pursuit of her.

Yashodhara and Siddhartha

We return to the teenagers in Kapilavastu, where we find tales of romance and arranged marriage. Our first story comes from the *Abhinishkramana-sutra.*

Back in the palace, Suddhodana is pondering how best to secure a daughter-in-law. His stubborn young son makes this prospect particularly daunting. A traditional, arranged marriage would surely backfire. Like any spirited teenager, Siddhartha is unlikely to go along with his father's plan for his future. In a passage any parent can relate to, we hear the king's innermost thoughts and catch him strategizing:

> If I do not go to the [prince] and consult with him about taking a wife, then I shall but provoke him to disobey and thwart my design; and again, if I do go to him and consult, then I fear he will take the subject deeply to heart, and in the end not fall in with my views. What then shall I do?[11]

In the end, Dad comes up with a skillful solution: set up an offhand scenario where Siddhartha meets every young maiden in the clan, one by one. Trusted spies will be posted strategically to observe any amorous encounters and report back to the king. Whichever maiden most strikes Siddhartha's fancy will be put forward as a marriage candidate.

The king orders a fabulous array of jeweled ornaments made of silver and gold, then sends messengers throughout the land proclaiming that in one week the prince himself will distribute these to all the Shakya maidens. The cry goes out for them to assemble:

Let all the ladies, therefore, come as they are bidden, to the palace gate![12]

On the appointed day, the young ladies arrive bedecked in all their finery, and the handsome prince, seated on a throne, receives them one at a time. So far, so good. However, the girls, though anxious to receive their gifts, are far too shy even to look at Siddhartha. With bowed heads, they quickly pass him by. Just as things are winding down and it seems that Suddhodana's plan may fail, Yashodhara shows up surrounded by a retinue of attendants. With confidence and swagger, she steps up to the prince, looks him in the eye, and says,

Your Royal Highness! What gift or costly ornament have you for me?

Uh-oh, the prince has run out of goodies. He tells her,

You have come too late.[13]

Yashodhara is not happy with this response. Banter ensues, until finally the prince offers her a costly signet ring off his own finger. She remains dissatisfied, although it is not clear why, even as he further offers her his priceless pearl necklace. She stomps off, and we're left with a *Jataka* tale to explain that the discord in their relationship dates from previous lifetimes. The story segues to the athletic tournament, described earlier, when Siddhartha finally wins her over. Marriage follows, though the plotline advances straight to their wedding night, where we're told,

They indulged themselves in every species of nuptial delight.[14]

And further,

Yasodhara, the daughter of the great Minister,
Whose fame was known in every land,
Selecting a fortunate day for her marriage,
Approached and entered within the royal precincts,
And afforded the Prince every sort of pleasure.[15]

In the *Lalitavistara,* the young couple's courtship story is similar but with significant added elements. Here the prince is in full Bodhisattva persona, which is reflected in his deliberations about a prospective marriage. Though allegedly not attached to worldly pleasures, he acknowledges that he must follow the lead of previous bodhisattvas and participate in ordinary married life:

> The wise bodhisattvas who came before me,
> All were known to have wives, children, and harems,
> Yet they were not enamored with desire, nor deprived of the bliss of
>   meditation.
> I too will emulate their merits.[16]

On behalf of the Shakyas, his father asks him to choose a bride from among the five hundred or so available maidens. The prince asks for seven days to decide and launches into a lengthy account of the qualities a suitable wife must have. Another list. As with the requirements for Maya, this list tips the scales toward sexism ("she should dress with modesty," "she should lovingly obey"), although notably, attributes idealizing her body do not come up. The list mostly comprises qualities related to character, stipulating aspects of perfection that more or less align with Buddhist ideals of ethical body, speech, and mind. Bodhisattva or not, however, the prince does not fail to mention lovemaking: "She should be as adept as a courtesan in knowing the arts of love."[17] Most remarkable here is the practically unheard-of, stated disregard for caste or family, especially because it comes from the king.* Suddhodana makes the following declaration as he dispatches a messenger to take Siddhartha's list of requirements around the kingdom to find a match:

> Whether she is a girl of royal caste or priestly caste,
> Merchant caste or servant caste—
> Report to me whichever girl
> Possesses these qualities!
>
> My son is not enthralled
> By family or caste;

---

* A wholesale break with Shakya custom.

His mind delights in
Good qualities, truth, and righteousness.[18]

Demonstrated here is authentic Buddhism's egalitarianism, an absence
of bias that extended to women as well as caste and was modeled by the
Buddha throughout his teaching career. Also of interest in this story is that
Yashodhara is portrayed as literate.* From the messenger's letter, she reads
out loud the prince's list of desirable qualities and, with delight, claims her
candidacy:

> Since I have all of these suitable qualities,
> May this handsome and gentle Prince be my husband!
> If he consents, there should be no delay,
> Or I will end up with an inferior, ordinary man.[19]

The story then meanders through the jewelry and tournament episodes to
arrive at the point of marriage, where Yashodhara is named foremost wife in
Siddhartha's harem:

> In order to conform to worldly conventions, the Bodhisattva
> dwelt among 84,000 women and showed himself to partake of the
> amorous games with pleasure. Among the 84,000 women, the Sakya
> girl [Yashodhara] was consecrated as the foremost wife.[20]

In a startling postscript, the chapter concludes with a lengthy description
of Yashodhara's first challenge as principal consort. Harem protocol
apparently required that women veil their faces.† Yashodhara refuses to do
this, to the dismay of both her parents-in-law and the other harem women:

> She did not cover her face. So people criticized her and spoke badly
> of her, saying, "A new wife is supposed to be covered, but this one is
> always exposed."[21]

Responding to their criticism, Yashodhara squares off in front of everyone

---

* In the *Lalitavistara,* her name is Gopa.
† This detail is not mentioned in other stories.

and in wise, elegant verse reprimands them for the shallowness of their thinking:

> A noble being shines when uncovered,
> Whether sitting, standing, or walking,
> Like a precious gem beaming,
> Radiant on the pinnacle of a standard. . . .

> A noble one without evil
> Shines perpetually,
> Whereas an immature being who commits evil
> Never shines no matter what [she] wears. . . .

> Those who control their bodies thus control all physical faults;
> Those who control their speech never confuse their words;
> Those with guarded senses are mentally composed and serene.
> What good is it to cover the face of such beings?

> Others may be covered in a thousand garments,
> But if their minds are revealed to lack shame and modesty
> And if they have no good qualities and lack truthful speech,
> Then they move through the world more naked than naked.

> There are those who conceal their minds and restrain their senses,
> Who are satisfied with their husbands and do not pine after others.
> When they shine unconcealed, like the sun and the moon,
> What good is it to cover their faces?

> Furthermore, the great sages, those who know the thoughts
>   of others,
> And the assemblies of gods all know my thoughts.
> They know my discipline, qualities, restraint, and carefulness;
> So why should I veil my face?[22]

With that speech, she sets the record straight about who's boss in the harem. Even more startling is the response from Yashodhara's father-in-law. Indeed a great man, Suddhodana, is so overjoyed by her rebellious words that he offers her gifts of fine clothing and costly jewels, declaring,

> Just as my son is adorned with good qualities,
> His bride too is radiant with her own qualities.
> That these two pristine beings have come together
> Is just like butter and clarified butter.[23]

That he, the king and patriarch, is seen to rejoice at Yashodhara's stubborn defiance, not to mention breach of protocol (in the context of a *harem*, no less) is truly noteworthy. Needless to say, examples of women asserting themselves are rare in early Buddhist literature, but even rarer are instances of men praising them for it.

From the Sinhalese tradition, we're told that Siddhartha and Yashodhara married under more constrained circumstances. As the prince turns sixteen, Suddhodana decides it is time for the young man to marry. With aggression not seen elsewhere, the king demands Yashodhara's hand for his son from her father, Suprabuddha, king in Devadaha.* Suprabuddha refuses, though his unwillingness has nothing to do with Siddhartha's qualifications. He says the prince will break her heart, indicating that he has heard Asita's prophecy. Suprabuddha reasons that since Siddhartha is destined to become a recluse, he will be abandoning Yashodhara eventually, and she will become a widow. Thus, he refuses to send his daughter back to Kapilavastu with Suddhodana's messengers. Yashodhara, meanwhile, hears of this exchange and vehemently defies her father. She will marry none other than Siddhartha, she declares, even if he were to become a recluse the day after their marriage. A solution may be hatching except the prince, who has had nothing to do with the proceedings until now, agrees with Suprabuddha, saying he has no desire for the kingdom and is fine with losing Yashodhara. Not exactly a passionate love story. Undeterred, Suddhodana sends forces to Devadaha, takes Yashodhara by force, and declares that she will be Siddhartha's principal queen.† This peculiar story ends with a gem—a description of Siddhartha and Yashodhara's wedding:

---

* Not to be confused with Maya's father.

† This is an extremely rare example of aggression on the part of Suddhodana and the Shakyas.

> [The king] placing [the bride and groom] on a mound of silver, . . .
> poured the oil of consecration upon them from three conches, one
> gold, another of silver, and the third a shell opening to the right
> hand; after which he bound upon their heads the royal diadem and
> delivered over to them the whole of his kingdom.[24]

The last remark is curious and echoes Maya and Suddhodana's wedding.
It's never well explained in the texts, but the marriage ceremony appears to
mark an essential level of royal investiture for the heir apparent.[25] This would
further explain the king's seeming obsession with Siddhartha's marriage. We
saw a similar obsession earlier when King Simhahanu vigorously pursued a
wife for the sixteen-year-old Suddhodana. Suddhodana reigns until death
as an old man, but his concern over his successor is a recurring theme up to
the end.

Yashodhara in the Jataka *Tales*

We learn more about Yashodhara and her relationship with her husband
from *Jataka* tales that appear in the Sanskrit tradition. As with most
past-life stories, they don't add much, if any, useful detail to the this-life
biographical narrative, but they can be helpful in illuminating themes and
emotional content that have already been introduced. As we shall see here
and again later on, Yashodhara, more than any other figure in the Buddha
legend, is remembered (or forgotten) with ambivalence. She is also assigned
more *Jataka* stories than any other female figure, which may provide clues as
to what that ambivalence was all about.

There is always tension in her stories, as if the truth of her historical
story, whatever that may have been, strains against an idealized Buddha
legend, as if she were the miscreant whose character must be harmonized or
redacted to make the narrative flow. But should we be surprised? Like her
husband, Yashodhara was only human. Her life was clearly very challenging.
The *Jatakas* display a complex composite of her character: loving wife, angry
wife, adulteress, courtesan, murderess, as examples (Siddhartha is no angel
in these stories either). We'll look at a few of these tales that tie back to the
narrative of the youthful Yashodhara and Siddhartha, beginning with a love
story. This is called the *Siri Jataka*.

Once upon a time in an imaginary town there lived a brahman who was the master of all the religious texts, which he taught to five hundred young brahman disciples. Renowned for his superior knowledge, the brahman was invited to travel a great distance across the sea to perform a certain sacrifice for a rich merchant. Deciding to send a proxy instead, he asked his disciples who among them would like to undertake this arduous journey. That disciple, he said, would receive as payment the master's beautiful daughter, Siri, in marriage. This was great news to one clever, energetic young student because he was already deeply in love with Siri. He readily volunteered. His teacher gave him a letter to deliver, and soon he departed on a ship to cross the great ocean. The voyage was uneventful, and when the disciple was ready to return, the rich merchant gave him a large parcel containing precious gems, gold, and silver to be given in gratitude to the brahman master. Once again the disciple set out by boat, but this time, misfortune struck. The package accidentally fell into the sea and was lost. There was no way he would be winning the lovely Siri now. Upon reflection, he determined the only solution was to drain the sea entirely of water. Standing on the shoreline, he took a copper bucket and began in earnest to empty the ocean. Soon enough, the water goddess became alarmed and, appearing in front of him, asked him just what he thought he was doing. As he tried to explain, she berated him for his foolishness and asked him to stop immediately lest he harm all the water creatures. However, his love for Siri was irrepressible. He said,

> I would not desist even before a raging fire; I would overturn the earth and moon and stars.[26]

Impressed, the goddess retrieved the precious package for him. The young brahman returned home and happily won his beloved Siri. He, of course, would later be reborn as Siddhartha, and Siri was a past life of Yashodhara.[27]

A second story hearkens back to the jewelry giveaway where Siddhartha irritated Yashodhara when he ran out of ornaments at the end of the event and had nothing to offer her. Much less savory than the previous story, it provides an example of the sometimes weird or ghoulish plotlines typical of the *Jataka* genre. This tale is framed as told by the Buddha later in his life to his disciples to explain why Yashodhara remained so displeased with him after the jewelry incident. He says it was not the first time and recounted the following past-life tale.

Long ago, in the city of Benares, a jealous king banished his son from the kingdom. Taking his wife with him, the prince built a grass hut in a forest in the Himalayas where they lived on roots, fruits and the flesh of deer and wild hogs. One day when the prince was away, a cat caught and killed a fat lizard, which he threw down in front of the princess. Disgusted, she would not touch it. When the prince came back, he asked her where the dead lizard had come from. She told him, and he rebuked her for not cooking it, then set about skinning and cooking it himself. Finally, he hung it on a tree branch. The wife took a pitcher and went out to fetch water, promising to prepare a meal when she got back. Meanwhile, she began coveting the cooked lizard, thinking that it might be delicious after all. While she was gone, the prince reflected that the lizard had disgusted her, and she was not even willing to touch it, much less cook it. Therefore, why should he share it now that he had cooked it himself? So he ate the lizard. The princess returned and asked what had happened to it. Prevaricating, the prince replied that the lizard had jumped up and run away. The princess was smarter than that, knowing that a cooked lizard tied to a tree could not run off. So she became sorrowful, concluding that because he had lied to her, the prince must not love her anymore. Not long afterward, the king died, and his ministers fetched the prince and princess from the forest to return to rule the kingdom. At his investiture, the new king lavished every sort of treasure on his wife—jewels, necklaces, and the finest raiment. When she did not seem satisfied, he gave her even more. Finally, perplexed, he asked her why nothing could please her. Because of the lizard, she replied, and reminded him of his falsehood about the lizard running away. So concludes the *Jataka of the Lizard.* Of course, the prince and princess here are past lives of Siddhartha and Yashodhara. Just a story, but one can't help but notice that she is the one cast in a negative light when he is the one who fibbed![28]

Junior Wives

That Siddhartha had more than one wife is no secret in the early literature. Stories of additional wives, even additional weddings, appear patently in the Sanskrit sources. However, much less is said about these women than about Yashodhara, and the details are often confusing and contradictory. The Pali sources name only one wife, Yashodhara, although most of the additional wives named in the Sanskrit sources also appear in the Pali sources, just not as wives. It should be noted that the term *wife* can be used loosely in the stories in the sense that all women in a royal harem are sometimes referred to as wives of the patriarch. Harem wives may also be referred to collectively in the texts as "consorts" and sometimes "dancing girls." Suddhodana's harem wives are sometimes called his "queens," and Siddhartha's are his "princesses." However, in addition to his harem, it would appear from the stories that Siddhartha likely had three official wives: one chief wife and at least two junior wives.[29]

For many, it might seem unpalatable to think of the Buddha in his preenlightenment years as having had a harem and multiple wives. While this version of events goes against the grain of the conventional Buddha legend, it should not be surprising. Polygamy was commonplace during the Buddha's era and de rigueur in royal households during that time. The practice is widely referenced in Indian Sanskrit as well as Buddhist Sanskrit literature.[30] We already know that Suddhodana had two wives—the Buddha's mother, Maya, and her sister, Mahaprajapati—in addition to his harem. Two kings who appear later in the Buddha legend, King Bimbisara and King Prasenajit, are described as having similar large, polygamous households.

Note that this is the historical period and region that gave rise to the *Kama Sutra*,* a classic Sanskrit handbook on the arts of love and lovemaking that gives detailed pointers on the etiquette and responsibilities of the patriarch, principal wife, junior wives, and harem. It is written as a guide for both women and men. Millennia later, and culturally a universe apart, readers can discover a trove of insights into sex and love in relationships and family life during this ancient time. For example, the following passage explains when a cowife is needed:

> The addition of a co-wife takes place when the first is frigid, promiscuous or a bringer of bad luck; if she cannot have children or repeatedly only has daughters; or if the husband is fickle-minded and capricious. The first wife should preclude this from the beginning

---

* About 400 B.C.E.–200 C.E.

by demonstrating her devotion, virtue and proficiency. If she cannot have children, she herself urges the husband to take a co-wife.[31]

There are also tips for the junior wife:

> [The junior wife] attends more on the husband in private but does not tell him how she herself suffers because of the co-wife's hostility to her. Secretly she tries to get some special token of the husband's esteem, telling him that she indeed lives for such support. But, after getting it, she never reveals it to others out of pride or anger, for a woman who betrays the husband's confidence earns only his contempt.[32]

From this larger context, we are invited to enter the imaginations of the Shakya people—and the storytellers of the time—and abandon prudish hang-ups about who the young Buddha was or, rather, who we might want him to have been. Clearly some of the stories of Siddhartha's manhood and harem life are over the top, but such is the nature of legend. To wit, the *Abhinishkramanasutra* tells us that an added reason Suddhodana built three palaces for Siddhartha was to provide separate residences for each of his three principal wives. In each palace, the princess wife would preside over her own harem as principal consort, and a schedule was set up such that the pleasure-seeking prince could visit the ladies in each palace at different hours of the night.[33] Perhaps there is a Buddhist lesson here about the trappings of desire, or perhaps it is just vivid storytelling!

While several legends recount that Siddhartha had multiple wives, they generally don't tell us much about them. The one exception is Kisa Gautami, a woman who appears consistently in the stories, whether named as a wife or not. Hers is a complicated, probably conflated, story that we will examine in detail below. Sometimes the wives' names are familiar from other contexts. For example, Utpalavarna is named as Siddhartha's junior wife in at least two legends, but she is most commonly remembered as a nun. Another name that appears as belonging to one of Siddhartha's wives is Gopa. In the *Lalitavistara,* her character appears to be a conflation with Yashodhara, since there she is Siddhartha's chief (and only) wife. The stories generally fit those found elsewhere about Yashodhara, although the *Lalitavistara,* which concludes with the Buddha's enightenment, does not mention her pregnancy or son, Rahula.

In other sources, however, Gopa is named as a wife *in addition* to Yashodhara. There is one brief story about her. Gopa and Siddhartha meet when he stops his chariot one day to speak with her as she stands on the terrace of her home. Clearly they are attracted to each other, which the gossipy townsfolk immediately report to the king. Without further ado, Suddhodana sees to their marriage.[34] The Kangyur has it variously that Siddhartha's three wives are Yashodhara, Gopa, and Mrigadja, and elsewhere Yashodhara, Gopa, and Utpalavarna. In the Sanskrit *Sanghabhedavastu,* they are Yashodhara, Gopika, and Mrgaja; while in the *Abhinishkramanasutra,* the three wives are Yashodhara, Manodhara, and Gautami. The *Mahavastu* only names Yashodhara as a wife, yet there is a reference to Siddhartha having four wives when he renounces the kingdom.[35]* Some Pali sources suggest additional wives but do not name them. Clearly the topic of the Buddha's multiple wives is a tangled skein that invites more research. None of the legends are shy about referring to Siddhartha's harem or harems and his thousands of "dancing girls" or consorts. The Pali canon makes an oblique reference to Siddhartha's active harem life when the Buddha tells his disciples of his youth:

> In the rains palace I was entertained by minstrels with no men among them. For the four months of the rains I never went down to the lower palace.[36]

The Mysterious Kisa Gautami

A young woman by the name of Kisa Gautami† appears in both the Sanskrit and Pali legends. While there is no connected biography of her, she is clearly a very important figure in the Buddha's life story. In the Pali sources, she is mentioned variously as both a nun and a laywoman. Some Sanskrit legends state clearly that she was Siddhartha's junior wife. Laying all the stories side

---

* J. J. Jones (*The Mahāvastu*) translates *dvitiya* as "female companions," which makes no sense, but Monier-Williams (*A Sanskrit-English Dictionary*) translates *dvitiya* as "wife."
† Pali: Kisa Gotami.

by side, there are many inconsistencies, and at least two different characters emerge. We are left with a tantalizing mystery that is worth pursuing. Were there two women with the name Kisa Gautami? Which one was the alleged wife of the Buddha? What pieces can we put together to learn more about her? This is a juncture where we must have patience with the stories and not expect more from them than they can give us. We only have fragments to work with here, but the following investigation sheds light on the mysterious Kisa Gautami and brings us to a startling new supposition.

We begin by looking at the two core stories that frame our problem. Both are well known within Buddhist traditions, and in both accounts, the central figure is named Kisa Gautami. The first story, *The Mustard Seed*, has also become a popular parable outside of Buddhism. In this story, Kisa Gautami is born into a poor family in the town of Shravasti. Because she is very thin, she is called "lean" (*kisa*) Gautami. Due to her lowly birth, she is treated cruelly and called "a nobody's daughter." Later, however, when she marries and bears a son, the townsfolk pay her more respect. Tragically, the boy dies as a toddler, and Kisa Gautami becomes distraught with grief. Fearing rebuke and crazed with sorrow, she carries her son's corpse on her hip from door to door, begging for medicine that would restore him. "What's the use?" people say with contempt when they see the child is dead. Finally a kind man, noting her despair, directs her to the Buddha. "Go to the town and bring me a mustard seed from a house where no one has died," is the Buddha's reply to Kisa Gautami's anguished request for him to revive her son. Now hopeful, she goes from door to door once again, but this time there is no house to be found that has not experienced death. Over the course of her search, her psychosis clears as she realizes that the "medicine" the Buddha is offering can help her state of mind but not bring back her son. With new understanding, she leaves her child lovingly in a charnel field saying, "This is the law: All is impermanent!" Upon returning to the Buddha, she requests ordination and becomes a nun. We learn more about the nun Kisa Gautami in a poem attributed to her in the *Therigatha*, which will be examined later in this discussion.

The second story—we'll call it *The Balcony*—appears as a brief but significant episode in almost all the legends, both Pali and Sanskrit. It is inserted into the narrative shortly before Siddhartha's Great Departure from Kapilavastu. There is much more variation in this story than in *The Mustard Seed*, including the complication that the leading lady goes by two different names. The thumbnail story goes like this: Kisa Gautami is a lovely Shakya princess who is the same age as Siddhartha in Kapilavastu. At the time of the story, the prince is at the end of his rope, having just witnessed the four sights of old age, sickness, death, and a holy man, and is on the verge of renouncing worldly life forever. On his final ride back into town with his charioteer, Kisa Gautami spots him from an upper balcony of the palace and calls out to him. The following is from the Thai variant, originally in Pali:

> Happy the parents of the Prince Siddhartha, for he will keep all sorrow from them.
> Happy the wife of the Prince Siddhartha, for he will make her heart glad, and keep all sorrow from her! [37]

Hearing her words, the prince tosses her a costly necklace in reply and rides on. In most Pali versions, this seemingly flirtatious exchange serves to remind the prince of the bondage of worldly life and reinforces his resolve to leave home. Kisa Gautami, on the other hand, receives his gift with delight and interprets it as an expression of his love. In the Sinhalese variation, she further believes it demonstrates his intention to make her a principal queen alongside his wife, Yashodhara.[38] Clearly there is some double entendre in this exchange, and Kisa Gautami and Siddhartha are on very different pages.

Note that Kisa Gautami thinks that the handsome young prince should make her his wife. In the Tibetan Kangyur, this is exactly what happens, although here her name is Mrigadja ("born of a deer").* In the balcony scene, the people of Kapilavastu observe Siddhartha's gesture of tossing her the necklace and report to the king that his son appears to favor the young maiden. Suddhodana sees to their marriage immediately, and Mrigadja becomes Siddhartha's wife, apparently his third after Yashodhara and Gopa. The text asserts that the wedding takes place seven days before Siddhartha's Great Departure. A similar balcony scene appears in the *Mahavastu* but ends quite differently. Here the maiden, called Mrigi, calls out to Siddhartha from the balcony, making her amorous intentions clear, but the prince does not throw a necklace or even acknowledge her. Piqued by his indifference, Mrigi is not happy. The text says,

---

* Mrigadja, Mrigi, and Mrgaja are all variants of the same name and no doubt refer to the same wife.

She was peeved and said to herself, "I have sung the praises of the prince in the midst of all this multitude, yet he does not deign even to look at me."[39]

In the *Abhinishkramanasutra,* there is no balcony scene, but we learn a great deal more about Kisa Gautami (shortened to Gautami*) as Siddhartha's wife. In a detailed story not found in any other legend, we learn about their courtship and marriage. Gautami appears as a vibrant and strong-minded young woman who, like Yashodhara, displays admirable agency in setting her own agenda. Clearly the bards relish the spunk of these two characters. The delightful, laugh-out-loud story goes like this:

Gautami is the only daughter of Dandapani, a wealthy nobleman in Kapilavastu, renowned for his grand palace and vast holdings of land, cattle, and jewels. Suitors throughout the land are pursuing Gautami for her singular beauty and grace (perhaps also her dowry). Hearing of her fame, Suddhodana sends a messenger to Dandapani, asking him to give his daughter in marriage to Siddhartha. Meanwhile, Dandapani has had similar requests from Siddhartha's peers Nanda[†] and the nasty Devadatta, the latter threatening the king with retribution if he is not the chosen suitor. Dandapani is distraught, thinking there will be trouble no matter which suitor he chooses. Perplexed and sad, he can do nothing but brood, while trying to find a way out of his dilemma. Gautami comes upon her father in this state and three times asks him the reason for his sorrow. Three times Dandapani refuses to respond. She says,

> Dear father, you ought to let me know the cause of all this, not try to conceal it from me!

Finally he relents and tells her about her many suitors. Without hesitation, Gautami takes matters into her own hands and announces she will select her own husband:

---

* Not to be confused with Mahaprajapati, who sometimes goes by that name.
† It is not clear if this is meant to be Siddhartha's half-brother.

Dear father! Don't be distressed! I will arrange this matter myself. I will give my father no further trouble than to ask for a man to follow my directions and make my intention known, and then I will select the husband of my choice.[40]

A proclamation goes out across Kapilavastu declaring that the Shakya princess Gautami will be choosing a husband in seven days. Suitors should assemble at her palace so she can make her choice. When the day arrives, all the Shakya citizens—led by their king, Suddhodana—turn out in festive attire for this exciting competition. A lovely passage describes Gautami and her circle of women as she prepares that morning to greet her suitors:

> Very early on the morning of the seventh [day, Gautami] arose, and bathing her person she proceeded to decorate herself with the choicest jewels and the most costly robes; around her head she wore a [garland] of the loveliest flowers and surrounded by a suite of maidens and accompanied by her mother, she proceeded to the place of assembly.[41]

The tables have turned. Now it's the guys, not the ladies, who primp and preen in order to present themselves as potential mates. Decked out in their finest robes, anointed with perfumes, and ornamented with fabulous earrings and sparkling gems, the young men mill about, anxiously awaiting Gautami's arrival. Everyone but Siddhartha, that is. Unimpressed, he shows up in ordinary attire, with simple earrings and three small flowers in his hair. Lounging casually, he hangs back.

Now Gautami enters accompanied by her all-female entourage. She carefully scans each of the five hundred contestants as her mother inquires,

Whom will you select of all these as your husband?

Gautami's response is as startling as it is funny:

> Dear mother! It seems to me that all these youths are very much decorated with ornaments. As to their persons they appear to me more like women than men. I, indeed, as a woman, cannot think of

selecting one of these as a husband, for I cannot suppose that any youth possessing manly qualities, fit for a woman to respect in a husband, would dress himself out as these have. But I observe that Siddhartha, the Prince, is not so bedizened with jewels about his person, there is no love of false appearances in his presence, I do not think that he is of the effeminate disposition that these [others] are—my heart is well affected to him. I will take Siddhartha as the husband of my choice.[42]

And so the princess selects her prince. Other gender surprises appear in this story as Gautami announces her choice of husband in consultation with her mother, not her father, and then publicly humiliates the unfortunate young gentlemen for appearing silly and effeminate. The story goes on to relate that Gautami and Siddhartha take their wedding vows on the spot:

> Then Gotami in her right hand holding a beautiful wreath of [jasmine], advancing past all the youths in succession went straight up to Siddhartha, and having reached him she stopped, and then taking the [jasmine] wreath, having fastened it around the neck of Siddhartha, she gently put her arm upon the back of his head and said, "Siddhartha! my Prince! I take you to be my lord and my husband!" Then Siddhartha replied, "So let it be—so let it be, even as you say." At this time Siddhartha in return took a [jasmine] wreath and fastened it round the neck of the maiden Gotami, and spoke thus—"I take you to be my wife; you are now my own wife."[43]

This detailed story further describes Suddhodana's joy and the rejoicing of the Shakyas at the wedding of their prince to Gautami. The band strikes up, and the citizens of Kapilavastu dance and sing in the streets, throwing their caps in the air. Meanwhile, surrounded by five hundred dancing girls, Gautami proceeds with her new husband to his palace, where "entering into the inner apartments she partook of the joys of wedded life."[44]

This story is followed by a lighthearted *Jataka* tale in which Gautami is portrayed as a magnificent tigress that chooses the lion king (a previous incarnation of the Buddha) as her husband from among all the other mighty beasts who would be suitors. This charming story is noteworthy for the gentlemanly nature of all the competing males. Rather than battling each other for her hand, they agree to abide by the tigress's decision in a fair contest. Once again Gautami displays mirth and wit as she makes her choice.[45]

Circling back to the discussion of the two different women known as Kisa Gautami, the characters and stories obviously could not be more different. In *The Mustard Seed* story, she is described as a destitute young mother of lowly birth from Shravasti, while in *The Balcony* scene, she is an aristocratic Shakya maiden in Kapilavastu who goes on to marry the prince. In the first story, she did not know the Buddha previously and would be quite a bit younger than he is—probably by at least thirty years, since he appears well established in his ministry at the time they meet. In the second story, Kisa Gautami is identified as Shakya and unmarried, and she and Siddhartha are peers. Further, the women are said to be from towns that are quite far apart. Lastly, but significantly, the name Gautami (Gotami) is odd for the character in *The Mustard Seed*, since from her story, she would likely not be of the Gautama clan. There is absolutely nothing to tie these two characters together except the same name, which begs the conclusion that they are two different women. Horner notes the discrepancies and draws the same conclusion.[46] Kisa Gautami of the *The Mustard Seed* will not be discussed further here, but it should be noted there is added confusion around her character in the *Therigatha* and in Tibetan folktales found in the Kangyur, where she is conflated with the nuns Utpalavarna and Patacara. The importance of distinguishing the two Kisa Gautamis will be made clear as we further explore the significance of the young woman who appears in *The Balcony* episode.

Kisa Gautami as Mrigi in the Mahavastu

Reading these stories is like sifting through sand for shards that speak for voices long lost. Occasionally, uncommon pieces surface, and even more occasionally several pieces fit together that suggest a larger, entirely new pattern. This is what happens in relation to the Kisa Gautami character who flirts with Siddhartha in *The Balcony* episode and also appears as one of his wives. We now return to her story in the *Mahavastu*, where we find significant new clues about who she was in the Buddha's life story. Recall that her name is Mrigi here, and she became quite annoyed when Siddhartha ignored her flirtation from the balcony. We learn more about her in that scene because she is introduced as follows:

Mrigi, a Shakyan woman, was the mother of Ananda.[47]

Mother of Ananda? That detail is only provided in the *Mahavastu*. Further investigation reveals that there is one more mention of Mrigi in that text, and again she is called the mother of Ananda. The second occurrence appears later in the chronology, when the Buddha's ministry is established. Here Ananda is a young man who wants to leave home to take ordination with the Buddha, but Mrigi won't let him. The reason for her refusal is not cited, but the *Abhinishkramanasutra* variant of the same scene gives the following explanation:

> On account of some jealous feeling his mother had encouraged in her breast, because of the Buddha's exceeding beauty, when he was living at home.[48]

That certainly sounds like old baggage from the harem. Put together, Mrigi's brief appearances here and in *The Balcony* episodes suggest that her feelings of resentment toward Siddhartha carried over when he became the Buddha. Obviously, there is a lot of stretching in drawing these conclusions, as most of the story is missing. But the evidence we have points to a relationship between Mrigi and Siddhartha characterized by discord.

Many questions arise. First, for those who are not already familiar with the Buddha's biography, who was Ananda? A beloved figure in early Buddhism, he was the Buddha's devoted disciple and personal attendant for the last twenty or so years of the Buddha's life. Because of their close relationship, Ananda was always present for the Buddha's teachings, and because of his excellent memory, he was able to recall and recite each discourse verbatim after the Buddha's death, giving rise to the earliest sutra transmissions and authoritative Buddhist literature. The legends say virtually nothing about Ananda's family background other than that he was a Shakya relative, usually identified as a cousin from Kapilavastu, the son of one of Suddhodana's brothers. Drawing from Sinhalese sources, Hardy says Ananda was the Buddha's nephew.[49]

Given the (scant) evidence so far, there appears to be an elephant in the room. The following conjecture admittedly steps outside already generous methodological boundaries in bringing a new theory to light. If Kisa

Gautami, aka Mrigi, was Ananda's mother, then who was Ananda's father? No one but her husband, young Siddhartha, emerges as a candidate. The theory suggested here is that Ananda was the Buddha's biological son. As a prince with multiple wives and a harem, it only makes sense that Siddhartha, like his father and other noble patriarchs of this era, would have had multiple children by different women. It appears from these story fragments that Ananda may have been among them. It also would have been no secret—and probably no big deal—among the Shakyas if Ananda was a child born of Siddhartha's harem.

From Mrigi's side, however, as junior wife (or significant consort) and the child's mother, it may have been a very big deal indeed. Not only may she have fallen prey to jealousy as a subordinate wife (especially if she was as highborn as Yashodhara), but her son, while loved and cared for in the palace, would have had no hereditary standing. This situation would suggest grounds for her resentment. That decades later the Buddha chose Ananda as a personal attendant may be testimony to his former tie to Mrigi and their son, perhaps a gesture of making amends. It would also speak to the tremendous affection and loyalty historically chronicled between Ananda and the Buddha. In any case, if it is true they were father and son, that important detail has been wiped from the records. A possible exception appears in the *Buddhavamsa*. While it is never a good idea to look at past-life stories for evidence, the eighteenth previous Buddha's wife was named Kisa Gautami and their son was named Ananda.[50]

The idea of Ananda as the Buddha's son certainly invites further research. There are more hints in the stories: for example, in the Kangyur, Ananda is said to have been born conatally with Rahula. At the moment, there seems to be no coherent opposing theory, just very little data at all about Ananda (and Mrigi). For conservative Buddhists, the idea may seem absurd. It definitely takes some getting used to, but finding a new pattern can also help explain old ones. It would shed light on why the Buddha's senior disciples during his ministry were jealous of Ananda's seemingly unearned access to their great teacher and why they gave him such a hard time after the Buddha's death. It would also help explain the many inconsistencies surrounding Ananda's age that appear in the Pali canon and the biographical legends. It's not clear why this is so and why we don't know more about Ananda generally. There is significant biographical background on the Buddha's chief disciples

Shariputra and Maudgalyayana, for example, even though they were from a different region, caste, and clan. But for whatever reason, storytellers in the oral tradition and/or later monk editors may have tweaked his age and other details to bury the storyline that Ananda was the Buddha's son. There are many ways the theory makes sense and breathes fresh insights into tired old assumptions. More than that, it refreshes the Buddha's life story overall with a new brushstroke of humanity. How heartwarming that it may have been his own son who attended the Buddha so lovingly in his later years.

Mrigi Gautami: A Reconstructed and Imagined Biography

Wife of the Buddha and mother of Ananda, Mrigi, aka Kisa Gautami, has emerged as a new character in the Buddha legends. Given the evidence, it is fitting to create a composite of her and her story from what we know thus far. First, to avoid further confusion, let's sever her connection once and for all with the sad mother in *The Mustard Seed* by giving her an entirely new name: Mrigi Gautami. This might not be far from what her name actually was, since Mrigi appears as her given name in the *Mahavastu* (similarly in the Kangyur and *Sanghabhedavastu*), while the moniker "Gautami" ties her to the existing stories and the Shakya clan. The following "biography" is simply an imagined graft of stories already recounted and possibly provides a starting point for learning more.

Mrigi Gautami was born to an aristocratic Shakya family in Kapilavastu. As a maiden of sixteen, she had a crush on the young prince Siddhartha and, like other Shakya maidens, had her eye on becoming his wife and queen. On the day he distributed ornaments, she eagerly awaited her turn but was jealous when he showed favor to Yashodhara. She also attended the tournament where Siddhartha demonstrated his athletic prowess, outshining all the other Shakya men, but she became distressed to see that again the prince had eyes only for Yashodhara. The final straw came when Siddhartha and Yashodhara married, as now Mrigi Gautami's hopes of becoming Siddhartha's chief wife and queen were dashed.

Undeterred, she adjusted her intention to becoming a junior wife and one day told her father to arrange a gathering of all the young Shakya men so she could make her choice of husband. This time things went her way. Siddhartha and Mrigi Gautami married, and she moved into his harem.

But old feelings die hard. Mrigi Gautami could not stand seeing the prince spending time with his other consorts, especially Yashodhara. She was consumed with jealousy and longed to be her husband's favorite. Siddhartha seemed indifferent to her and visited her in the harem only at the appointed times. One day she spotted him from a palace balcony as he was riding back into Kapilavastu. Seeing an opportunity to catch his attention and impress him in front of all the townsfolk, she called out, loudly praising him with a thinly veiled, if not sarcastic, compliment that he was indeed a wonderful husband. However, Siddhartha kept his head down and rode past, leaving her humiliated and furious. She did not see him again until they made love later in the harem. Seven days later, Siddhartha went forth, leaving his life as a Shakya prince forever. Bereft of a husband, Mrigi Gautami gave birth to his son in the harem and named the child Ananda, meaning "bliss."

She loved her beautiful son but worried about his future. Because she had been one of Siddhartha's junior wives, Ananda would never have standing in the royal lineage or even be officially recognized as Siddhartha's son. These disappointments continued to fuel her unhappiness and resentment. Further, Siddhartha's harem was dissolved after he left, leaving her and her son (as well as the other harem women and children) with an uncertain future. As a highborn Shakya woman, she could choose to remain with her son in the women's quarters of the king's palace under the patronage of Sud-dhodana, but it would be too sad to stay there, especially with Yashodhara close by. What made the most sense was to return to the women's quarters in her father's home where she grew up and where she once again would be under his protection.* There she could raise Ananda alongside his grandparents and among cousins in familiar surroundings. Back at home, she could also consider her options for remarriage.

Two decades later, Mrigi Gautami's heart was broken all over again when she learned that Ananda, like so many young Shakya men, wished to go forth and take ordination with the Buddha, his father. After much argument and unhappiness, she finally, grudgingly, agreed. Now bereft of all family ties, Mrigi Gautami, like so many Shakya women, looked to Siddhartha's mother, her former mother-in-law and queen, Mahaprajapati for solace

---

*Evidence suggests here that her father may have been Amritodana, Suddhodana's brother.

and leadership. Seeking a spiritual life together, she and five hundred other women made the trek to Vaishali to request ordination from the Buddha. As a nun, perhaps Mrigi Gautami's passions would finally be quelled. Of course, once Mrigi Gautami had gone forth, she would still get to see her beloved son, Ananda, from time to time.

As a postscript, there is a lengthy poem in the *Therigatha* attributed to Kisa Gautami. Such poems are thought to have been utterances of the nuns, which were later written down and preserved in the *Khuddakanikaya* of the Pali canon. There is much confusion and debate around the attribution of this poem, although the author is generally identified as Kisa Gautami of *The Mustard Seed* story. For our purposes, one passage in the poem stands out because it echoes the sentiments of our peevish Mrigi Gautami:

> Being a woman is suffering,
> that has been shown by the Buddha,
> the tamer of those to be tamed.
>
> Sharing a husband with another wife is suffering for some,
> while for others, having a baby just once is more than
> enough suffering.
>
> Some women cut their throats,
> others take poison,
> some die in pregnancy
> and then both mother and child experience miseries.[51]

There is much more to learn and imagine about Mrigi Gautami. Hers is a story of an ordinary woman who lived an extraordinary life that yielded an even more extraordinary legacy. Never mind her disappointing marriage; the gentle son she brought into the world is remembered as second only to the Buddha in his contribution to the birth of the new faith. Mother of Ananda, Mrigi Gautami deserves to take a seat alongside the other venerable mothers of Buddhism.

4

The Great Departure: A Family Affair

For more than two decades, the question had been looming over the Shakyas: would Siddhartha succeed his father as king, or would he reject his royal patrimony to pursue the spiritual life of a mendicant? We already know the answer to that question, but back in Kapilavastu, the tension was mounting. Suddhodana had done everything right for his son—built the palaces, set up the harems, arranged the marriages. Represented by their council of elders, the Shakya people applauded these measures, as they were equally invested in seeing that their beloved prince be happy and assume his rightful inheritance. At this point, young Siddhartha had been provided with every imaginable emblem of wealth and pleasure according to the noble customs of their caste and his position as heir to the kingship. All eyes were on him. What more could he possibly want? How could he even think of leaving now that he had the perfect life? A passage from the *Lalitavistara* extols the splendors of his princely privilege:

> The exquisite and perfect mansion where the Bodhisattva lived was a source of supreme pleasures and joy. In his palace his body was always pure and stainless, he was adorned with flower garlands and jewelry, and his limbs were scented with the finest and most sweet-smelling oils. . . . He wore stainless white clothes of the finest quality. . . . His bedding was made of divine fabrics of the finest thread. . . . There on his perfect couch, he lay surrounded by his wonderful retinue of consorts, who all resembled divine maidens. . . . [They] woke up

the Bodhisattva with beautiful and soft songs accompanied by the melodious tones of flutes.[1]

Much to everyone's distress, however, Siddhartha continued to display dissatisfaction and give off mixed messages about his intentions.

At this point in the Buddha's life story, he was in his late twenties.* More than a decade had passed since his marriage to his principal wife, Yashodhara. Other than tales about his courtship methods and wives, the legends hold virtually no details about him as a young adult. The twenties are a formative time for any young man, but those years in the life of the Buddha-to-be are left almost solely to our imagination. The Sanskrit tradition recounts that he was educated in writing and mathematics, but it is unclear where or at what age. Stephen Batchelor has suggested that perhaps he was away part of this time because Suddhodana, in preparing his son for the monarchy, would have wanted to remove him from the provincial backwater of Kapilavastu and expose him to the bustling commercial and political center of Shravasti to the west. Perhaps too, Siddhartha traveled even farther to study at the great university of Taxila in present-day Pakistan, which lay at the crossroads of major trade routes and the cosmopolitan cultures of the Greek and Persian empires. If this were the case, it could account for the Buddha's erudition and dissociation from the prevailing brahmanical ideology later during his ministry.[2]

Yet there is no known literary or iconographic evidence to support these intriguing hypotheses. Surprisingly too, storytellers were not inspired to spin heroic yarns about Siddhartha as a young man in the prime of his life. Perhaps after all, he stayed home, and life in the palace (or three of them) was just that humdrum. Of course, it's entirely possible that there were plenty of stories about Siddhartha as a young man that thrived in the oral traditions but never made it into the written record. Or perhaps stories included in the early written record have been lost or were redacted over time as irrelevant or, for whatever reason, at variance with the editor's purpose.

However, many stories emerge again in the legends as Siddhartha prepared to renounce his kingdom and leave Kapilavastu. It's noteworthy that there is a heightened focus on women in this final chapter of Siddhartha's life at home. This shows up in different ways, particularly as consorts became the

---

* Legends are fairly consistent that Siddhartha left home at twenty-nine.

royal family's last line of defense in their battle to dissuade the prince from his religious calling. Eros had to be the answer, since fortifications, armed guards, and trenches around the palace hadn't worked. There really was a sort of male-female split in strategy here, as the men attended mostly to tactical military maneuvers and the women to sex in their conjoined efforts to keep the prince at home. But we'll see that the role the women played was much more nuanced than this. As it says in the *Mahavastu*,

> Nobles have a hundred arts, brahmans two hundred, kings a thousand, but a woman's arts are countless.[3]

Tension in the Palace

While all the legends recount Siddhartha's spiritual evolution, it is mostly through the Sanskrit tradition that we gain an understanding of his family system and how his decision to renounce his home and kingdom impacted not just himself but the entire cast of characters we have already come to know: his wives, father, mother, friends, and the Shakya people. We become party to their emotional lives as well as his, especially in this final chapter at home when it becomes increasingly clear that Siddhartha would be cutting all ties to loved ones. Mythic elements remain, but now more than ever, we also find very human emotions shining through the narrative. For the most part, the women's stories are not separate but intertwined with the overall drama of Siddhartha's departure as it unfolds.

It is during this time that Abhaya, the goddess of Lumbini's grove who paid homage to Siddhartha at birth, returns to help the family. She appears to Suddhodana, who is heartbroken that his beloved son prefers meditation to the pleasures of palace life. The prophecy that the prince will renounce his royal inheritance is unfolding before his father's eyes, and the king is doing everything in his power to subvert it. For her part Abhaya sees the bigger picture and advocates for the prince's destiny, no doubt seeing the supreme benefit Siddhartha will someday bring to humanity. Gently addressing Suddhodana, she is both prescient and kind:

> Your majesty, reflect about your son. For he has no passion for the joys of any of the senses. Ere long he will break all the bonds of craving and leave none remaining. He will go off to the forest of penance,

and will develop his thought, which is yet quite limited. And now, O King, Siddhartha, though of royal lineage and surrounded in his beautiful palace by a throng of women, reviles what in his body is impermanent, ill, and unsubstantial.[4]

Besides her wise counsel, Abhaya's remark about the impermanence of the physical body is significant. As mentioned earlier, this important Buddhist teaching has often been genderized to focus on females. In her perception of the prince's quandary, Abhaya acknowledges the erotic pleasures available in the palace but clearly states that Siddhartha's revulsion stems from his experience of his own body—not the women's—as dissatisfactory, impermanent, and insubstantial. The distinction is significant within a Buddhist context and points to the Buddha's original teaching.

Despite Abhaya's good intentions, Suddhodana openly displays his grief at his son's decision to take up the religious life. We don't hear from Mahaprajapati in this next story, but the king speaks for both parents when he begs his son not to leave. He says that Mahaprajapati, too, would die of a broken heart:

> Pray do not do so, my lotus-eyed and charmingly beautiful son. Great grief would I suffer if I were bereft of you. Your mother as well as I would go to unwelcome death. What sort of special bliss is this then that for its sake you would leave me, your people and your kingdom? . . . Live the way your father lived, my son and be content, as long as I live or as long as she, your mother, will live. For seeing you go away, of a surety I will die.[5]

In this touching story, father and son engage in a lengthy debate in which Suddhodana desperately offers the prince anything he wants if only he will stay home to follow his royal destiny—or at least delay his departure until later in life when he would have his own son and heir to succeed him. In the *Buddhacarita,* Siddhartha appears to agree, but negotiations break down over his caveat that the king must then promise to bring about an end to old age, sickness, and death. Presented with an existential challenge far beyond the powers of any father's wealth or influence, Suddhodana responds with exasperation:

Give up this idea which goes too far. An extravagant wish is ridiculous and unfitting.[6]

In the *Mahavastu* version of this episode, Siddhartha poses eight requirements of his father. One of them stands out among the rest: he asks "that this harem of women . . . and my numerous kinsfolk do not disappear." Indeed, Siddhartha's lifetime familiarity with the women of the palace has provided fodder for both his worldly attachments and his philosophical insights. His words reflect that he has already experienced the dissatisfaction of worldly desires and the pain of loss and change. With dawning wisdom, his request is not about clinging to sensual pleasure and family but rather acknowledging their transient, and thus unsatisfactory, nature. As Horner has observed, passages such as these underscore the humanity of the young Bodhisattva as they demonstrate his keen familiarity with worldly attachments and the temptations of desire.[7]

But looking deeper, the expression "harem of women" in the context of Siddhartha's life would not refer simply to sexual liaisons, but also to his loved ones. As we've already seen, the women's quarters, first in his father's palace when he was a child and later in his own palace as an adult, largely defined his social world and relationships. His attentive father notwithstanding, women formed the primary influences in his early life. (Recall how the Shakya people indignantly noted that Siddhartha had spent excessive time with women to the extent that he had not formulated the conventional skills of a young man, much less a prince.)

The children of the harem would also be part of this social context. Not only did Siddhartha grow up with his mother, nurses, and Suddhodana's consorts in the women's apartments of his father's palace, but this is where the women of his father's harem raised their children too. However we define family, it must have felt like one to Siddhartha, especially since the harem children, as (presumably) Suddhodana's progeny, would have been the prince's half-siblings and everyday playmates. As such, this environment, as a microcosm of worldly life, was his primary frame of reference growing up. Further, whatever the luxuries of palace life, he would not have been completely sheltered from the sufferings of old age, sickness, and death living in the seclusion of the women's quarters. Not the least of which, as a boy, Siddhartha must have witnessed the dangers of childbirth, since maternal and infant mortality would have been as commonplace there as in the villages and countryside, the risks and dangers hardly mitigated by privilege.

Siddhartha's poignant request that his "kinsfolk do not disappear" sounds like a tender sentiment arising from anguish in his past. Could he be evoking the loss of Maya, the mother he never knew? Regardless of how much Siddhartha was loved as a child, the tragedy that marked his entry into the world must have affected him deeply as he grew up. The Buddha myth would have us believe that Siddhartha never knew death until just before his Great Departure, but surely Maya's death at his birth was a truth he lived with his entire life. It is ingenuous to take the myth of young Siddhartha's naïveté literally without accounting for the common knowledge, then as now, that death marked his life from its inception. Indeed, the death of his birth mother may well have played a significant role in fueling his insights into the suffering that arises from life's impermanence. Perhaps, too, it contributed to the inner turmoil that led him to renounce worldly life altogether in pursuit of greater truths.

Returning to our story, Suddhodana, ever the clueless, loving father, cannot take his son's philosophical brooding seriously. He is convinced that simply infusing *more* women and pleasure into Siddhartha's life will surely put an end to such thinking. It is a classic parent-child disconnect, although in this antediluvian scenario, we're talking about consorts and harems rather than car keys and smartphones. In the *Mahavastu,* the exasperated king gestures toward the harem women, saying to Siddhartha,

> Here is a noble sight for you, my son ... fair, faultless, loving women, with eyes bright as jewels, with full breasts, gleaming white limbs, sparkling gems, firm and fine girdles, soft, lovely and black-dyed hair, wearing bright-red mantles and cloaks, bracelets of gems and necklaces of pearls, ornaments and rings on the toes, and anklets, and playing music on the five musical instruments. Delight yourself with these my son, and do not yearn for the religious life of a wanderer.[8]

Father and son go on to have a curious conversation about sex and women:

> The prince said, "See father, a man may have an awareness of a woman and be excited, disturbed and intoxicated by it." The king

said, "What is your awareness of a woman like?" The prince said, "It is an awareness of [delusion]."[9]

Flummoxed, Suddhodana once again brings the conversation back to erotic pleasure. He is convinced that seductive consorts alone hold the power to distract his son from these foolish musings. As a last resort, he finally says,

> Are you not then as a man excited by a woman's beauty? What is your view on things?[10]

The answer is not what he hopes to hear, of course. The Bodhisattva now launches into a metaphysical homily on the defective trappings of worldly existence. Their exchange becomes more intransigent as the dialogue progresses. Suddhodana becomes distraught at his son's mulishness and sheds a flood of tears. Finally abandoning the debate in anguish, the king turns back to the consorts. After all, it is their job to keep the prince happily preoccupied. As professionals in the arts of love, their reputations are on the line. Repeatedly the king cajoles them to intensify their seductive efforts:

> Divert, delight and amuse the prince well with dance and song and music so that he may find pleasure at home.[11]

And so the ladies go overboard, and the prince's harem transforms into a celestial pleasure realm. Alas, as we know, it did not deter the prince a bit.

Perhaps the most famous episode in the Buddha legend comes at this point in the narrative. As we have seen, the early storytellers took Siddhartha's evolving psychological process and spun it into a colorful parable that could easily be understood by their audiences. The prince is described as embarking on an outer, rather than an inner, journey of insight. Looking for diversion from his cooped-up life in the palace, Siddhartha enlists his faithful charioteer, Chandaka, to take him on four separate excursions outside the palace walls. On these occasions, he observes the four sights: old age, sickness, death, and a religious saint—just what the brahmans had warned the king about years earlier. Taken together, these four sights turn the prince's mind finally and irrevocably to the religious life. Sometimes these outings are described as surreptitious; however, generally the prince simply wishes to journey by day to a pleasure park at some distance from Kapilavastu to amuse himself. His father and the Shakyas are well aware of his intention but are worried that the more Siddhartha sees of the outside world, the more he will get rebellious ideas in his head. Asita's prophecy that he will eventually renounce the kingdom has vigorously driven their actions to date. The whole point of giving him three palaces with three wives and three harems had been to ensure that he had all the worldly delights a young prince could want. So far that seemed to have been working. The legends all have it that Siddhartha never ventured outside the palace walls and had no inkling of what lay beyond. Neither had he witnessed suffering and pain, much less experienced them. Now this was going to change.

In one lovely story in the *Buddhacarita,* the consorts' music inspires the prince to venture forth from the palace to explore the outside world. Day after day in the harem he has listened to songs that rhapsodize the beauty of the nearby forest groves for their soft grasses, the trees resounding with birdsong, and lotus ponds abounding in blossoms and fragrance. Finally, "like an elephant confined inside a house," he resolves to see for himself these sublime places "beloved of the womenfolk." The king reluctantly makes preparations for the journey, ensuring that any signs of human suffering are swept from view. What is charming and exceptional about this story is the excitement of the young Shakya women because they have never before seen their prince. Their feelings are revealed in a selection of verses:

Hearing the news from their servants . . . the women obtained leave from their elders and went out on to the balconies in their desire to see him.

They gathered together in uncontrollable excitement, obstructed by the slipping of their girdle-strings, as they put their ornaments on at the report, and with their eyes still dazed by sudden awakening from sleep. . . .

Unquiet reigned in the windows then, as the women were crowded together in the mutual press, with their earrings ever agitated by collisions and their ornaments jingling. . . .

> Then with its palaces full to bursting with young women, who threw the lattices open in their excitement, the city appeared as magnificent on all sides as Paradise, with its heavenly mansions full of Apsarases.[12]

Siddhartha is elated by the festive welcome he receives from his people and experiences an awakened sense of purpose. However, his pleasure is short-lived. Soon he catches sight of a decrepit, senile old man, and the truth of aging hits him like "the crash of a thunderbolt." Overwhelmed with confusion and sadness, he is unable to proceed as planned and returns to the palace. His mind plunges even deeper into turmoil as he subsequently goes out three more times and sees the remaining sights.

In the *Lalitavistara,* Suddhodana listens with trepidation to his son's request to visit the pleasure park. So deeply does he love Siddhartha that his impulse is to grant the prince everything his heart desires. But remembering Asita's prophecy, the king knows the danger of letting his son see the outside world. He also knows how obstinate his son can be. At this point, Suddhodana realizes it is a no-win situation, since refusal to allow the journey would run the risk of inciting the prince's defiance and making matters worse. Upon reflection, the king arrives at an ingenious solution: he'll grant permission for his son's excursion as long as the harem women go along. As in the palace, it will be their job to keep him amused at all times and ensure that his mind remains properly focused on amorous delights. So preparations are made for the prince's outing to the park. The entire city is beautifully festooned for the occasion, and the road on which the prince is to travel is swept clean and sprinkled with perfumed water and fresh flowers. Four army regiments line the way, as scores of resplendent consorts ride with the prince's retinue, colorfully bedecked in their finest jewels and seductive attire. We can imagine them waving gaily to the crowds as their procession passes through the streets. Once again, the prince's excursion is on display to the entire population of Kapilavastu. The four sights of old age, disease, death, and a holy man are induced magically, however. Despite the crowds, only Siddhartha and his charioteer can see them.[13]

The story continues as heightened anxiety grips Kapilavastu. It's becoming increasingly clear that the prince's mind is turning to spiritual concerns. First we hear about the distress of the Shakya people:

All the Sakyas are worried and keep guard day and night;
The great noise of the powerful army is heard everywhere.
The city is in turmoil and full of terrified cries: May the Gentle
   One not depart!
If the holder of the Sakyas lineage leaves, this royal line will be
   broken![14]

Renewed instructions are issued to the harem:

You must never stop your songs and music;
You must make him stay, so captivate his mind with your games of
   pleasure.
Demonstrate all your many ways of female trickery and make a
   good effort;
Watch over him and create hindrances so that the Gentle Being
   does not depart![15]

Even the palace birds, normally joyous, are despondent:

The swans, cranes, peacocks, mynas, and parrots do not make any
   sounds.
They sit on terraces, by palace windows, on gateways, parapets and
   pedestals;
Depressed, unhappy, and miserable, they hang their heads and
   remain silent.[16]

Gloom settles over Kapilavastu:

The whole city is disturbed and overcome with lethargy;
Nobody has any desire for dancing, singing, or making merry.
Even the king is severely depressed and given to brooding:
He wonders: "Oh no, will the Sakya lineage, of such fortune, now
   be destroyed?"[17]

The legends leave no doubt that Siddhartha's departure for the religious
life was traumatic and sorrowful for his people. Immeasurable freedom lay
ahead for him and many others, yet for the Shakyas an indelible sadness was
left behind.

We turn now to the *Abhinishkramanasutra,* where this sequence of the four sights has a different nuance. Here we feel Siddhartha's vulnerability, even fear, as he approaches the epiphany of his renunciation. It begins in the palace as he revels in hedonism without any awareness whatsoever of his bodhisattva nature or destiny. He displays neither resistance to leading the good life in the harem nor the slightest inclination to give it up. We're told he is totally enslaved by his "animal passions." This troubles a tutelary god who has been charged with watching over him. This is a nonbrahmanical male god, not the protectress Abhayadevi we heard from earlier, although the figure may originally have been female. Impatient, this unnamed god decides that time is being wasted, and it's long overdue that the prince wake up and get on with fulfilling his karmically driven moral imperative to become a religious leader. In some of the strongest language yet, he says,

> This [Bodhisattva] too long a time is indulging himself with worldly pleasures, dwelling in his palace and partaking of the five enjoyments of sense. We must not permit these lusts to cloud and besot him, his mind and senses to be darkened and deluded; quickly! quickly! quickly! flies the time. [The Bodhisattva] must be taught now to recognise the just limits of such things, and that he ought at once to let them go and leave his house. . . . If I do not take some preparatory step in this direction, and incite him to flee from these things, it will be too late.[18]

Using magical powers, the god causes the prince to conceive a desire to tour the gardens outside the city, then he conjures in sequence the four sights intended to turn the prince's mind to religious matters. As before, Suddhodana is alerted. He again proclaims that the entire town be festooned and swept clean of any adverse sights, but in this case, he does not call upon the consorts.* Siddhartha goes forth with his charioteer as before. This time, it is just the two of them, with the guardian god lurking invisibly above. With each of the unfortunate sights of old age, sickness, and death, the prince

---

* An odd, anomalous gender detail appears at this point in the narrative: as Suddhodana festoons the gardens, the trees with male names are decorated with the men's ornaments, while the trees with female names are decorated with women's ornaments. There is no further context for this remark. An intriguing garden design!

is profoundly startled and disturbed. We see a very human side to him in this story, unlike in the *Lalitavistara,* where the dialogue always reflects the prince's bodhisattva self-awareness. So discomfited is the prince after the first three outings that each time he comes home, he returns directly to his carnal addictions in the harem as if taking refuge in what is familiar and comforting after a frightening experience:

> And so the Prince still remained in the indulgence of his animal passions, without any reflection.[19]

As in all of the legends, the turning point finally comes during Siddhartha's final outing when he encounters the gentle mendicant. The saint's dignified demeanor draws the prince's attention and prompts many questions he asks the simple man. Overwhelmed with awe and respect, Siddhartha has found a new role model for his life. The seed of awakening has been nourished in his mind, and so begins his final journey of investigation into the way out of worldly desire and pain.

With new resolve, the prince returns to the palace and forthwith announces to his father and the assembly of Shakya ministers that he will renounce his birthright to seek liberation. The worst-case scenario as predicted by the seer Asita has finally come to pass. Suddhodana dissolves in tears and sorrowfully beseeches his son to reconsider:

> Then [the king], having heard these words, trembled as a tree shivers that is struck by the whole weight of an elephant's body, and the tears coursed down his cheeks, while he gave way to his grief in these words—"Alas! alas! My son, let not such thoughts as these prevail with you; for, my son, you are young, and the time for your becoming a recluse is not arrived. After a few years more, I shall give up my kingdom and retire to the forest, and then you, my son, will succeed me. Let not my son think of giving up the world at his tender age!"[20]

Distressed, the ministers also implore the prince to change his mind, impressing upon him his sovereign responsibility to king and kingdom. It almost works—but then it doesn't. Overcome with doubt, Siddhartha wavers in his determination. Returning to the familiar, he hastens to the inner chambers of the harem. The ladies are delighted to see him, of course, and they swiftly ply him with seductive music and dance and indulge him with familiar sybaritic pleasures. This time, however, the prince is unmoved. His animal passions have quelled. Sitting quietly, surrounded by the women, his mind remains absorbed with his encounter with the peaceful saint. Gradually Siddhartha's thoughts cease their habitual agitation and the thirty-two beautiful marks of a buddha begin to emerge on his body. The women are awestruck. Surely he is a god, they say. Soon enough, by the power of the prince's concentration, their minds, too, become tranquil. The music and erotic dancing cease as the harem quiets down. Like the prince, the consorts are no longer incited by gratification of the senses. The harem, as a nexus of samsara, has begun to transform. Indeed, Siddhartha has reconnected with his Bodhisattva calling and found his first disciples.

Mahaprajapati Takes Charge

Mahaprajapati reemerges in the legend during this time of family crisis. Once again, these stories appear only in the Sanskrit sources. In the first story, we find her fully engaged in palace efforts to prevent the prince from leaving. However, her role here is not so much as mother or queen, but as chief consort in the king's court and advisor to the ladies of Siddhartha's harem. While Suddhodana's job is to marshal the military solution to keep their son at home (adding patrols of infantrymen, chariots, elephants, and so forth), hers is to mobilize the consorts, rousing them to new heights of seductive powers. Time to pull out all the stops, she tells them, to keep her son, their husband, at home. In the *Abhinishkramanasutra*, we find a humorous passage where she lectures the consorts on their responsibilities, reminding them that their own sexual gratification is also at risk. No prince, no pleasure, she tells them. They will be losing more than just their jobs and reputations if the prince leaves home:

> Mahaprajapati Gotami within the palace assembled all the women of pleasure and upbraided them with their want of influence over the mind of the prince—"Let none of you," she said, "fail to provide amusement for him night and day; let there be no interval of darkness, and never be without wine and burning perfumes; let there be guards at every door to prevent ingress or egress. For, remember, if the prince escape, there will be no other pleasure within the palace." [21]

This scene is further dramatized in the *Lalitavistara*. Here Mahaprajapati is not just enlisting the ladies' seductive skills, but also asking them to arm themselves with weapons lest Siddhartha try to escape. These methods are intended only to thwart him, of course, as no harm should ever come to their beloved prince. We hear the urgency in Mahaprajapati's voice as she directs the women to prepare quickly for his arrival:

> Light bright lamps and fasten all jewels to the peak of the banners!
> Hang garlands of pearls and illuminate this entire palace!
> Play music, sing songs, and stay awake and alert through the night.
> Guard the prince so that he cannot leave without anybody knowing.
>
> Arm yourselves! Carry in your hands weapons—
> Swords and lances, bows and arrows, and two-pointed spears—
> To guard our beloved prince.
> Everyone must be on high alert.
>
> First shut all doors, then lock them tight
> And place door bolts firmly across the door panels.
> Unless you must, do not open any door,
> Otherwise this noble being might escape.
>
> Adorn yourselves with necklaces of jewels and pearls;
> Wear flower ornaments, half-moon ornaments, and chains.
> Adorn yourselves with belts, rings, and earrings;
> Take care to fasten your anklets well.
>
> Should this benefactor of humans and gods, who acts like a proud
>   elephant,
> Try to escape in a hasty manner,
> You should confront him in such a way
> That no harm is done to him.
>
> You girls with lances in your hands,
> Who surround the bed of this pure being,
> You must not slip into laziness,
> But watch him with eyes like a butterfly.

In order to guard the Prince,
Adorn this palace with bejeweled lattices
And take up your flutes and play them to your fullest.
Protect the Stainless Being through the night!

Keep each other awake
And do not rest.
Otherwise he may certainly leave his home behind,
Abandoning the kingdom and all his subjects.

If he were to leave home,
Then the royal palace would become a place with no joy.
The continuity of the royal lineage, which has endured so long,
Would become interrupted.[22]

Mahaprajapati expresses much more that just her personal grief at the thought of losing her cherished son. As queen, she has a strong sense of royal lineage and understands how devastating it would be to her husband and the Shakya people were the prince to abdicate his crown. Besides the issue of succession, all the Shakyas clearly feel deep affection for Siddhartha and the royal family. A wise and loving mother and queen, Mahaprajapati would have been keenly aware of the sorrowful omens looming over Kapilavastu, a cloud that would soon overwhelm not just her, her husband, and the palace, but the entire Shakya kingdom with the loss of their beloved Siddhartha.

In a second story, Mahaprajapati shares a prophetic dream with her son. Expressed in beautiful verse, it touchingly conveys a mother's unconditional love and acceptance, even in the face of loss. She knows her son is leaving and displays equanimity, even reverence, for Siddhartha's imminent journey:

My boy, who art beautiful as a mass of gold, in my dream I saw a noble bull, white, with an exceeding lovely hump, with an extra horn, whose very motion spoke of love, and it was sleek of body.

The bull bellowed most sweetly, and ran out of Kapilavastu, taking the path his heart was bent on. There is none that can beat his bellowing when he bellows—the noble bull that is like a heap of flowers.[23]

While the "bellowing" could refer to the sounds of dharma that continue to reverberate even today, perhaps here it is also a mother's gentle teasing of her son's willful nature. This dream, which appears in the *Mahavastu,* is told to Siddhartha, but unfortunately we do not hear his reply. In the *Abhinishkramanasutra* version of the dream, Mahaprajapati's words come across with more sadness. She appears anxious at the notion of losing her son and expresses feelings of helplessness that she cannot forestall his unfolding destiny:

> The Queen Mother Gotami … in her sleep had the following dream—she thought she saw a white ox-King in the midst of the city going on in a wistful way bellowing and crying, whilst no one in the place was able to get before it to stop it or hinder it.[24]

Brotherly Advice

Previously we met Siddhartha's close childhood friend Kalodayin, whom he knew throughout his life. As we already know, the relationship between Siddhartha and Kalodayin was characterized by extraordinary intimacy and trust. In the following story, that trust is extended also by Suddhodana, who summons Kalodayin (here cited as the son of chief minister Mahanaman) to petition his advice on how to keep the prince at home. The king asks:

> By what stratagem, … can we keep Siddhartha in the palace, and prevent him becoming a Recluse?[25]

While other Shakya men are busy reinforcing garrisons around the palace, Kalodayin heads straight for the women's quarters and enters the harem. (That he would even think of doing so, much less be allowed or invited, demonstrates that he was considered an intimate member of Suddhodana's— and Siddhartha's—household.) Like Mahaprajapati, Kalodayin chides the ladies for their (perceived) failure in keeping the prince adequately entertained. Dejected and demoralized, the consorts stare silently as he goes on lecturing them, even citing stories of legendary seductresses who were presumably more skillful than they. Their enthusiasm renewed, the ladies try—and fail—again to seduce Siddhartha: striking erotic poses, talking salaciously to him, even making "bird whistles" to engage his attention.

One consort removes a sprig of jasmine from her headdress and fastens it seductively to the prince's breast. Nope. His mind remains firmly settled on the wretched exigencies of old age, disease, and death. Women's wiles stir him not one bit.

Kalodayin, now frustrated, finally sees the futility of the consorts' efforts. Switching tactics, he tries to reason with the prince instead. Logos not Eros is his stratagem now, although the subject remains sex and women. Just as Suddhodana talked to his son man-to-man about sex, so now does Kalodayin speak to Siddhartha in brotherly confidence about how he should play his cards with the ladies:

> Great and holy Prince! ... I wish to speak plainly on the present occasion, and I ask you to bear with me—as with a friend. I observe that your Highness is wrong in not yielding to the importunities of the ladies of your palace; but that you rather hate, avoid and dislike their society. But why should you think it wrong to act according to our natural tendencies? The very first principle of a woman's being is to allow her the privilege of loving some one, and seeking the gratification of her desire. Respect to a husband is won only by being capable of participation in pleasure. If your Highness persistently refuses to indulge yourself in these objects of desire, then the world, rich and poor, however well they may speak of you with flattering lips, as courteous, will find it difficult to honour you at heart.[26]

Kalodayin is shaming Siddhartha. A real man brings pleasure to a woman, he says. The consorts will not respect him if they do not mutually participate in sexual gratification. A woman with beauty but no carnal enjoyment is "like a tree without flowers." Perhaps worse, Kalodayin warns Siddhartha that his reputation within the kingdom is at stake. As much as the Shakya people generally may wish to flatter him, they will not ultimately respect the prince if it were known that he does not sexually satisfy his harem wives. Siddhartha counters, of course, that women's beauty—indeed, all worldly enjoyments—are ephemeral by nature and thus of no ultimate value:

> Udayi! only regard these women in another light! See them as they will be when they are old, their skin wrinkled, their beauty faded

and gone . . . How much more stupid of a man in such a place and surrounded by such companions to be merry and amorous![27]

Sexism notwithstanding (a woman's fading beauty is used as an example of impermanence throughout Buddhist literature), Siddhartha once again stands firm in his resolve to abandon all worldly attachments. His family has struck out trying to stop him. Suddhodana, Mahaprajapati, the consorts, and now Kalodayin have all failed in their efforts to dissuade him from renouncing worldly life and abandoning the kingdom.

A variation of this story about Kalodayin's attempted intervention consumes an entire chapter in the *Buddhacarita*. It takes place after Siddhartha's experience of the four sights. Here, on orders from Suddhodana, the palace charioteer whisks Siddhartha directly to a pleasure park on the outskirts of town after their encounter with the religious mendicant. Awaiting them there are scores of consorts with strict instructions from the king to distract the prince with sexual pleasures. "Their eyes dancing with excitement," they rush to greet him, "as if he were a bridegroom arriving."[28] However, so overcome are the women by the power of Siddhartha's beatific radiance that they hang back shyly, hands folded in reverence. Once again, Kalodayin is in charge, and events are not proceeding as planned. Seeing the ladies' hesitation, he first praises their extraordinary skills, which are apparently capable of captivating the most "lust-free" ascetic or even gods normally accustomed to the charms of the celestial maidens. How could the consorts hold back now, behaving as ordinary brides or wives? Duly chastened, the ladies set about trying to seduce the prince:

> Thus these young women, to whose minds love had given free rein, assailed the prince with wiles of every kind.[29]

In the ornate, erotic style of classical Sanskrit poetry, we find colorful accounts of just what this entailed:

> Then some of the young women there, pretending to be under the influence of intoxication, touched him with their firm, rounded, close-set, charming breasts . . .

Some walked up and down so as to make their golden [girdles] tinkle and displayed to him their hips veiled by diaphanous robes.

Others grasped mango-boughs in full flower and leaned so as to display bosoms like golden jars.[30]

Unfazed as always, the prince is only driven deeper into reflection on the transitoriness of youth and beauty. It is now that Kalodayin takes him on, escalating his arguments while citing devotion and friendship to both Siddhartha and the king. The prince, he asserts, is ungrateful for the many pleasures that have rightfully come to him. Siddhartha counters that he is being misjudged, claiming that impermanence, not pleasure, is at issue. He says,

It is not that I despise the objects of sense and I know that the world is devoted to them; but my mind does not delight in them, because I hold them to be transitory.

If the triad of old age, disease and death did not exist, I too should take pleasure in the ravishing objects of sense.[31]

As before, the brotherly comrades are at an impasse. Disheartened, everyone packs up and returns to the palace.

The Harem as Muse

While Siddhartha seems to be very much alone in waging his struggle for freedom, we must recall the tutelary deity watching over him in the *Abhinishkramanasutra* who has the prince's best interests—indeed, the best interests of all sentient creatures—at heart. This god (appearing as several brahmanical gods in other stories) is well aware of Siddhartha's destiny and wishes to help free him from the mire of samsara as soon as possible so that others may benefit from his (still latent) bodhisattva awakened wisdom. Difficulties in Kapilavastu are tame compared to those of all humanity. It's time for Siddhartha's sojourn as an ordinary human being to come to an end so that he can turn his mind to rescuing sentient beings from the ocean of samsara's misery.

All the legends refer to various sorts of divine intervention at the time of Siddhartha's Great Departure, especially during the episode of the four sights when the prince is out touring with his charioteer. However, further divine methods are employed in the harem, where the paradigm now shifts. Here deities leverage the ladies' power to make Siddhartha *leave* Kapilavastu and his life as a prince rather than stay home—in direct opposition to his family's efforts. So far, accounts of the harem women and activities have been matter-of-fact and told with candor, even warmth and humor. The women are typically portrayed as beautiful, erotic, refined, and empowered. They are expert in all the sensual arts, including music and dance as well as lovemaking. Descriptions of the harem conjure images of harmony and beauty, as well as sensuality. That the family has called upon the consorts as the last line of defense in keeping their beloved prince at home is an affirmation of the women's perceived power and place in the larger family system. (As we've seen, Buddhist double entendre abounds—the harem's power is also a metaphor for desire's stranglehold over our minds). Yet all the legends tell us that however brilliantly Siddhartha's consorts may have executed their seductive skills, they ultimately failed in securing the prince's lasting allegiance. But wait. Their power swings both ways. Now the tutelary gods step in to use the ladies' sway in igniting Siddhartha's passions, not for worldly pleasure, but for the spiritual life. They turn the tables in the harem.

The following account is familiar to even the most general readers of the Buddha legend. Indeed, it's typically the only harem episode in the popular, made-for-Westerners version. To varying degrees, it appears in all the early Pali and Sanskrit legends, and unfortunately—depending on the version— is largely blighted by misogyny. It's too bad that more positive renditions of harem life in the Buddha legend are not better known and understood. The episode goes like this: It is Siddhartha's last night at home. Utterly disheartened by the unsatisfactory nature of worldly affairs, he returns to the harem and, ignoring the seductive charms of the dancing women, falls asleep. The gods meanwhile have cast a spell over the palace, and soon the ladies too (forty thousand according to the Sinhalese version) are sleeping soundly. The harem transforms in dreadful ways. Through divine magical powers, the women appear passed out in vulgar, slovenly fashion, their clothes falling off and their bodies splayed in sexually suggestive poses. With matted hair and jewels awry, they are drooling, dribbling, and grinding their teeth. It is, indeed, a hideous scene.

[Some women] ... helplessly lost to shame ... lay in immodest attitudes, snoring, and stretched their limbs, all distorted and tossing their arms about.

Others looked ugly, lying unconscious like corpses, with their ornaments and garlands cast aside, the fastening knots of their dresses undone, and eyes moveless with the whites showing.

Another lay as if sprawling in intoxication, with her mouth gaping wide, so that the saliva oozed forth, and her limbs spread out so as to show what should have been hid. Her beauty was gone, her form distorted.[32]

Siddhartha awakes and, by the eerie light of the lanterns, perceives the women thus. Gone are his beautiful harem wives and enchanting abode overflowing with sensual delights—sources of comfort and pleasure his entire adult life. Now the harem appears ghastly and repulsive, resembling a charnel ground full of rotting, stinking corpses. Like a man who sees his house is on fire, Siddhartha only wants to get out. In desperation, he says,

How impure the world! how false and deceiving!
And nothing more so than woman's appearance;
Because of clothes, and the decoration of jewels,
The fool is filled with mad desire.
But if a man bring himself to consider
All these charms are but a phantasy, unreal as a dream,
And so put away ignorance, and do not permit himself to be
    deceived,
That man shall obtain deliverance and a body free from
    contamination.[33]

Clearly this is a no-win situation for the ladies. Beholden to their patriarch, they're all dressed up according to the desires and fantasies of men. This makes them attractive—until it doesn't. Then it's the same men's projections, now altered, that make the women appear repulsive and the root of delusion that leads to samsara's bondage. Greater Buddhist lessons aside, women repeatedly take the dubious prize of being the metaphor in the crosshairs of samsara's miserable reality. Even so, there may be an upside here. Taking a broader view of all these harem stories, women clearly hold the power whether the narrators saw it that way or not. Although their goals are antithetical, first Siddhartha's family and then the gods turn to the women of the harem as the strongest weapon in their arsenal. While the "positive" efforts (i.e., seducing the prince) failed, the "negative" ones (i.e., becoming repulsive) did not. Siddhartha was not meant to remain in samsara. If it was women's power that once kept him there, it was also through women's power that he was ultimately set free. It must be mentioned that in the *Lalitavistara* version of this episode, the women per se do not repulse Siddhartha. Rather, it is by witnessing their "disgusting" states that he is induced to meditate on the truth that his body is just like theirs—in alignment with the Buddha's intended teaching, as discussed earlier. From this insight, he sees that all physical bodies have the same shortcomings and are ultimately susceptible to the decrepitude of old age, sickness, and death. A gender distinction is not being made in this variant so much as the women's display is used to prompt Siddhartha's meditation on a universal truth.[34]

But let's take another look at the "disgusting" harem story and tweak it a bit. The following revised version does not appear in any of the ancient legends, but since those early stories arose from the cultural context and imaginations of contemporaneous androcentric storytellers, it's reasonable to posit an update or at least a refreshed version based on our own contemporary—and in this case, female-friendly—values. Religious fossils shed light on the past but need not be held sacrosanct in the present, especially in the Buddha legend where this misogynist scene has been mindlessly reiterated for millennia. The following story is suggested as an alternative to the "disgusting" harem scene that appears in the traditional version of events.

This proposed tweak is surprisingly minor and remains true to elements of the overall narrative. It goes like this: Instead of a male god or gods orchestrating the final intervention in Siddhartha's harem by having the women appear repulsive, let's switch gender and suppose for a moment that it was a goddess, specifically Abhayadevi, whom we have already met. She has been a loving presence in Siddhartha's life since he was born, attending his birth as Maya held the branch of the *shala* tree and soon after receiving him in the temple where she acknowledged his superior destiny. Recently she appeared again to Suddhodana to counsel him in his grief that Siddhartha will go forth, affirming that his son will soon leave the "throng of women" in the harem and turn to a life of contemplation. True to her name, Abhayadevi has always been Siddhartha's protectress, an unseen wisdom presence guiding him toward the fulfillment of his fate. It's not much of a stretch to imagine that her next step would be to help the emerging Bodhisattva in his struggle to leave home and embark on his spiritual quest. So in this newly imagined story, she appears in the harem to speak to the consorts. Just as Mahaprajapati held forth with the ladies on strategies to incite Siddhartha to stay, so now Abhayadevi exhorts them on how to help him leave:

> Ladies, listen up! You must stop confusing Siddhartha with all your seductive wiles. Our beloved prince must fulfill his destiny and go forth to become a buddha for the benefit of others. Time is of the essence. The moment has come for you to shed your lustful ways and help him leave the life of pleasure behind. Use your superior skills to shock him with the dark side of his addictions. Let's transform the harem into a repulsive charnel ground so he will no longer see a reason to stay. Only then will he arrive at his own wisdom and sever all attachments to worldly desire.

The rest of the story proceeds as already described. The ladies splay themselves grotesquely about the harem, but that is now their intention. In this way, they come across not as repulsive, but as wise and skillful. Without attachment to appearance, they deliberately provide the necessary illusion to help set Siddhartha free. This version looks much the same as the traditional account, but it is no longer framed by misogyny and, significantly, still concludes with Siddhartha's intended epiphany. Accomplishing what the male gods could not, Abhayadevi's approach invokes the sacred feminine, where darkness and light are not the problem, but seeing them as separate is.

Another wonderful and much lesser known story about the harem in these final hours is found in the *Lalitavistara*. Once again, the deities are working their divine magic as Siddhartha lounges on his couch among the consorts. No ordinary gods, however, these are enlightened buddhas who've decided that it's time for the Bodhisattva to get on with his spiritual mission. In this story, the awakened ones transform the harem into a blissful liminal realm where the powers of celestial sound become the agent of their intervention. Gone are the pulsing, erotic rhythms of dancing girls. Now in the guise of celestial muses, the consorts gently ply their musical instruments as the harem brims with sweet melodies flowing like nectar from the divine realms. The women's quarters resonate with exquisite music that gradually transforms into the sounds of dharma itself. While not perceptible to ordinary beings, the celestial buddhas call out to the Bodhisattva through this mystical sound in beautiful protracted verse that exhorts him to action:

> Virtuous One, quickly leave this fine city
> And practice the conduct of previous sages.
> When you reach the right place on the earth,
> You shall awaken to the incomparable wisdom of the victorious ones.
> In the past you gave away your wealth and riches,
> And even your hands, feet, and dear body.
> Great Sage now is your time;
> Open up the limitless river of Dharma for sentient beings.[35]

These melodious verses extend over an entire chapter. They remind the Bodhisattva of his many past lives in which he accumulated the abundant merit that brings him to this crossroads in his current rebirth. They serve to jog his memory, as it were, so that he will resume his overarching mission of rescuing sentient beings from samsara's misery.

The ironic role reversal for the consorts is noteworthy. In the most ordinary sense, their first job has always been to pleasure the prince, engaging his senses fully in all measure of physical and psychological gratification. More recently, they've been charged with the critical—and as we know, futile—task of subverting Asita's prophecy that the prince would renounce his kingdom. Failing that, they are then cast as disgusting, which we're told has actually been the case all along. No wonder Siddhartha would want to leave. However, in this story, the ladies no longer define the life Siddhartha chooses to reject. His journey of transformation is not a solitary one; it touches the women too. As he has the potential to transform, so do they. No longer temptresses, they appear rather as muses emanating the wisdom that proscribes temptation. Conjoined with Siddhartha's destiny, the women are divine messengers entrusted with the sacred message of dharma that finally sets him free. In this harem account, sexual activity (lust, delusion) subsides as dharma (expressed through sublime music) dawns. The transformation is beautifully portrayed as a process shared with, and simultaneously experienced by, the women.

Throughout this chapter in the *Lalitavistara,* the narrator has reminded us that Siddhartha has been fully aware of his bodhisattva nature the whole time; his activity in the harem—indeed, his entire rebirth as prince of the Shakyas—is simply a skillful display orchestrated for the benefit of ordinary beings. From this viewpoint, his human emotions such as confusion, lust, or despondency are just de rigueur demonstrations of his bodhisattva behavior. This story further highlights that the final jumping-off point for all bodhisattvas past and present is their harem. Not only have they all had harems, but the reason they linger in samsara is not because they are enjoying sensual pleasures, including sex, but because they begin their mission by emancipating the women they care for.

Unfortunately, a faith-based belief in bodhisattva intention has too often been co-opted in present-day Buddhism by the delusions of some unscrupulous male Buddhist teachers who use similar "harem" paradigms to frame—and justify—their own sexual misconduct among trusting students within their communities. Where these ancient stories may be intended as religious metaphors to illustrate or inspire an understanding of dharma, it is a perversion that they may be used in ways that contribute to greater delusion and suffering, particularly the abuse of women. To use them as license to behave badly blights the tradition and furthers the struggles of Buddhist women seeking equal footing in an already densely androcentric religious system. In short, it is misguided—in this case, harmful—to view stories, rather than dharma itself, as blueprints for personal behavior.

Let's return briefly to the previous story. According to the *Lalitavistara's* version of events, the consorts have accumulated untold positive karma in past lives that has brought them to their present auspicious relationship with the Bodhisattva. The chapter concludes as Siddhartha assumes his unobstructed identity and manifests numerous miracles that open the gates of dharma for their benefit. His desirous attachment to the women has transformed into a profound wish to benefit them in this and all their future lives. Now it is the Bodhisattva's voice that emanates spontaneously through the musical instruments, as he gives the consorts their first teaching in how to free their minds and hearts from the pain of worldly attachments. In this way, the women of the harem (here, eighty-four thousand) all mature in their personal journeys to unexcelled perfect awakening. Once again we find a story where women were the Bodhisattva's earliest disciples.[36]

Yashodhara's Dreams

Anxiety is running deep in Kapilavastu as Siddhartha prepares to leave. By day, his family tries to stop him, and by night, they are sleepless with nightmares. Mahaprajapati, as we know, awoke with distress after dreaming that her son had fled the city as a white bull. Suddhodana also had a bad dream: with a sharp pain shooting through his heart, he awoke in his harem after dreaming that his son had been abducted from the palace during the night by a host of gods.[37] Yashodhara too is fraught with nightmares as she anticipates the loss of her husband. The Sanskrit tradition goes on about this in great detail.

A brief version appears in the Kangyur, where Yashodhara awakens anxiously after dreaming that Siddhartha has abandoned her. Recounting her dream, she beseeches him never to leave her: "Oh, my lord, where e'er thou goest, there let me go, too." But he misunderstands her in an exchange that includes another Buddhist pun. Taking her words to mean that she wishes to go where there is no more sorrow, meaning nirvana, he reassures her, "So be it; wherever I go, there mayest thou go also." As it turns out, this is prophetic: much later in their lives, Yashodhara becomes a renunciate and disciple of the Buddha. This is certainly not what she meant at the time of her dream, however.[38]

In the *Abhinishkramansutra,* Yashodhara is tossing and turning in her sleep. Siddhartha, lying next to her in bed, rouses her with great concern and tenderly tries to comfort her. He says,

> Yashodhara, beloved! Why are you so restless and alarmed? Your breathing indicates distress, and your heart is oppressed; what is it affects you that you start so? My Yashodhara is not in a [cemetery] nor in a place for burning bodies, nor amidst the mountains, or in a desert; but you are in the city surrounded by guards, in the King's palace, well protected; there are no wild beasts here, or robbers to frighten you; but in this place there is peace and safety and no cause for alarm! But yet I see my Yashodhara's heart is greatly affected, filled with doubt and anxiety; tell me then, as you have just awoke, the cause of all this?[39]

Yashodhara awakens. Terrified and choking with sobs, she relates numerous apocalyptic visions that came to her in her sleep: the earth shook while the sun, moon, and stars fell from the sky; her beautiful headdress ornaments, along with her finest jewels, were torn off and scattered; her body became naked and ugly; her hands and feet fell off; furniture overturned; mountains burst into flames; and the wind blew down beautiful trees in the palace gardens. Further, the guardian spirit of the city raised his voice in lamentation, and Kapilavastu became a wasteland as vegetation withered and wells dried up. Indeed, the sun itself lost its glorious light, and the world was plunged into darkness.

Reflecting silently on Yashodhara's agitated words, Siddhartha realizes that they clearly foretell his imminent departure and the emotional devastation that will soon befall his family and homeland. However, he chooses to reassure her and responds that there is nothing to worry about. Dreams, after all, are illusory:

> Dear wife! . . . Dreams are but the empty products of a universal law; return dear wife, to your rest! You are young in years and your body delicate and soft, let not such anxieties as these molest you or cause you distress![40]

Siddhartha further proceeds to pacify his wife by making love to her.

In the *Lalitavistara,* Yashodhara's* dream episode is similar, but here Siddhartha appears in full bodhisattva persona and turns the occasion into an opportunity to give her a dharma teaching. Once again, they lie in bed together and she awakens terrified. After recounting to him the many ill omens that appeared in her dreams, she begs him for reassurance:

> Lord, what is going to befall me? Please tell me the meaning of these dreams!
> My memory is confused, and I cannot see clearly. My heart is aching![41]

Siddhartha responds that nothing bad is going to happen to her and then proceeds with a lengthy interpretation that takes each ill omen and turns it into some positive prognostication for her future. For example,

---

*Here her name is Gopa.

When you dreamed that the trees are uprooted
And you cut off your hair with your right hand,
It shows that you, Gopa, will quickly cut the web of afflictions
And free yourself from the web of viewing conditioned phenomena.

When you dream that the sun and the moon fall to the ground
And that the stars fall as well,
It shows that you, Gopa, will quickly conquer the enemy of
    afflictions
And will become worthy of offerings and praise from the world.[42]

Unfortunately, he also says,

When you dream that your pearl necklace is torn
And that you are naked and your body mutilated,
It shows that you, Gopa, can soon leave your female body
And swiftly attain a male body.[43]

The voice of an androcentric narrator shines through. It is held in some
Buddhist texts (though not taught by the Buddha himself) that enlightenment is not possible (or just very difficult) in a female body. According
to this bias, being born female puts one at a distinct disadvantage when it
comes to soteriological matters. The best bet for any woman striving for
release from samsara, therefore, is to achieve rebirth as a male. So in this
story, in an effort to cheer Yashodhara up, Siddhartha delivers the "good"
news that omens foretell she will soon be a man!

In the *Mahavastu*, Yashodhara's dream is more uplifting. As before,
she wakes up and recounts her experience to Siddhartha: A mighty cloud
suddenly engulfed Suddhodana's palace accompanied by a burst of rain, a
clap of thunder, and a brilliant flash of lightning that lit up the three worlds.
Following this, an ocean of rain—incomparably cool, clear, and pure—
softly pelted the entire earth. This time, the god Brahma appears to provide
an explanation, assuring Yashodhara that her dream augurs well for herself
and all beings:

This lovely-eyed son of Suddhodana, like a cloud raining on the three
worlds, will bring relief to those who are scorched by the great fires

of passion, by bringing to birth immovable dharma, and compassion beyond compare.[44]

Siddhartha's mind, too, was restless before he left. The legends tell us that he had five dreams, which he recounted to his disciples later as the Buddha. Not at all frightening, these dreams were in the nature of marvelous miracles presaging his future accomplishments and the great benefit the Buddha would soon bring to humanity.[45]

The Great Departure

The time had finally come for Siddhartha's departure from family and kingdom. Preordained by his actions in previous lives and prophesied by the sage Asita in this one, the prince's destiny was rapidly advancing toward the inevitability of his full and complete awakening. Quite a difference from life so far in Kapilavastu, but one Siddhartha was clearly ready for since no measure of the life he had once enjoyed was now satisfying. Despite the excessive privilege he experienced from birth, the foibles of human existence far outweighed its pleasures. This—together with undue pressure from his parents, wives, and kingdom—was pushing him to the edge. Rather than keeping him at home, the din of expectations seems to have secured his resolve to leave. Bodhisattva aside, it's a tale familiar to many families, past and present, where a beloved son (or daughter) spurns the life others expect of him in order to pursue his own purpose. Siddhartha says,

> I would rather be cut in pieces, limb by limb, and piece by piece; I would rather be burnt in a fiery furnace; I would rather be ground to pieces by a falling mountain, than forego for one instant my fixed purpose to become a religious recluse, or to return again to my home. For, alas! All earthly pleasures are transitory and perishable—this alone endures.[46]

The Pali sources offer a consistent account of Siddhartha's departure from home. Reeling from the sight of the disgusting women draped about his harem, he decides forthwith to call his guard to saddle his horse. It is late at night and everyone, including his wife, Yashodhara, is fast asleep. According to these sources, she had given birth to their son, Rahula, that very day. With the last vestiges of attachment, Siddhartha decides to make a final visit to her apartments to see his son and bid her farewell. However, so deeply are mother and child sleeping—Yashodhara reclining on a couch scattered with white jasmine flowers and holding the infant Rahula in her arms—that Siddhartha chooses not to awaken them. His resolve is still shaky, and she might prove an obstacle to his departure. Quietly closing the door, he determines that when he sees them next he will be a buddha.* According to the Thai variant, he says,

> How can I continue to live thus . . . how can I live loving my wife and child, and at the same time escape the evils of circling existence? It is impossible! If I remain with them I shall never attain omniscience. I will away at once; and when I have attained all knowledge I can return to visit my relations.[47]

With this declaration he descends to the palace courtyard to meet his servant Chandaka and mount his horse. In these Pali tradition scenarios, the servant is portrayed as mostly wordless and compliant as he carries out the prince's instructions. A more developed relationship comes across with the horse, Kanthaka—a magnificent steed the color of white conch and eighteen cubits in length—who is anthropomorphized throughout the stories. Kanthaka is said to be delighted as Siddhartha caresses him and speaks to him as one would a beloved pet:

> Well, Kantaka, you must assist me tonight, that by your aid I may be enabled to release all sentient beings from the perils of existence.[48]

At the stroke of midnight they depart. So thunderous is mighty Kanthaka in flight that the gods magically hold their hands beneath his hooves to muffle the sounds of Siddhartha's escape. As with many auspicious occasions in Buddhist lore, it is said to have been an effulgent moonlit night:

> The lovely full moon shone without a speck; and the earth, flooded with its rays, appeared like a sea of gleaming white milk.[49]

---

* This story line is continued in chapter 6.

The Sanskrit tradition relates these episodes somewhat differently and with more detail. We've already seen how Yashodhara plays a big role through her dream sequences, which exhibit her anxiety at the prospect of being abandoned by her husband. Siddhartha's harem, too, is treated with much more depth at the time of his departure. In the Sanskrit texts, there is no final visit to Yashodhara's quarters to say good-bye to wife and son; instead the prince's biggest concern is taking leave of his parents, particularly his father. In the *Lalitavistara,* out of filial affection and duty, Siddhartha seeks out the king and quite touchingly asks his forgiveness. Waking Suddhodana in his chambers, the prince says,

> My lord, now the time is right for me to leave home;
> Please do not hinder me and don't be distraught.
> My king, may you, my family, and the people of the kingdom
>   forgive me.[50]

A familiar dialogue ensues in which the emotional king implores Siddhartha to reconsider. In the end, with abiding parental love, he gives his son his blessing:

> Then go and benefit and liberate beings. I rejoice in that.
> May all your wishes be fulfilled.[51]

Other sources similarly express the strong father-son bond. As Siddhartha gallops through the eastern gate of the city on Kanthaka's back, he perceives his sleeping father and calls out,

> Father! Though I love thee, yet a fear possesses me and I may not stay.
> I must free myself from the fear of conquering time and death, of the
>   horrors of age and death![52]

As Siddhartha turns away from his wives in the palace, he pledges himself to a lifetime of celibacy:

> This for me is the last night on which I will have lain with a woman.[53]

That Siddhartha is assisted and escorted by countless deities and supernatural beings in making his escape is noted in all the legends, though here again we learn more from the Sanskrit sources. The celestial maidens strike up their beautiful melodies and sing the praises of the Bodhisattva as he takes off. To facilitate matters, the gods use their magical powers to cause the entire palace and city of Kapilavastu to fall asleep.

> In the city, all men, women, and children
> Became tired and fell asleep, abandoning their chores.
> The horses, elephants, oxen, parrots, cranes, peacocks, and mynas
> Became tired and quickly slept, not noticing anything.

> Armed with lances hard as [diamond], and mounted on elephants,
>   horses, and chariots,
> The Sakya youths who kept guard also fell asleep,
> As did the king, the princes and the royal pages.
> The retinue of consorts, completely naked, were asleep and oblivious.[54]

Generally the gods are jubilant that the Bodhisattva is finally embarking on his journey to liberate humanity. Leading the way for Siddhartha, who is astride his horse with Chandaka hanging on to Kanthaka's tail, are grand processions of celestial beings holding torches aloft to illuminate the heavens, as every sort of celebratory offering in the form of flowers, jewels, incense, perfumes, banners, and so forth rains from the sky. The heavens rejoice with the sounds of music as gods and celestial maidens call out their praises and encouragement to the prince.

Noteworthy, however, are the exceptions to the rejoicing. As already mentioned, an occasional tutelary god appears in the Sanskrit traditions. So far we've seen the goddess Abhayadevi appear in the *Mahavastu* and a male god of uncertain name in the *Abhinishkramanasutra,* both of whom serve to guide and assist Siddhartha toward his destiny. Occasionally these legends also note female guardian spirits (*yakshis*) of the palace, the city of Kapilavastu, and natural elements such as trees or rivers. As might be expected, the *yakshis* spring into action at the time of Siddhartha's Great Departure. Rather than rejoice, however, we find that mostly they are sad. Unlike the celestial beings who are gladdened that the Bodhisattva is finally on his way, these earthly spirits reflect the sentiments of Siddhartha's family and the Shakya people. Those that inhabit the harem of the palace begin to weep at the prince's departure, their tears falling as rain upon Kapilavastu. Chandaka is confused about which deity is affecting the weather and queries Siddhartha,

> "Prince, drops of rain are falling. Why is the god making it rain?" The bodhisattva replied: "The god is not raining, but because of my departure, the deities who dwell in the harem of the palace are crying; their tears are falling down everywhere." And Chandaka, his own eyes filled with tears, heaved a long, emotional sigh, and remained silent.[55]

The guardian *yakshi* of Kapilavastu similarly expresses sadness. In the *Mahavastu,* her name is Nagaradevata. While the Shakya people sleep, she rises above the city and sorrowfully calls out to Siddhartha as he rides off,

> O [Mighty One], O [Mighty One], look at me. O lion, O lion, look at me. O most elect of beings, look at me; O leader of the caravan, look at me.[56]

Hearing her cry, Siddhartha turns to take one final look at his homeland. Rather than waver in his decision, however, he reasserts his vow to attain awakening:

> Though I were to fall into hell and get poisoned food to eat, I shall not again enter this city before I have gone beyond old age and death.[57]

In the *Lalitavistara,* the town's guardian deity—in this instance, male— invokes Siddhartha in more extreme terms. Speaking on behalf of the Shakya people, he foretells the ruination of the kingdom without the prince. The town will wither and die, the god says, without the life force brought by their prince:

> If you leave . . .

> You will take away the vitality and power from this entire city;
> Like a wasteland, it will shine with beauty no more. . . .

> The might of the Sakyas on this earth will come to nothing,
> And the royal family line will be interrupted.
> The hopes of the assembly of Sakyas will be dashed entirely
> If you, the great tree of merit, depart.[58]

Undeterred, Siddhartha reiterates his resolve and perseveres in his journey.

The relationship between Siddhartha and his servant, Chandaka, is notable in this context and hearkens back to the earlier discussion where it was suggested that they grew up as close friends, perhaps half brothers, in Suddhodana's harem. As with Kalodayin, the familiarity and trust between Siddhartha and Chandaka is pronounced in the Sanskrit stories. In the *Buddhacarita,* for example, an entire chapter is devoted to Chandaka's important role in the prince's Great Departure. We know that the two young men were the same age, since it is mentioned repeatedly that they (and for that matter, Kanthaka the horse) were conatal. Siddhartha himself often refers to their exceptional bond with great affection. That a servant would be featured in such an auspicious context highlights the importance Chandaka was given in the early Buddhist traditions.

Chandaka is distressed when Siddhartha calls out from the harem ordering his favorite horse to be saddled up in the middle of the night. Such a request is unprecedented, and Chandaka knows something unsettling is about to occur. Not at all servile in these Sanskrit stories, he tries to dissuade the prince from his plan to leave the palace. As with Kalodayin in the harem scene, Chandaka speaks directly and frankly to Siddhartha, much more as a brother or cherished friend than a servant.

> O, prince, it is now midnight. What need of a horse is there at such a time? Thou hast a mansion like the abode of Kuvera.* So be happy in it. Why dost thou call for a horse? Thou hast a harem as fair as the [celestial maidens]. Be happy in it. . . . O, prince, this is no time for a horse. This is the time for lying on royal beds. What need is there of a horse just now?[59]

---

* The god of wealth.

There is little here of the obsequious attendant found in the Pali stories. Like Kalodayin earlier, Chandaka urges Siddhartha to abandon thoughts of leaving. Why not just enjoy the manly privileges of princely life, particularly his harem wives? In the *Lalitavistara,* the related passage goes on for ten pages. Chandaka is inconsolable and weeping as he wrangles with the prince, lobbing one argument after another. By now Siddhartha has heard enough and just wants to get under way.

The *Abhinishkramanasutra* focuses on a different theme at this point in the storyline. Here Chandaka trembles with fear when he hears Siddhartha call for his horse. After all, like all the Shakyas, Chandaka is under orders from the king to quash any attempt by the prince to flee. As much as he loves Siddhartha, his loyalties are being challenged. His feelings of responsibility and affection for the royal family, especially his patriarch, Suddhodana, shine through in this episode. In a very personal, brotherly exchange, Chandaka challenges Siddhartha from a different angle. He cites the king's advanced age and the unutterable heartbreak Suddhodana would feel if the prince were to carry out his purpose. Siddhartha responds with touching testimony to his own love for his father and family:

> My love to my father is not less than his to me, nor do I love all my relatives less; but I feel my heart filled with awe and fear in consideration of the misery awaiting them all if they continue in this condition of birth and death, and I desire to find out the Law of [Dharma] to prove my love to them to be greater even than theirs, for I aim to rescue them and all men from their misery, and every future consequence of it.[60]

Here, as in so many places in the biographical legends of the Buddha, we can feel Siddhartha's abiding love for his family. It is not due to indifference that he leaves them; rather, his profound love compels him to seek greater answers. He wishes to find freedom from suffering beginning with himself so he might then bring those truths to others, including his loved ones.

The theme of family is carried through the moment of Siddhartha and Chandaka's parting when, after riding through the night, the prince dismounts his steed for the last time. Shedding his royal diadem and ornaments, Siddhartha hands them over to Chandaka to return to the king.

Further, he entrusts Chandaka to take back a message of reassurance in which he affirms his decision to become a seeker of truth, asks his loved ones not to grieve, and pledges to return home once he has awakened to supreme wisdom. It is interesting to note the discrepancy in the legends as to whom his message is directed. While most legends name his parents or Suddhodana and Mahaprajapati specifically, several sources additionally name Yashodhara, the Shakya people, and, in one instance, Siddhartha's sister, presumably referring to Sundarinanda. More extensive accounts also have Siddhartha tenderly referencing Rahula in this episode with the wish that his son be well cared for in his absence, as he will not see Rahula again until he has become a buddha.

For his part, Chandaka continues to be brokenhearted. In the *Buddhacarita,* he goes so far as to rebuke the prince, naming Siddhartha's family members in turn as reasons to reconsider:

> O mighty prince, you should not desert . . . your loving aged father, who yearns so for his son.

> Nor should you forget, like an ingrate kind treatment, the queen, your second mother, who exhausted herself in bringing you up.

> You should not abandon, like a coward the sovereignty he has obtained, the virtuous princess, mother of a young son, devotedly faithful to her husband and of illustrious lineage.

> You should not abandon, like a vicious man his excellent repute, the young son of Yasodhara, worthy of praise and best of the cherishers of fame and *dharma.*[61]

Siddhartha reminds him that death eventually separates everyone from their loved ones, and with this, he specifically references his loss of his mother, Maya:

> My mother bore me in her womb with pains and great longing. Her efforts have been fruitless. What am I now to her or her to me?[62]

Despite distancing himself emotionally and physically from his loved ones, Siddhartha has kind parting words for Chandaka. In the *Abhinishkramana-sutra,* he addresses him affectionately and as kin:

No further conversation do I purpose [sic] to hold;
You know my heart and my love to you;
I am now freed from the love due only to relatives.
Take the horse Kantaka and depart.[63]

Chandaka and Kanthaka are deeply moved at the moment of parting from their beloved prince. Ever weeping, Chandaka begs to accompany Siddhartha on his quest and become a recluse himself. In the Pali tradition, the horse is so devastated that he drops dead from grief on the spot.

At this point in most of the legends, Siddhartha exchanges his royal vestments for those of a hunter, who happily sheds his filthy rags at the prince's bidding. Usually the gods orchestrate this scenario, but in Sanskrit variants, we learn that women were involved. Here an old woman had been entrusted with a humble cotton garment prior to the Buddha's birth. It was worn by ten successive buddhas over previous lifetimes, and now it is given to her with express instructions to save it for the son of Suddhodana, who would someday become the next great buddha. However, soon after receiving the garment, the old woman is dying, so she entrusts it to her daughter. When the daughter, too, feels her death approaching, she gives the garment to the guardian spirit of a nearby tree. The god Indra observes all this from his celestial perch and, at the proper time, sweeps down and steals the robe, assuming the appearance of the hunter who exchanges clothes with Siddhartha. The rest of the story merges with the usual accounts, which all say that Siddhartha's princely vestments became enshrined as a sacred relic in the godly realm. Noteworthy here is not just the participation of women but also that of a sacred tree in providing the Bodhisattva's first ascetic garb.[64]

Sadness in Kapilavastu

It must have been with great relief that Siddhartha finally said good-bye to Chandaka, at long last severing all ties with home. So much emotional turmoil had led up to this moment (plus lifetimes of accumulated merit, according to the Sanskrit sources). Now he could turn his mind to the peaceful practices of a religious recluse. Many years later, the Buddha described this time in his life to his disciples.

While I was being delicately brought up, this thought occurred to me: "Now this life at home is too full of hindrances. The way of religious life is in the open air. It is not possible for one living at home to live the holy life that is utterly bright, blameless, pure and clean. Let me then now go away from home into the homeless state."

Then monks, against the wishes of my sobbing and weeping parents, I left my sumptuous home and the universal kingship that was in my hands. And now, being a wanderer from home into the homeless state I withdrew towards the city of Vesali.[65]

Shedding the identity of Prince Siddhartha, this newly minted wanderer became known to fellow anchorites as Shakyamuni ("Sage of the Shakyas") or often simply Gautama, his family name and the postdeparture moniker that will henceforth be used for him in this narrative. It was now that he donned a lifelong cloak of celibacy, never again becoming a householder or returning to the libidinous ways of his youth. There is a curious and anomalous mention in the *Lalitavistara* that Gautama took his first two meals as a renunciate with women hermits, both of them of the brahman caste. The first was named Saki, and the second was called Padma. We learn nothing more about them.[66]

Meanwhile, back in Kapilavastu, the palace is in chaos. The morning after Siddhartha's escape, the magical sleep cast over the city lifts, and Siddhartha's consorts awake to find him missing. Distraught, they search every room in the palace until finally, unable to locate him, they each begin to wail, "I do not see the prince! I do not see the prince!" Now Yashodhara is awake, and she too comes unhinged. Falling to the floor, beating her chest, tearing her hair, and casting off her jewels, she cries, "Alas, we have been deceived! Where did [the prince] go?" Hearing the ruckus, the king gets the news that his son, Chandaka, and the horse are nowhere to be found. Fearing that Asita's prophecy has finally come to pass, he laments, "Alas! Alas! My son— my dear son!" Mahaprajapati, along with her daughter, hears the outcry and, collapsing to the ground, she beseeches the king, "Your Majesty, get my son back quickly!" Suddhodana orders the gates of the city to be sealed and dispatches soldiers who search—in vain, of course—for the prince.[67] Despite her own misery, Mahaprajapati tenderly comforts Yashodhara during this time:

Daughter of the Sakyas, do not cry.
The supreme noble one among men has said in the past:
"I will liberate this world from birth and old age."[68]

Before long, Chandaka is on his way home to Kapilavastu. Miserable and heartbroken, he carries with him the heraldic ornaments of Siddhartha's princely status. He must deliver them to the king together with the disastrous news that the prince is gone for good. Following the Sanskrit tradition, Chandaka makes the journey with the faithful Kanthaka, who is equally despondent. The two require eight arduous days to return, even though the outward journey with Siddhartha had effortlessly taken only one night. As they arrive at the gates of Kapilavastu, they find their once-resplendent city deserted and depressed, "like a sky without the sun."[69] The gardens have withered and fountains have dried up, as if afflicted by sadness on account of the prince's absence. Kanthaka neighs in recognition as he trots through the city gate, which sets off a flurry of excitement and renewed hope among the Shakyas. Even the palace birds perk up with hope that they may soon see their beloved prince again. Townsfolk amass in doorways, and the palace women—including Yashodhara and Mahaprajapati—crowd the balconies, crying out that Siddhartha has returned. Soon enough, of course, their hopes are dashed:

Those ladies of the palace, their hearts overwhelmed,
Looked through the windows to see the Prince returned.
But seeing the horse and the servant only,
The tears fell in thick succession from their eyes.
Casting away their jewels and their choice garments again,
Their head dresses and other decorations scattered,
With both hands raised above them in the air,
See how they weep! Hearken to their sad lamentations![70]

A variant in the *Lalitavistara* asserts that Yashodhara does not appear on the balcony but remains in her apartments, certain that the prince has not returned. She remembers her husband's vow that he would not be back before attaining enlightenment.[71]

The truth hits home that their prince is not coming back, and the Shakyas are devastated all over again. Taken together, the Sanskrit texts go on for pages in elaborately emotional detail about the grief of the Shakya people, particularly the palace women, as they mourn the loss of their prince.* The *Buddhacarita* is known for its dramatic poetic style, but no less descriptive are passages in the *Abhinishkramanasutra* and the *Lalitavistara*. While clearly and beautifully conveying the emotionality of this sad occasion for Siddhartha's family, these passages generally do not add much to the overall narrative. Here we'll look at highlights, focusing on portrayals of the women.

Chandaka is met with consternation as he enters the palace. Returning noble ornaments to the seat of sovereignty is a customary ritual that honors a warrior slain in battle. The symbolism is not lost on the king when the groomsman presents Siddhartha's jewels and diadem, incontrovertible evidence that the prince has abdicated the throne and will not be coming back. In some legends, there is even a moment of panic that the prince has been killed, a misunderstanding that Chandaka quickly clears up. The ladies of the palace—including Mahaprajapati and Siddhartha's junior wife, Mrigi Gautami—are witness to this dramatic scene. Overcome with anguish, they ply Chandaka with questions over the fate of their beloved son and husband.[72] Upon seeing her husband's ornaments, Yashodhara collapses in a faint. The consorts immediately tend to her, anxiously dousing her with water and crying out,

> May our Sakya princess not die now!
> It would be too much to bear if we lost two loved ones![73]

Three Shakya princes try to lift Siddhartha's magnificent ornaments but cannot, as they were forged for a body as mighty as a god's. Unable to bear the sight of this, Mahaprajapati exclaims,

> When I see his ornaments lying there, my heart is pierced with pain.
> I think it is better therefore to throw the ornaments into the pond.[74]

This was done, and the lake remained a sacred site to the Shakyas.

---

*For the most part, the Pali sources do not address this interval in the Buddha's biography.

Mahaprajapati's emotional distress is dramatically evinced further in the texts. After hearing Chandaka's report, she is overcome with grief:

> Like a cow bereaved of its calf, [she] uttered every kind of lamentable cry, unable to control herself she raised her hands and said, "My son! My son! Alas, my child!"[75]

Her lament is about not just her longing for Siddhartha, but also her motherly worry over how he will fare in the forest. Raised with every manner of luxury, how is Siddhartha going to manage sleeping on the hard ground and begging for his food? It is incomprehensible to Mahaprajapati that the delicate boy she held, bathed, and nurtured for twenty-nine years would choose rags and alms over the lavish privileges of his upbringing. Scandal over his departure is one thing, but as a mother, she has practical and logistical concerns for his health and safety. Lovingly she agonizes,

> His feet are soft with a beautiful network spread over the toes, tender as the fibre of a lotus or a flower, with the anklebones concealed and wheels in the middle of his soles. Shall they tread on the hard ground of the jungle?

> His powerful body is accustomed to sitting or lying on the palace roof and has been adorned with priceless clothes, aloes and sandalwood. How will it fare in the forest in the heat, the cold, and the rains?

> He is ennobled by race, goodness, strength, beauty, learning, majesty and youth, and so fitted to give, not to ask. Is he to practise begging alms from others?

> He has been sleeping on a spotless golden bed and awakened at night by the strains of musical instruments. How then shall he lie in accordance with his vows on the ground with only a piece of cloth interposed?[76]

It is ironic, of course, that Mahaprajapati would express these concerns when later in her own life she makes the same decision to abandon royal privilege and enter the contemplative life. Her tender feet will also bleed as she walks barefoot, dressed in dusty rags to the city of Vaishali to beseech her son, the Buddha, to grant ordination to herself and five hundred Shakya women. As we shall see, her son's journey is by no means a solitary one, as over time she and every member of the family is moved to follow their own inner path literally and figuratively in his footsteps.

As always, the harem women are portrayed as full participants in the royal family drama. All of them are wives, after all, to either the grieving father or the absconded son. As Mahaprajapati and Yashodhara lament, so do the other women. The description of these scenes appears overwrought but lovely in its imagery:

> Then all the ladies of the Palace seeing Mahaprajapati in this condition, and hearing her lamentations, themselves gave way to unrestrained grief; they wept and wailed as the cried "Alas! alas! where is our Lord? Alas! alas! where is our Prince?" and in this way they gave vent to their feelings—some rolled their eyes with grief, some looked at each other and wept, some smote their bodies, some smote their breasts, some twined their arms around each other, some tore their hair, some wandered disconsolate hither and thither, weeping and wailing the while, just as the stricken deer wanders at random through the brake, the poisoned arrow in his side—so did they wander to and fro, weeping and bending their bodies in grief, as the wind bends the tender palm—others, like the fish on the ground, writhed in anguish on the earth; thus in every way they showed their grief at the loss of the Prince.[77]

According to the *Buddhacarita,*

> Some of the . . . women, bereft of their brightness and with drooping arms and shoulders, seemed to become unconscious through despondency; they wailed not, they dropped no tears, they sighed not, they moved not, there they stood like figures in a picture.

> Other women, losing self control, swooned from grief for their lord, and with streams pouring down their faces their eyes watered their breasts . . . as a mountain waters the rocks with its streams.

Then with the women's faces whipped by the water from their eyes
the royal dwelling resembled a pond with dripping lotuses whipped
by rain from the clouds at the time of the first rains.[78]

A touching scene from the *Mahavastu* shows the consorts in a whole
new light. Here the faithful steed Kanthaka has arrived at the palace,
exhausted and starving from his journey. Bereft of his beloved master, he
is wasting away from grief. Seeing his beleaguered state, the ladies quickly
set upon the horse, affectionately plying him with sweetmeats mixed with
honey and other regal food. But Kanthaka cannot eat. All he can do is weep.
This poignant passage relates how the women do their best to nurture him,
hoping to revive his health and once indomitable spirit:

> Some women of the palace with their regal and costly garments
> of cloth, silk and wool wiped Kanthaka's tears. Others stroked his
> head, others his neck, others his back, others his shoulders, others his
> forelimbs, others his joints, others his tail, and others his hoofs. Some
> held morsels of honey to his mouth, others fodder of various kinds,
> others . . . sweetmeats, others regal drinks in vessels of gold and silver
> studded with precious stones. But Kanthaka would not feed.[79]

Despite their loving efforts, Kanthaka pines away from grief. In death,
he is celebrated by the royal family and honored by the king. Almost all
the legends say that due to his devoted service to the prince, he embarks
directly from his horse incarnation to one of the heavenly realms, where
he assumes the form of a god. There we find that harems are de rigeur in
heaven as on earth, because he enjoys the company of thousands of dancing
celestial maidens. Sometime later, Kanthaka is reborn as one of the Buddha's
disciples.[80]

A key figure who has a lot to say about Siddhartha's absence is
Yashodhara. To some extent, her lamentations very much mirror those we
have already seen expressed by her mother-in-law and the palace consorts.
However, overall, her reaction is more complex and nuanced than their raw
grief. Carrying the torch of the principal wife of the heir to the throne, she
is very angry. As Siddhartha's beloved chief consort with whom he shared
a deep romantic bond, she also feels betrayed. In the *Buddhacarita,* as the

mother of his child, she is outraged that he would abandon her and their son. The rawness of her emotions is beautifully expressed in many of these verses through ornate, metaphoric style. This emotional dimension in the Buddha legend is only found in the Sanskrit sources.

When Yashodhara first sees Chandaka and Kanthaka return to Kapila-vastu, her impulse is to fall upon them in a rage. She blames them both for absconding with her husband and robbing her of their life together. In the *Mahavastu,* she throws her arms around the horse's neck and cries out,

> O Kanthaka, where have you taken the prince? What offence have I given you and Chandaka that you should take the prince away when I was sleeping blissfully? I and the sixty thousand women of the palace are bereaved.[81]

Her rebuke in the *Buddhacarita* is much more vehement. Choking with tears, she demands an explanation from the groomsman and horse, accusing them of ruining her life and her family:

> Yashodhara, her eyes reddened with anger, her voice choking with the bitterness born of despair, her bosom heaving with sighs, and tears streaming down with the grief she was enduring: [spoke] . . .
>
> "Why do you weep here today, you brute, after doing me an ignoble, unkind, unfriendly deed? . . .
>
> "For through you . . . my lord has gone never to return. . . .
>
> "For your imprudence and so-called friendship have wrought great ruin on this family."[82]

Chandaka moves to defend them both, explaining the magical circum-stances surrounding the prince's escape. He and Kanthaka really had no power over the events as they unfolded, he tells her. The gods orchestrated everything from the sleeping consorts to the bolted gates spontaneously swinging open to allow them to pass. He says,

> I vainly tried to arouse you, oh! Lady, from your sleep. I fruitlessly attempted by force to awake you and the others from their torpor

. . . but in vain . . . all my efforts were useless! O lady! . . . this was the work of the Gods. I dared not oppose it.[83]

Inconsolable, Yashodhara's anger now shifts directly to her husband where, in the *Buddhacarita* account, she berates him in absentia. Here she invokes her rights as his wife and his responsibilities as her husband. By abandoning her, she says, Siddhartha has breached the sacrament of their marriage. Further, he has ignored the ancestral tradition of a king taking his wife with him if he departs for contemplative forest life. What kind of "dharma" is that? Here the poet Ashvaghosa is setting up a pun between the word *dharma* in the worldly sense, referring to proper conduct, and *dharma* in the religious sense, referring to ultimate truth and in this case, the Buddha's teachings. In the following verses, Yashodhara is sarcastically accusing her husband of violating dharma in pursuit of dharma. Simply put, she is implying that he is a hypocrite:

> If he wishes to carry out *dharma* and yet casts me off, his lawful partner in the duties of religion and now husbandless, in what respect is there *dharma* for him who wishes to follow austerities separated from his lawful partner?

> Surely he has not heard of our ancestors . . . who took their wives with them to the forest, since he thus intends to carry out *dharma* without me.

> Or else he does not see that in the sacrifices it is both husband and wife who are consecrated and purified by the precepts of the Veda and who will enjoy together in the hereafter too the recompense of the rites; therefore he has become miserly of *dharma* towards me.[84]

She even intimates that he has chosen austerities so that he may one day be surrounded by beautiful celestial maidens in Indra's heaven! Before collapsing with exhaustion, Yashodhara finally asserts that at least Siddhartha should have stayed home for the sake of their beautiful infant son, Rahula.

A softer, more philosophical version of events is related in the *Lalitavistara*. Here Yashodhara's love for Siddhartha elevates her expression of sorrow. Her grief mingles with an understanding of his purpose and insight into why he had to leave. Alone in her musings, she wonders tenderly, "When you left my bed, where did you go?" She vows to join him by practicing austerities in the palace until she sees him again. What unfolds is a beautiful love poem in which she recalls the sweet sensuality of his body while revealing her awareness of his bodhisattva nature:

> Alas, you gave me joy!
> Alas, noble man whose face is like the spotless moon!
> Alas, my most noble of men!
> Alas, you with excellent marks, so stainless and splendid!
>
> Alas, my wellborn man with a perfect body,
> Well formed and tapering, you are unequalled.
> Alas, my lord full of supreme qualities,
> Venerated by humans and gods alike and full of compassion.
> . . .
>
> Alas, my sweet tasting man, with lips like the bimba fruit,
> With eyes like a lotus and skin of golden hue.
> Alas, my dear one with spotless teeth,
> As white as cow's milk or snow.
>
> Alas, my dear one with a beautiful nose, beautiful eyebrows,
> And the stainless circling hair between your brows.
> Alas, my dear one with shoulders so well formed,
> With a waist like a bow, legs like a deer, and rounded hips.
>
> Alas, my man with thighs like the trunk of an elephant,
> With fair hands and feet, and with copper-colored nails,
> All these beautiful attributes were formed by your merit
> And delighted the king.[85]

To Chandaka, she now says,

> Chanda, I am miserable, for I had been showed a treasure.
> Yet now since it is like my eyes have been gouged, restore my sight!

Chanda, the victorious ones always teach
That one's parents are to be honored.

If [Siddhartha] abandoned them, needless to mention
That he would abandon the pleasures of love with a woman!
Alas, to separate from those we love
Is like watching a play—nothing endures![86]

Chandaka kindly counsels Yashodhara not to weep but to rejoice that her beloved husband will soon be awakening to supreme enlightenment. Before long, she will witness him being honored by mortals and immortals alike. His excellent deeds will illuminate the worlds. And since she loved and respected her husband, Chandaka assures her that she, too, will one day attain supreme enlightenment. He says, "I believe that you shall become just like him, the most noble being!"[87]

This sampling of passages about Yashodhara reveals the varied ways she is remembered and characterized by different Buddhist traditions. Unlike the Buddha's mothers Maya and Mahaprajapati, who appear more or less consistently as beneficent figures, Yashodhara displays a range of very real human emotions. What wife (or husband) does not feel angry and betrayed by a spouse who abandons her? It is to the credit of the narrators and storytellers of these particular stories that such emotional displays have been retained, not redacted or entirely stereotyped. Yashodhara's abandonment in the Buddha legend has fueled many conversations among contemporary Buddhist women. A section on Yashodhara's pregnancy that follows in chapter 6 will address this topic further.

A discussion of Chandaka's return to Kapilavastu would not be complete without checking in with Suddhodana, who has spent the entire time doing damage control surrounded by swooning, weeping women. As he did when Maya was pregnant, the king is said to have adopted ascetic practices upon learning of Siddhartha's Great Departure. By propitiating the gods, he hopes to secure his beloved son's safety and swift return to the kingdom.[88] Palpable here, as throughout the legends, is his profound, abiding love for the prince. Overcome by emotions, "as if in a delirium,"[89] Suddhodana is disconsolate with grief and confusion. Alarmed by their king's unprecedented loss of constancy, his ministers step in to counsel him and fortify his spirit. Just as Abhayadevi once gently reminded Suddhodana of Siddhartha's noble destiny, so the ministers point out that Asita's prophecy had come to fruition. There is nothing to be done about it:

> [Siddhartha's] state of mind was predestined; call to mind the words of the seer Asita of old. For it is not possible to make him stay happily even for a moment [either in heaven] or in a [king's] rulership.[90]

It's hard to believe, but Suddhodana still does not give up. According to several of the Sanskrit stories, he dispatches two ministers (or a minister and the head priest) to find Siddhartha in the forest and bring him home. Entire chapters in both the *Buddhacarita* and *Abhinishkramanasutra* are devoted to this futile exercise. However, far more powerful than his father's worldly attachment is Gautama's own resolve to pursue his spiritual purpose with unwavering diligence and discipline. In his mind, the path forward is clear and unshakable. To the ministers who eventually find him meditating under a tree, he proclaims,

> The sun may fall to the earth, Mount Himavant may lose its firmness, but I will not return to my family as a worldly man who has not seen the final truth and whose senses are drawn towards the objects of pleasure.

> I would enter a blazing fire, but I would not enter my home with my goal unattained.[91]

5

En Route to the Bodhi Tree

*T*he hush of the forest was Gautama's closest companion for the next six years. In the course of his wanderings, he came across fellow seekers of truth but always broke away, preferring to follow a solitary path and the guidance of his own inner wisdom. From time to time, he would remain briefly in the company of hermit pandits, only to discover the limitations of their philosophical teachings and push on. This was certainly a switch from the life he had known as Prince Siddhartha, wrangling with family expectations and the buzz of advice givers, servants tending to his every whim. Even more extreme, now he was alone and celibate, whereas throughout his life to date he had been surrounded by the women of his family and court—first growing up in the women's quarters of his father's palace and later as a noble patriarch with his own wives and harem. The luxuries of palace life had been replaced by the extremes of asceticism. Mahaprajapati's motherly worries about her son's welfare as a forest-dwelling recluse proved to be well founded, as he now slept on the hard earth, his body subject to the afflictions of heat, cold, and rain.

But Gautama did not look back. "The thing is done!" he exclaimed.[1] Indeed, his heart was buoyed by the changes he had made and the promise of the path that lay before him. The goal of full awakening was clearly in his sights, and so he thrived as he stepped away from Kapilavastu and the bonds of his past. Rather than weaken from the privations of mendicancy, his body was robust—becoming radiant like the full moon and distinguished by the thirty-two marks of a bodhisattva:

His body bereft of all its jewels, nevertheless emitted a soft and dazzling light, like the beams of the sun piercing through a dark cloud, and spread all around the brightness of its glory.[2]

It continues,

Graceful and perfectly at ease in every step,
Advancing like the King of the great Oxen,
His body perfectly adorned with every distinctive sign,
Every single hair properly disposed,
The thousand-spoked discus beneath the soles of his feet,
The curling circle of white hair between his eyebrows,
Keeping his strength as one aiming to be self-dependent,
This can be no other than the Great Lion among men.[3]

So captivating was Gautama's lustrous form that the brahman hermits practicing their religious rituals in the forest were startled at the sight of him, unsure if he be god or human. Birds and beasts gathered around in loving admiration as he sat motionless in meditation under shade trees. Country folk, too, stopped and stared in awe at his beauty when they spotted him on his wanderings. We hear their words and glimpse a vivid scene of ordinary life during these ancient times:

There were various people scattered about on the mountain side, some gathering shrubs and roots, others collecting the dry dung of the ox, others engaged in hunting, others tending their herds, others traveling along the way. All these afar off beheld the Bodhisattva sitting under the shade of the tree, his body as glorious as a bright golden image. At the sight they were filled with a strange feeling of reverence, and one spake to another thus—". . . Believe me this is no ordinary person; whence has he come, and how did he arrive . . .?" . . . So they were all in doubt who this could be that shone so gloriously, as the brightness of the sun and moon in the midst of the mountain, and in whose presence the flowers . . . opened and displayed their sweets. At least, they said, this is no mortal man, for never yet did man possess such beauty, and shed abroad such glory as this man.[4]

Thus did Gautama launch his new life. As ever, the legends are prone to idealizing him while also asserting his humanity. These two motifs are never untangled in the stories, but together they speak to the complexity of describing (and understanding) Gautama's profound transformation during this time. As one brahman exclaimed,

> It seems to me that this is no other than a child of Heavenly birth, thoroughly acquainted with the human heart.[5]

We'll resume the narrative, which begins after Siddhartha has taken leave of his horse and charioteer.

A Mendicant Begins His Journey

The itinerant Gautama has just arrived seeking alms at the major city of Rajagriha within weeks of his departure from Kapilavastu.* The sight of him creates quite a stir, as the nobility of his bearing is belied by his humility. Townsfolk gather, and the crowds jostle to get a closer look at this beautiful, serene man dressed in the robes of a mendicant and proffering an alms bowl as he silently makes his way through their streets.

> When men and women see him,
> They cannot get enough of him.
>
> . . .
>
> People move out of his way, only to follow behind him.
> They ask, "Who is that being whom we have never seen before
> And whose luster makes the whole city shine?"
>
> Thousands of women stand on their roofs
> And in their doorways and windows.
> Filling the streets, they leave their houses empty;
> Dropping all other tasks, they only stare at this perfect man.

---

* A distance of about three hundred kilometers as the crow flies.

> All business and shopping come to an end;
> Even those in the bars stop drinking.
> They cannot stay in their houses or in the streets
> As they behold the form of this perfect man.[6]

All the commotion attracts the attention of Bimbisara, their king, who observes the bustling scene on the streets from his palace balcony. Intrigued to learn more about this beguiling mendicant, he makes his way to Gautama and inquires if he be god or human.* Gautama says,

> Maharaja! I am no god, or spirit, but a plain man, seeking for rest, and so am practicing the rules of an ascetic life.[7]

The two men engage in a spirited debate, arguing the pros and cons of worldly versus religious life. They are the same age, but when Bimbisara learns of Gautama's noble heritage, he sounds a lot like Suddhodana as he tries to dissuade his new friend from his asceticism, even offering to share his own kingdom and harem. He worries that Gautama will expose himself to unbearable hardships as a recluse, not to mention the dangers of wild beasts lurking in the forest. Ever steadfast, Gautama is indifferent to this last opportunity to turn away from his intention and proceeds to give Bimbisara a teaching on life's real dangers: old age, sickness, and death. Soon the two men take leave of one another on the friendliest terms. Gautama prophetically promises to return one day to Rajagriha to teach the highest dharma to Bimbisara and his people. Years later, he would give many teachings there, including (according to Mahayana tradition) the quintessential Heart Sutra from the heights of Vulture Peak that rises above the town.[8]

A turning point comes in the legend now as the hard truth of Gautama's choices begins to hit home. Nowhere is this more vividly expressed than in the moment when he stares into his alms bowl and is disgusted by what he sees. The former prince who was "most delicately brought up" is faced quite literally with the revolting fruits of his resolve to forsake privileged royal repast for an ascetic's daily fare. Mendicants cannot choose what they eat,

---

* In the Sinhalese text, Bimbisara recognizes Gautama as an old family friend.

only partake of what is deposited by others in their alms bowl. This was the supreme test, demonstrating to onlookers (hidden nearby) that Gautama was, in fact, an ordinary man and not some kind of god or supernatural spirit. Only an ordinary human being subject to normal bodily cravings would succumb out of necessity to eating such vile food. Gautama proves to be quite human, as the disgusting mess in his bowl turns his stomach. Nonetheless, he is hungry and must eat. As described in the Burmese legend,

> He could not swallow the first mouthful, which he threw out of his mouth in utter disgust. Accustomed to live sumptuously and feed on the most delicate things, his eyes could not bear even the sight of that loathsome mixture of the coarsest articles of food collected at the bottom of his [bowl].[9]

Reproaching himself for his weakness, Gautama directs his awareness inward and seeks to analyze his way out of this dilemma. The Sinhalese legend provides a detailed, poetic account of his mental process, as well as a decent understanding of digestion! Gautama reflects to himself,

> Siddhartha! Thy body is not of polished gold; it is composed of many elements and members; this food entering into the house of my body, will be received into the mortar of my mouth, where it will be pounded by the pestle of my teeth, sifted by the winnow of my tongue, and mixed with the liquid of my saliva, after which it will descend into the vessel of my abdomen, and pass into the oven of my stomach, there to be again mixed with the water of my gastric juice, and reduced by the fire of my digestive faculty; the fan of my wind will blow this fire; in sixty hours (a day) this food will turn to excrement, and be expelled. This food is therefore clean and pure in comparison with that into which it will be converted. Siddhartha! Thy body is composed of the four elements, and this food is the same; therefore, let element be joined to element.[10]

With this reflection Gautama overcomes his disgust and swallows the food. Never again, we are told, does he experience such aversion, thereafter adopting equanimity with regard to ingesting any food offered him.

But Gautama's bodily challenges are just beginning. Departing Rajagriha, he soon arrives at the banks of the Nairanjana River in the district of Uruvilva,* where he decides to remain to undertake focused religious austerities rather than continue his nomadic roaming. He has had enough unsatisfactory philosophical teachings from brahman hermits and wants to begin seeking the truth for himself. No need to keep wandering about—he feels ready to settle down and direct his full concentration inward through extreme physical and mental practices. Years later, the Buddha describes to his disciples why he chose this special place for his retreat:

> I saw woods that were delightful, lovely, secluded, sequestered, remote from turmoil, remote from men, and growing in seclusion amid charming lakes. Round about were herdsmen's villages, not too far away nor yet too near, but accessible; a level tract and the river Nairanjana with its pure water flowing still and clear between beautiful banks.[11]

An abundance of tortoises and fish could be seen splashing about in the river, and lofty trees amid lush greenery were said to be suggestive of enlightened thoughts.[12] According to the Sinhalese legend, this area along the river was an ancient holy site even at the time of the Buddha, where over earlier centuries, generations of yogis had performed arduous practices standing in the rushing river with water up to their chins. Retrieving sand from the river bottom, they would later throw it down before an assembly of fellow ascetics to demonstrate proof of their penances. Over time, so much sand had accumulated along the banks of the river that regional kings designated the area sacred ground. It was here that Gautama joined in the tradition of the ancient yogis and commenced a six-year period of increasingly harsh austerities.[13]

While to date Gautama had been solitary in his wanderings, a company of five fellow forest dwellers attached themselves to him at this time, striving to emulate his practices so they, too, might attain his enviable religious stature and eventually supreme awakening. In the ancient Eastern tradition of discipleship, they stayed by him during the period of his six-

---

*Near present-day Bodh Gaya.

year retreat, serving him in ways such as sweeping and cooking. Some stories say simply that they all met up along the way as kindred spiritual seekers, but according to several Pali sources, the five young disciples were sons of the Shakya brahmans who participated in the council that prophesied the infant Siddhartha's destiny shortly after his birth. Paralleling the story of the seer Asita, these elders were saddened that they would not live to hear the Buddha's great teachings, so they advised their sons to become ascetics and seek out Gautama's highest wisdom once he renounced the kingdom.[14] An intriguing variant also appears in the Kangyur, where the young men had been sent directly by Suddhodana and Suprabuddha (Gautama's maternal grandfather) as attendants to minister to the prince's needs while he lived as an ascetic. Always worrying about their beloved prince, the two kings originally sent five hundred men, but Gautama only retained these five—three from his father's family in Kapilavastu and two from his mother Maya's Koliyan line in Devadaha.[15]

Thus did Gautama set up a retreat spot near the banks of the Nairanjana River and commence the final practices that were to bring him to the cusp of his longed-for goal of full awakening. The *Mahavastu* offers a unique description of the exquisite forest landscape surrounding him during this time of retreat. The following selected verses express the exuberance of nature, likening its playful abundance to feminine sensuality and fecundity:

> Here . . . is the rare beauty of the lotus; there the forest is [washed] by a mountain stream, and there the hermit's retreat echoes all around to the songs of cuckoos, parrots and peacocks.
>
> . . .
>
> Here, stirred by a gentle breeze, the branches of various bright flowering trees caress one another like women in play.
>
> Here, the swaying forest branches in bloom bend under the weight of their burden, like calf-bearing cows with the weight of their bellies.
>
> Here is a flowery spot covered with freshly-blown flowers, like a newly wedded bride lying at her ease, decked out in a cluster of jewels.[16]

Gautama clearly sets his intention as he begins his retreat:

I shall live with both body and mind withdrawn from sensual pleasure, and with my thoughts of them, my fondness for them, my feverish longing for them and my attachment to them subdued. Although I undergo unpleasant, bitter, cruel and severe feelings which torment my soul and my body, I shall be capable of the state of [superior] men of knowledge, insight and enlightenment.[17]

The stories of what transpired during Gautama's retreat are as diverse as the traditions and storytellers who ventured to tell them. As the accounts become less about his daily activities and more about the changing psychological context, we find a renewed mix of imagery and symbolism layered into the narratives. In this way, our own imaginations are challenged to reach deeper into the stories, beyond both fanciful and literal meanings. To the extent that the Buddha's life story can be experienced as allegory, it is during this period of his extreme austerities and aftermath that we find episodes framing the profound transformation that is about to take place and the foundation of his later dharma teachings.

Gautama's Extreme Austerities

Gautama begins his fast by taking only one jujube fruit (about the size of a small date) per day. Deciding over time that he needs to curb his intake even more, he graduates to a daily grain of rice and from there to a single sesame seed. The Thai account asserts that he feels even this is too much of a distraction from his meditative concentration, so thereafter he eats only if a fruit falls within reach as he sits cross-legged under his tree. In the rigorous style of advanced yogis, Gautama eventually pushes his human limits to the furthest extreme and stops eating entirely. Abandoning all interest in his physical state, he meditates without interruption and allows nothing to deter him. Some stories say he remains unmoving for the entire six years, during which time he is impervious to both bodily needs and changing conditions in the world around him.

The Bodhisattva remained sitting cross-legged for six years. He simply sat the way he was, without forsaking his activity. When the sun was shining, he did not seek shade. When the shade fell on him, he did not move into the sun. Never did he seek shelter from the wind, the sun, and the rain. He never chased away mosquitoes, bees, and poisonous snakes. He did not defecate, urinate, spit, or blow his nose. Neither did he bend his limbs or stretch them out. He never lay down on his belly, side, or back.[18]

Unfortunately all this austerity came at a price. Gautama's robust, healthy body soon becomes emaciated and weak. The radiance that had surrounded him upon entering the forest life has vanished. Gone, too, are the thirty-two marks of a bodhisattva that had manifested since his departure from home, harbingers of his awakened destiny. His body shrivels and loses its golden hue. The village folk, previously in awe of Gautama's venerable bearing, are dumbfounded by the changes:

> Oh my! The mendicant Gautama has turned black! Have you seen, he's so dark! The mendicant Gautama has the color of the madgura fish!* Previously his complexion was so beautiful, but now it has all changed![19]

The Buddha later acknowledged to his disciples that his body had been "ruined" during this time:

> My rib cage resembled the sides of a crab, and it looked like a collapsed stable with rafters exposed on either side. My spine appeared like a braided tuft of hair. My skull looked like a cracked gourd. My eyeballs appeared like a stars in a sunken well. . . . I tried to [stand up], but my body was so hunched over that I fell every time. When I finally managed to get up . . . my body hair, its roots rotten, came out of my body. Previously my complexion had been beautiful and smooth, but now this radiance had disappeared because of exerting myself in extreme austerities.[20]

And so Gautama's austerities bring him dangerously close to death. His body becomes such a miserable, forsaken heap that village children think he is a demon and pelt him with dung and dirt. Taunting him further, they stick straw in his ears, which then juts out his nostrils, and stick straw in

---

* Similar to a catfish.

his mouth, which then pokes out his ears.[21] This sorry sight catches the attention of the gods who, as we know, have been very invested in the Bodhisattva successfully fulfilling his karmic destiny and becoming an awakened buddha in this lifetime. They have had a hand in his journey every step of the way since birth. The notion of Gautama dying before his goal has been accomplished concerns them greatly. According to the Pali legends, the gods force-feed him the "sap of life" surreptitiously as moisture through the pores of his skin. This just barely keeps him alive, but because he is eating no solid food, his body continues to darken and further lose its strength. Meanwhile, Gautama does not waver in his resolve to remain in meditation until he has attained the truth he seeks regarding freedom from suffering and the cycle of birth and death. Alternate accounts in the Pali canon and Sanskrit sources relate that Gautama spurns the gods' offer to feed him magically, feeling it would be hypocritical with respect to his vow to fast. He is determined to achieve his goal completely on his own. In the *Mahavastu*, the forest goddesses offer to magically restore his strength, but Gautama refuses them for the same reason—to accept their assistance would be a "deceit."

Finally at the extreme of starvation, Gautama, the mighty prince who once had the strength of ten thousand elephants, is so depleted that he collapses and is taken for dead. Now the gods are alarmed and dispatch a messenger to Suddhodana in Kapilavastu to deliver the bad news. A variant in some Pali sources says that it is a goddess who does this. Some stories say the king has been updated all along by spies who have been reporting back on his son's welfare. They tell the king,

> Your majesty, the prince is dead as a result of his severe austerities and meager diet. He no longer inhales and exhales but lies like a log of wood.[22]

Suddhodana is skeptical. "Did my son become a buddha?" he asks. When he learns Gautama did not, the king is confident that his son must still be alive. He has complete faith in the miracles at Siddhartha's birth and the prophecy that his son would become either a universal king or an enlightened buddha. It is impossible for his son to be dead if neither has yet transpired. Recalling the prince's profound meditation under the rose-apple tree, Suddhodana pronounces that Gautama is alive and must simply be immersed in deep concentration. The gods double-check and find that the king is right. The the ailing hermit has indeed revived.

An extended version of this episode is found in the *Abhinishkramana-sutra,* where Suddhodana takes action as the worried, loving father. Distressed by the news of his son's deteriorating condition, he dispatches the ever-trustworthy Kalodayin to search for the prince and bring him home. Having traveled to the banks of the Nairanjana River, Kalodayin finds the ragged, emaciated Gautama asleep on the ground. Shocked by the decrepit state of his childhood friend, he cries out,

> Alas! alas! That one so beautiful and full of grace should ever come to this![23]

At first Gautama does not recognize Kalodayin, but then, summoning all his strength, he roundly dismisses the notion that he might give up his quest for enlightenment, saying to his friend,

> May my body be ground to powder small as the mustard seed if I ever desire to return to my home! If indeed I die before the completion of my vow, then, Udayi, take back my bones to Kapilavastu and say, "These are the relics of a man who died in the fixed prosecution of his resolve"; but as it is, go tell my Royal Father that I am resolved to persevere. . . . Go, then, Udayi! Return home, for there can be no further communication between us.[24]

Kalodayin brings the prince's tidings back to the king, who is overjoyed to hear firsthand that his son is alive. By this time, Gautama's fame as a great ascetic has spread throughout the land. As beautifully expressed in the Burmese legend, his acclaim resounds, "like the sound of a great bell hung in the canopy of the skies."[25]

Perhaps the most remarkable story that comes from Gautama's near starvation appears in the *Lalitavistara,* where we find a rare account of a feminine presence during this time. Here again, the gods are very distressed to see the prince's emaciated state. Fearing that he is dying, they turn in desperation not to Suddhodana, but to Maya. Finding Gautama's mother in her heavenly realm, surrounded by a retinue of celestial maidens, they report the terrible news that the prince is about to die. As any mother would, Maya departs immediately for the Nairanjana River. Arriving at midnight, she finds her son cadaverous and unconscious on the ground. Choking with tears, she lovingly sings to him,

> When I gave birth to you, my son, in the Lumbini Grove,
> Without support, like a lion, you took seven steps on your own,
> You gazed in the four directions and said these beautiful words:
> "This is my last birth." Those words will now never come to pass.
>
> Asita predicted that you would be a buddha in this world,
> But his prediction was wrong, as he did not foresee impermanence.
> My son you have not yet had the joys of a universal monarch's splendors,
> And now you are passing away in this forest without attaining awakening.
>
> To whom can I turn to about my son?
> To whom shall I cry out in my pain?
> Who will give life back to my only son,
> Who is barely alive?

Awaking in confusion, the Bodhisattva responds,

> Who are you? You cry so heart wrenchingly,
> With disheveled hair and your beauty impaired,
> Lamenting your son so intensely
> And throwing yourself on the ground.

Again Maya sings to him,

> It is I, your mother, O Son,
> Who for ten months
> Carried you in my womb like a diamond.
> It is I who now cry out in despair.[26]

Gautama now consoles his mother, affirming that Asita's prediction, consistent with the predictions of the gods and previous bodhisattvas, will come to pass. Maya should not despair, he says, but rejoice because soon her son will become a fully realized buddha. An ordinary man, Gautama determines to achieve his goal through his own unshakable resolve without the help of others. He reassures his mother,

> It is possible that the world may break into a hundred pieces, and the jewel peak of Mount Meru may fall into the ocean. The sun, the moon, and the stars may fall to the ground. Yet although I am an ordinary person, I will not die. Therefore do not bring misery on yourself. Before long you shall behold the awakening of a buddha.[27]

Maya is overjoyed to hear her beloved son's response. In reverence, she circumambulates him three times while sprinkling him with flowers. Then, as divine music beckons, she returns to her heavenly abode. Here again, we see Maya's enduring love for her son. Although she has forsaken her human form, she has never ceased looking after him.

On Finding the Middle Way

As so often happens on a spiritual quest, the answer eventually comes, but it's not the one the seeker is looking for. After six years, Gautama did awaken to truth from his austerities, but what became clear to him was not the cessation of suffering and the cycle of birth and death, but rather the futility of his approach. Mortification of body and spirit achieved mortification of body and spirit, but it did not lead Gautama to his goal of a higher truth that could set him and others free from the painful web of worldly existence. Gautama realized that however much self-denial may quell passions and craving, it does nothing toward the cultivation of profound insight. After all, if hunger led to awakening, there would be lots of enlightened beings, animals as well as humans. Gautama had been emulating the ascetic practices of the time, the result being the deterioration of his body, not the realization of deeper philosophical truths. Reaching this conclusion, he says,

> With these acts and methods I have not been able to manifest any true knowledge that would be higher than manmade teachings. This path does not lead to awakening. This path is incapable of eradicating the continuation of birth, old age, and death in the future.[28]

In the *Buddhacarita,* he asks,

> How can the result . . . be reached by a man . . . who is so worn out
> with the exhaustion of hunger and thirst that his mind is unbalanced
> with the exhaustion? [29]

Teetering on the brink of death, Gautama finally recognizes the vanity of
his efforts and wonders if there might be another path. Reflecting further,
he recalls the profound joy he experienced as a young boy meditating
under the rose-apple tree on the day of the ploughing competition. It was
an extraordinary state of bliss, free from the bonds of thought or sensual
attachments. Could this hold the answer? Years later, he described to his
disciples his mental process during this time of reaching the extreme of his
ascetic practices:

> I remember how, long since, before I had gone forth to the religious
> life, I was seated cross-legged on the ground . . . in the cool shade of
> a rose-apple tree. There I entered an abode in the first meditation,
> which is aloof from sensual desires and from sinful and wicked states
> of mind, is accompanied by applied and sustained thought, is born
> of solitude and is full of zest and ease. Could this, I wondered, be the
> way to enlightenment?
>
> And, monks, while I was thus indulging that memory, there came
> to me as a result the conviction that this was the way to enlighten-
> ment. But this way could not be won when the body was emaciated,
> weak, distressed and fasting. So I said to myself, "Let me now then
> take a hearty meal of boiled rice and [sweet milk]." [30]

And so with insight that the path to awakening could not be traveled in a
beleaguered human form, Gautama makes the decision to return to health
and wholeness. He resolves to strengthen his body with food and drink and
to resume bathing and caring for his daily needs. [31] It could be said that, in
so doing, he is coming into balance with feminine aspects of his psyche. An
analogy comes to him at this time that describes the extremes the course of
his life has taken—an image of a three-stringed guitar:

> One string, too tightly strained, gave a harsh and unpleasant sound;
> the second, not strained enough, had no resonance; the third,
> moderately stretched, gave forth the sweetest music. [32]

From mighty lion of the Shakyas to pathetic heap covered in dung, from pleasure-seeking prince to starving anchorite, Gautama at last had found a middle way. His insight that the correct path to awakening is not one of extremes was soon to become the cornerstone of his dharma teachings, often called the "Middle Way." Drawing a lesson from the metaphor of the guitar strings, Gautama returned to the practices of a renunciate but with moderation. He resumed seeking alms in the village and began to eat ordinary food. Soon his body returned to health, taking on its former golden aura and the thirty-two marks of a bodhisattva. As described in the *Nidanakatha,*

> He perceived that penance was not the way to enlightenment; and begging through the villages and towns, he collected ordinary material food and lived upon it. And the thirty-two signs of a great man appeared again upon him, and his body became fair in colour, like unto gold.[33]

Meanwhile, Gautama's five disciples concluded that he had given up his austerities due to weakness and, disillusioned with him as a spiritual role model, they abandoned him.

Meetings with Sujata

It has been a big change for Gautama that his life has been almost entirely devoid of women since leaving home. With the exception of his mother, who visited him as a celestial angel when he was starving, women hardly appear at all in the stories of this period in his life. The disparity makes sense, as it was normal for a *kshatriya* prince to be surrounded by wives and the women of his harem, while a religious recluse is celibate and solitary by nature. Companions, if any, would typically be men. But now, as Gautama turns back from death to moderation and continues his quest for enlightenment, female figures emerge again in the stories, together with powerful symbols of nurturance and the sacred feminine.

An intriguing and complex episode involving a woman now appears as Gautama breaks his fast. Sujata, the daughter of a wealthy chieftain from a nearby village, offers him a meal of rice milk. This scene is often portrayed in Buddhist art and has made its way into popular versions of the Buddha legend in the West, where we're typically told that her offering is the first nourishment Gautama takes after near-starvation and marks the end of his years of austerities. Symbolically, it illustrates his discovery of the Middle Way and his return to inner balance and a valid quest for enlightenment. Overall, however, the early Pali and Sanskrit legends recount this story somewhat differently. With minor variants, both traditions report that the Bodhisattva resumed eating food of his own initiative, as reflected in the earlier quote from the *Nidanakatha*. In these accounts, Sujata's offering is significant because it nourishes the Bodhisattva on the morning of the day of his enlightenment and sustains him for the duration of his forty-nine-day fast that marks its aftermath. The sequence of events is made clear in the *Mahavastu,* where the Buddha tells his disciples:

> And so, monks, I made a meal of soup of beans, pulse, and peas. Then, after I had gradually won back power and strength of body, I received sweet milk-rice from Sujata, the daughter of a village overseer, and at night, towards daybreak, I made my way to the river Nairanjana ... and then made my way to the *bodhi* tree ...[34]*

In the *Lalitavistara,* Sujata's offering breaks his fast *and* marks the beginning of his enlightenment journey, since the two events take place on the same day. Elsewhere we are told that in past lifetimes Sujata provided rice milk to all previous bodhisattvas-cum-buddhas on the morning of their awakening. Whatever the version, Sujata's participation in the Buddha's life story is significant—both for her participation as a woman on his path to enlightenment and for the symbolism of nurturance and motherhood she brings to the narrative. The variations of her story are worth relating. We begin with the Pali tradition where her characterization is more or less consistent.

Here, as a young maiden, Sujata had prayed to the local tree spirit that she would attain a worthy husband and that her firstborn child would be a son. She vowed that if her wishes were fulfilled, she would make an annual offering of rice milk and wealth in the form of alms to honor the local tree deity. Time passed, and her prayers were heard: she married a nobleman from Benares and gave birth to a beautiful son. Now, as the present story

---

* A variant in the Tibetan tradition says that the Buddha's first meal was colostrum, taken sometime before the rice milk offering.

opens it is an auspicious full moon day. Sujata decides to make her first rice milk offering to the tree deity. To that end and so that the very best milk would be procured, she had kept one thousand cows feeding in a meadow of the richest, most luscious grass. With the milk from these, she nourished five hundred cows, and with the milk from those, she nourished two hundred and fifty, and so on in diminishing proportions by halves until sixteen cows were milked to feed eight. These eight cows yielded the richest, sweetest milk imaginable, and this essence was to be used for Sujata's special offering.

On the auspicious morning, Sujata arises to milk the eight cows and witnesses twin miracles: the calves stay away from their mothers' teats of their own accord, and the udders stream milk spontaneously as soon as the buckets are in place. Marveling at these favorable omens, Sujata proceeds to make a fire and cook the rice milk, which boils in an unusual fashion without creating any smoke. At this point in the story, the brahmanical gods—not to be outdone by eight cows and a young mother—take an interest and show up. Brahma holds an umbrella over the fire, while Indra stokes it and other gods infuse divine nectar—apparently the same "sap of life" used previously—into Sujata's rice porridge. It's unclear why they need to do this when Sujata is managing just fine on her own, and milk by itself is the perfect, primal, life-giving substance. One can't help but see this as an early androcentric editor's unnecessary intrusion into an otherwise intact story that embodies beautiful, life-affirming symbols of the sacred feminine in an account about nourishing the Buddha-to-be.

In any case, Sujata is delighted by all the miracles and instructs her servant Purna to go quickly to the tree to make preparations for the offering, including sweeping and sprinkling flower garlands around the site. In the meantime, Gautama has risen after a night of vivid dreams foretelling that this very day he will become enlightened: "Verily this day I shall become a Buddha," he proclaims.[35] After receiving alms in the village, he stops to rest at the base of Sujata's sacred tree. All bodily signs of starvation have vanished, and he is resplendent with robust health and the thirty-two marks of a bodhisattva. The entire tree is illuminated by his golden aura. Purna is dazzled when she comes across him and determines that he must be the tree god come to accept Sujata's special offering in person. Rushing back, she joyfully relates the news to her mistress who is equally jubilant, thinking that she will soon meet the beneficent deity who has given her a son. So overcome is Sujata that she grants Purna her freedom on the spot and adopts her as an elder daughter, providing her with robes and ornaments suitable for her new position.

The theme of the Bodhisattva's day of awakening now becomes the focus of the story. Sujata still thinks she is making an offering to a tree spirit, but inspired by the morning's auspicious events, she decides to enhance the ritual offering. Although she does not overtly know the tradition that bodhisattvas are presented with a golden bowl on the day they become buddhas, Sujata sends for such a priceless vessel, which she uses to hold the specially prepared rice milk. She then adorns herself in her most costly garments and covers the golden bowl with a pure white cloth draped with garlands of sweet-smelling blossoms. She sets this ensemble on a golden tray, which she then carries on her head to the holy tree.

The Pali stories generally say that she approaches Gautama reverentially, setting the tray aside and bowing low, touching her forehead to the ground before offering him the rice milk. However, a variant in the Sinhalese story asserts that Sujata is accompanied by a procession of sixteen thousand festively dressed maidens and, upon seeing the Bodhisattva sitting cross-legged under the tree, her joy so overwhelms her that she approaches him dancing. One can just imagine Sujata and all sixteen thousand maidens dancing at this wonderful moment! Respectfully setting the golden bowl beside Gautama, she then offers him a basin, also made of gold, filled with perfumed water to wash his hands. At that moment, the ascetic's own crude earthen bowl disappears, and Sujata presents him with her precious offering of rice milk, expressing gratitude for the birth of her precious son: "The wish of my heart is accomplished; may your wish be accomplished as well."[36] With that, she departs. The Thai version adds that Gautama calls after her, "Your desire shall be accomplished," and she joyfully sings the words over and over, "My desire shall be accomplished," as she returns home thinking she has just encountered the marvelous tree spirit who gave her a son.[37] In the Burmese legend, there is a special sweetness in her parting words for the Bodhisattva:

> May your joy and happiness be as great as mine; may you always delight in the happiest rest, ever surrounded by a great and brilliant retinue.[38]

Even though she does not realize it at the time, Sujata has just become the last person, male or female, to provide a meal to Gautama the (soon-to-be) Buddha prior to his awakening. Thereafter the Bodhisattva takes the bowl of rice milk with him as he proceeds to the banks of the Nairanjana River and arrives at the sacred spot where thousands of previous bodhisattvas bathed on the day of their enlightenment. After bathing and dressing, he sits down facing east and eats Sujata's meal. Then, remembering the order of events from previous lifetimes, he throws the golden bowl into the river, exclaiming,

> If I shall be able today to become a Buddha, let this pot go up the stream; if not let it go down stream![39]

And off it goes upstream, "swift as a racehorse."[40] Filled with peaceful joy, Gautama spends the day meditating in a cool grove of *shala* trees and in the evening sets off for Bodh Gaya and the tree of enlightenment. As we have just seen, the Pali legends are unambiguous about Sujata's rice milk offering nourishing Gautama on his last day as an ordinary man prior to his awakening to buddhahood.

We'll now turn to the Sanskrit sources for variations on this tale of Sujata and the offering of rice milk. Unlike the Pali tradition's more or less uniform account, the Sanskrit stories differ widely—in some places appearing as curious fragments and elsewhere as detailed narratives. Taken together, the contrasting traditions provide a complex composite of her character and a variety of contexts for her special offering.

The story of Sujata found in the *Lalitavistara* shares many elements with the Pali version. The story opens, however, with a fresh detail. In addition to the five disciples serving Gautama during his six-year retreat, ten young village girls have similarly been visiting and assisting the recluse on a regular basis. All ten girls are named in this account, and Sujata is among them. After Gautama proclaims his intention to eat solid food again, the girls prepare appropriate meals and bring them to him at his retreat along the river. Soon the recluse regains his strength and resumes alms rounds in the village. Upon observing the return of his lustrous appearance, the village folk all hail his beautiful form.

Sujata now takes a central role in what appears to be a new story fused to the previous one. Here she is a young woman who has been concerned for Gautama's welfare from the outset of his arduous retreat. Each day for the duration of his austerities, she has made offerings to eight hundred priests with the prayer that he would survive his hardship. Knowing full well that his aim is to achieve enlightenment, she adopts a parallel program to help sustain him. Symbolically feeding Gautama with each offering to the priests, she utters the dedication prayer,

> May the Bodhisattva take my food and thereby truly attain perfect and completely unexcelled awakening![41]

After six years of this, the gods notify her that Gautama has ceased his austerities and urge her to take further action. Due to her abundant good karma in past lives, she is preordained to serve him. Sujata sets to work preparing the rice milk offering in the fashion of the one thousand cows milked to feed the five hundred and so forth, as described earlier. In observing miracles around the cooking pot, she prays that they foretell the Bodhisattva's imminent supreme awakening. According to the *Lalitavistara,* she brings the rice porridge in a golden bowl to Gautama where he is sitting along the river and offers it to him after reverentially making prostrations (in the prose version, she serves him outside her house). According to this story, the Bodhisattva regains his former strength and splendor upon consuming Sujata's excellent food. In this version, it is his first meal after the six years of austerities and has instantly restored him to wholeness. After bathing and meditating at the river, Gautama proceeds to the tree of enlightenment. All these events have taken place within the span of one day.

As we have seen in the preceding Pali and Sanskrit stories, Sujata's role in the Buddha's life is understood differently in the various traditions. First she appears as a simple mother and cowherd, providing rice milk to the Bodhisattva inadvertently, thinking she is venerating a tree deity. In this last story, her purpose is always to serve the Bodhisattva, ritually sustaining him over the course of his retreat and later knowingly providing him with the nourishment that will sustain him from the day of his enlightenment through the next forty-nine days. We learn more about Sujata in the following story from the *Abhinishkramanasutra,* where a similar episode is framed with the Bodhisattva encountering Sujata both before and after his six-year retreat.

The scene opens as Gautama first arrives as a wandering mendicant in Uruvilva, along the banks of the Nairanjana River. He takes up his morning alms round in the village and comes to the home of a village chief named Nandika. As is the custom for mendicants, Gautama stands silently at the door, waiting to be noticed. Nandika's beautiful daughter, Sujata, has seen the Bodhisattva approach and immediately her breasts begin to stream with milk from "joy and reverence." Addressing him without shyness, she says,

> Most excellent and illustrious Sir! what is your name, and of what family and tribe are you? who are your father and mother? and whither go you now? For in truth your Divine appearance has so affected me that the very milk from my breast exudes of itself![42]

The Bodhisattva responds by naming his parents and birthplace, then goes on to tell her that his mission is to attain the highest wisdom. Joyfully Sujata takes his alms bowl and fills it with every kind of choice delicacy and luscious fruit to be found in her house. Handing it back respectfully, she vows to stand by Gautama through his entire course to buddhahood and requests that in the future she may become one of his disciples:

> Most excellent Sir! I vow to minister always to your wants; and I pray that when you have attained the end of your present search that I may become one of your followers.[43]

Calling her "illustrious sister," the Bodhisattva assents to her request and departs. Settling in a peaceful spot by the river, he begins the six-year program of ascetic practices we have already learned about. In the meantime, Sujata has kept her vow to Gautama, not by feeding him (since he has forsaken food), but by giving generously each time a mendicant comes to her door seeking alms. Her intention is to accrue enough merit to become the future Buddha's disciple. As in the previous story, her life parallels his for six years as she dedicates each offering to the Bodhisattva's awakening. Gautama at last begins eating and determines that he is prepared to proceed toward enlightenment. He questions where he might obtain nourishment sufficient to sustain him for the forty-nine days required for the full course of awakening to take place. Now he returns to Sujata's door, appearing very much the radiant, robust ascetic she had met six years previously. This time she sends for a golden bowl and fills it to the brim with deliciously prepared rice milk (there is no mention of cows or elaborate preparations in this story). Noting that the superior quality of her offering is a symbol of enlightenment itself, he departs for the riverbank, where he eats it and later that day proceeds to the *bodhi* tree. The verse says,

> [Bodhisattva], having partaken of the choice food, as the laws of
> religion direct,
> The food which Sujata had piously prepared,
> Filled with joy, proceeded onward to the Bodhi tree,
> Determined to attain to Supreme Wisdom.[44]

A pause is in order here to point out that the Buddha's final meal prior to the momentous occasion of his enlightenment is food prepared by and offered directly from the hands of a woman. While this detail may appear unremarkable, today in some Southeast Asian Buddhist monastic cultures, monks are not allowed to receive food from the hands of a woman but must have it placed nearby on a cloth. While this prohibition does not appear in the Vinaya (monastic code) of the Pali canon, it is unfortunate that such a tradition has become ingrained, especially when it does not appear in the biographical legends or sutras that relate the Buddha's own values and practices.[45]

Of further note, it is a young, lactating mother who provides nourishment to the Bodhisattva on the morning of his enlightenment. The "birth" of the Buddha has commenced and Sujata's offering of milk essence, like colostrum for a newborn, will sustain him during the arduous days ahead. In the Pali tradition, Sujata's rice milk is given out of love for her infant son while simultaneously nourishing the Bodhisattva. In the Sanskrit traditions, she nurtures him in the gestational stage of his journey to awakening while aspiring to ultimate wisdom herself. Themes of motherhood are further developed in the following story from the *Mahavastu,* where we learn that in the larger, karmic scheme of things, Sujata has been the Bodhisattva's mother in countless previous lifetimes. The following story combines fragments from different accounts.[46]

As before, Gautama the ascetic arrives in Uruvilva begging for alms and soon ends up at Sujata's door. Rather than exuding milk from her breasts, this time she is overwhelmed with reverence immediately upon seeing him. It's not clear just why she has the following reaction, but Sujata then bursts into tears and begs Gautama not to leave her. Clearly a devotional element is suggested here, but as the story progresses, her outcry becomes the lament of a mother rather than a disciple.[47] As Sujata declares her reverence goddesses call out from the heavens that he is none other than the renowned prince of Kapilavastu, son of King Suddhodana. In confusion, Sujata chases him through the village, lauding his virtues while proclaiming that he has been exiled from his family and kingdom. By now, a crowd of village women are following both of them, all weeping piteously. In many ways, this odd passage and what follows is reminiscent of Mahaprajapati's earlier lament and the grief shared by the harem women when Siddhartha left home. In a symbolic sense, he is going forth once again, as he is about to leave the life of a wandering mendicant and reach his goal of enlightenment.

Sujata's lament extends over many beautiful poetic verses, all expressing motherly concern for Gautama's comfort and safety. In the following verses, she appears to be intimately familiar with his former life as a prince and, like Mahaprajapati earlier, expresses concern for the hardships of forest life:

> Thou wast brought up on savoury dainty foods, thy body thrived on diverse fine essences. How wilt thou live on a diet of roots and fruits and leaves in the forest with its tumbling mountain streams?
>
> Having been wont to sleep on a bed with feet of ivory and gold, with fine coverlets and strewn with flowers, how wilt thou live on a ground strewn with kusa grass and leaves?
>
> O noble man, in thy home thou wast wont to listen to the music of drum and tabour, but now will listen to the harsh, dreadful and roaring snort of the angry elephant.[48]

Sujata then goes on to offer a tender blessing, almost a benediction, for his well-being:

> May thou find a spot well furnished with roots and leaves and fruits, and a haunt of beasts that are gentle. O forest-wanderer, may the rock not torment thee when thou art thirsty and hungry.

> When thou art scorched by summer's heat mayst thou find an
> embowered grove with a spring of water. And when it is cold in thy
> mountain caverns, may there be a cloudless sun.
>
> May the [protectors] guard thy body . . . which delighteth heart
> and mind more than sun and moon.[49]

The narrative cuts away briefly to Gautama's six-year absence and then
continues with this story. He returns to Uruvilva for alms, where he again
encounters Sujata. This time she is standing at the foot of a tree holding a
bowl of sweetened rice milk. The narrator identifies her as the Bodhisattva's
mother from numerous previous births, yet she appears not to recognize
him. Offering him the rice milk, she says, "O holy man . . . why is thy body
so lean and worn out?" He asks her why she is giving him the rice milk.

> She who had been the mother of this pure being in a hundred births
> sweetly replied to him, "It is my wish. Let me have it so.
>
> "On the slopes of the Himalayas there is a city called Kapilavastu,
> which is renowned far and wide.
>
> "A prince of that city, the son of the Sakyan Suddhodana has left
> his people, renounced his kingdom, and gone into the forest.
>
> "For six years he has been a wanderer in the wild and fearful forest
> of penance. By this gift to him my vow is fulfilled.
>
> "May my purpose prosper through the life of austerity which the
> excellent man seeks. May I, too, go along that way with the most
> excellent Great Man."[50]

As this *Mahavastu* narrative continues, a celestial voice shouts out to
Sujata that the Shakya prince she is seeking stands before her now. Further,
he has renounced his "useless" austerities and is on his way to the *bodhi*
tree, where he will finally attain supreme enlightenment. Sujata weeps for
joy and, falling to her knees, joins her hands in homage to the Bodhisattva.
While Maya is not named, the following passage is reminiscent of her
anguish when she descends from heaven to speak to her starving son. These
could almost be Maya's words that Sujata now speaks:

> Lotus-eyed one, that thou hast arisen from thy grim austerities in
> the terrible forest, and seeing this, my heart which had been stricken
> with grief feels joy again.

It is six years since the beds I have slept in have brought me ease, for I was tormented by the arrow of grief as I thought of thy austerities.

But now the whole kingdom, thy people, thy father, thy loved ones and thy aunt will be glad and joyful when they hear that thy penance is over.

In the city of Kapila the houses will resound to the music of a hundred instruments, with throngs of men and women laughing beside themselves with joy.

Partake of this sweet milk-rice and become the destroyer of the conduit that formerly irrigated existence, and attain immortality, the griefless state.[51]

The Bodhisattva responds by affirming that she has been his mother for five hundred births and that she will attain buddhahood in the future.

A brief, third version of this story in the *Mahavastu* also clearly identifies Sujata as the Bodhisattva's mother in previous lives and states that she fed all previous bodhisattvas just before they proceeded to the tree of enlightenment. Her intention throughout these many eons has been to accumulate enough merit to become a buddha herself. In this story, she is overjoyed that by feeding Gautama she is nearing her goal. Just as Gautama is on his path to full and complete awakening, so too is she. The verses say,

She tendered him strength-giving food that was exquisitely flavoured and fragrant of smell. Then greatly stirred she formed a resolution saying, "May I become a Buddha accoutred with the [thirty-two] marks.

"Abandoning this base state of desire, may I live the pure, untarnished holy life. May I renounce the pleasures of sense, the source of ill, the root of passion, and follow after the Buddhas, who have destroyed defilements and are rid of lusts.

. . .

"And all the [bodhisattvas] worthy of offerings . . . may I be able to worship them all by reason of my incomparable enlightenment. No other desire whatsoever is mine."

. . .

And Sujata, conceiving a pure love in her heart for the Bodhisattva, again recalled to mind her former lives, and said, "Thousands of . . . Buddhas ate my food and went on to the foot of the *bodhi* tree."[52]

These varied stories of Sujata demonstrate wide-ranging representations of her as reflected in the different traditions: simple village wife and cowherd, mother of countless previous bodhisattvas, ambitious woman aspirant on the path to enlightenment. In all of these roles, she tenderly nurtures the Bodhisattva with life-giving rice milk. While at times she appears as a more mythic or symbolic figure than other women in the Buddha's life, Sujata's role is pivotal—not just as a mother figure, but as the only person who consistently interacts with Gautama during the critical final hours before his enlightenment. In no small way, she and the Bodhisattva are deeply connected. According to her wish, Sujata does go on to become the Buddha's first female disciple (discussed later). In Buddhist literature, very few women become or aspire to become buddhas. We see from these stories that Sujata deserves to be counted among them.

Two Sisters and the Rice Milk

An intriguing variant of the Sujata stories appears in several Sanskrit texts and is likely linked to the story of the ten girls mentioned earlier. Here Sujata's character is split into two sisters whose aim in feeding the Bodhisattva is unabashedly to win him as their husband. They are cast as innocent maidens from the same village named in Sujata's story, and their father is also a village chieftain. The two sisters here are named Nanda and Bala (elsewhere Nanda and Nandabala). Described as very beautiful, they learn of Siddhartha, the great prince of the Shakyas, revered son of Suddhodana and Maya, by reputation and long to marry him. The following story from the *Abhinishkramanasutra* offers curious elements not found in other accounts. Again, the narrative is framed by encounters with Gautama both before and after his six-year retreat.

The story begins with a brahman businessman from Kapilavastu lodging in the home of a village chieftain named Senayana in Uruvilva, near the Nairanjana River where Gautama is practicing austerities. Taking a walk in the woods one day, the brahman comes across Gautama and is overjoyed to recognize the beloved Prince Siddhartha from his hometown. This is early on in his austerities, and Gautama's response is to inquire whether the brahman would be willing to sponsor a daily meal of millet sufficient to support him for the duration of his retreat. Normally it is considered a great privilege to support a recluse pursuing religious practices, and indeed that has always been a key role of the laity in Buddhist cultures. This brahman, however, is cruel and selfish. What he sees is an opportunity to gain karmic merit through charity, while in his heart, he is really feeling very stingy. Accordingly he agrees to Gautama's request but ends up providing such a meager daily portion of millet that Gautama just barely survives. The story gives this as the reason why Gautama wasted away over the course of his six-year retreat.

When Gautama eventually ends his austerities and resolves to eat again, he asks the brahman to procure for him healthy food such as wheat, honey, oil, and milk. The brahman says he doesn't have such things but delivers the message to Senayana, who prompts Nanda and Bala to make an appropriate porridge. Their father persuades them that such a favorable offering might induce Gautama to marry them. The girls eagerly comply and take the porridge to Gautama, along with warm water for bathing, where he is meditating by the river. Bowing deeply in homage, they make their offering, which he accepts. After washing and completing his meal, he commends the girls for their meritorious charity and asks them if they would like anything from him in return. Of course this is the moment they have been waiting for. Together they proclaim their wish to marry "a certain beautiful Shakya prince, whose equal would be hard to find." Gently refusing their suggestion, Gautama explains he has given up all sense pleasures, whereupon the girls graciously wish him well in his spiritual pursuits and request that he return one day that they might become his religious followers. Just as he said to Sujata, the Bodhisattva responds, "Your wish shall be accomplished." The girls continue to bring him food each day until he fully regains his strength.[53]

Although the overt theme of motherhood is missing here, the sisters provide the nourishment that restores the Bodhisattva after his brush with starvation. In this example, their offering appears to be his first meal after his long fast and does not directly relate to his departure for the *bodhi* tree. While perhaps disappointed not to win Gautama as a husband, the young girls, like Sujata, request that he become their spiritual teacher. The story of the two sisters is very similar in the Kangyur and *Sanghabhedavastu,* although the curious prefatory passage concerning the cruel brahman does not appear in these texts.

Further Symbols of the Sacred Feminine

Another story that appears as Gautama emerges from retreat concerns his need for new clothes. After six years being exposed to the elements without washing, his mendicant robes have become filthy rags. Falling about his body in tatters, they are too unseemly and immodest for Gautama to wear, especially now that he is to resume seeking alms in the village. While the cowherd Sujata tends to his hunger, it is a washerwoman by the name of Gava who notices that Gautama needs fresh clothing. In this story from the *Mahavastu,* she is described as being overcome with devotion as she hangs a simple hempen rag-robe on a tree branch under which Gautama is meditating. She voices the wish that he use the robe once he has "achieved his purpose," to which Gautama silently signals his assent. Joyfully Gava bows down, and after circumambulating him three times out of respect, she departs. Not long afterward Gava dies, apparently in the presence of the Bodhisattva. Her heart is said to be completely peaceful because of her gift to him. Due to her great merit, she is born in one of the heavenly realms from which she continues to look after Gautama.* Soon, however, she notices that he has not yet donned her robe. This concerns her because it would mean her merit in giving it to him is incomplete. Accompanied by a retinue of heavenly maidens, Gava descends to earth and, taking the robe off the tree branch, offers it to him, saying,

> Lord, when I was a human being, with a heart full of faith I gave this hempen rag-robe to the Exalted One while he was practicing austerities, so that he should for my sake make use of it when he had achieved his purpose. As a result of that root of merit, when I passed away from among men I was reborn among the devas of Trayastrimsha. Well would it be if the Exalted One, taking pity on me, would now make use of the hempen rag-robe, so that thus my reward might be greater still.[54]

---

* Trayastrimsha Heaven, where Maya also resides.

At this moment, a multitude of gods descend from the sky and call out to Gautama that he should accept *their* special divine garment instead, not a paltry hempen robe given by an ordinary washerwoman. Declining the offer, the Bodhisattva accepts Gava's robe directly from her hands. Now the gods jeer at the Bodhisattva, one hundred thousand of them waving celestial garments while shouting,

> Ha! ha! hail! hail! As [the Bodhisattva] has renounced his universal sovereignty, are not our hearts glad that he has gotten him hempen rag-robes?[55]

Nonetheless, several gods assist Gautama as he sets out to wash, bleach, and darn his new garment. This is to be the robe he will soon wear upon taking his seat under the *bodhi* tree. This scene is reminiscent of the earlier story that took place after Siddhartha's Great Departure, where his first robes of mendicancy were entrusted to a woman who also died shortly thereafter. In that story, the robes eventually made their way to the Bodhisattva after Indra stole them from a tree spirit. These curiously entwined themes of women, garments, and death are found again in the following account from the *Lalitavistara,* where a variant of the story of Gava the washerwoman appears.

The story opens as Gautama ends his austerities and decides it's time to replace his aged robes. It turns out that one of Sujata's former servants, a woman named Radha, has just died and her body is lying in a charnel ground covered with a hempen shroud. Indifferent to taboos surrounding charnel cloth, Gautama decides to adopt this garment as his mendicant robe.[56] Just as he is reaching for it, the gods begin to heckle him:

> Here is a descendant of a great royal clan. He has abandoned his kingdom of a universal monarch, and now he turns his mind to a dusty rag. What a sight! Friends, this is really amazing![57]

So loud is the heavenly clamor that news of Gautama's alleged indignity makes its way all the way up through the celestial worlds to the god Brahma in the highest realm. However, the Bodhisattva is nonplussed and looks to wash the humble garment before putting it on. Several gods offer to help him, but retaining the discipline of a renunciate, Gautama spurns their assistance and goes to the river to wash it himself. Still feeling weak from his austerities, he attempts to climb back up the riverbank but is obstructed by the jealous, evil demon Mara. Hearing his cry for help, the goddess of a nearby tree intercedes by bending her branches low so he can pull himself up. Now settled quietly, Gautama sews the rag into proper mendicant attire. He has benefited not only from Radha's cloth in this story, but also from the ever-watchful kindness of a tree goddess.

Many miracles take place along the Nairanjana River at this point in the legends. In the *Lalitavistara,* the waters flow with divine fragrances and flowers infused by the gods. This version also says that Sujata gathers the Bodhisattva's remnant hair and beard cuttings, thinking they must surely be sacred.* A river goddess appears in some stories, identified as the *naga* princess, or daughter of the king of the river.† According to the *Abhinish-kramanasutra,* she emerges from a fresh spring that bubbles up from deep within the earth. As Gautama emerges from bathing in the river, she quickly furnishes him with a special seat woven of reeds, where he takes his place and proceeds to eat the rice milk porridge provided by Sujata. The same scene transpires in the *Lalitavistara,* but there the *naga* princess offers the Bodhisattva a throne encrusted with jewels. As he later arises and begins his advance toward the *bodhi* tree, she carries his seat off to her palace in the underworld, where it becomes a sacred object of veneration.[58]

An intriguing final story at the river appears in the *Buddhacarita,* where the *naga* princess and Sujata are conflated into one character. The episode opens as Gautama emerges after bathing in the river and again struggles to climb up the bank. The trees bend their branches low "in adoration" to give him a helping hand. At this moment, the Sujata character, here named Nandabala, arrives.‡ Overcome with joy, she humbly approaches the Bodhisattva and offers him the bowl of rice milk. The conflation with the river goddess becomes apparent in the poet's lovely description of her

---

* It sounds as though he must have cut his hair after his six years of austerities. This is an unusual reference, since conventionally the Buddha's hair and beard are said never to grow again following his first haircut after his Great Departure.
† *Naga* refers to serpents or snakelike nature spirits who dwell in the underworld, particularly waterways.
‡ A further conflation with the variant about the two sisters.

appearance, likening her to Yamuna, a sacred river in India. Not only is she deep blue in color, Nandabala is wearing shells:

> She was wearing a dark-blue cloth and her arms were brilliant with white shells, so that she seemed like Yamuna, best of rivers, when its dark-blue water is wreathed with foam.

> Her delight was enhanced by faith, and her blue-lotus eyes opened wide, as, doing obeisance with her head, she caused him to accept the milk rice.[59]

Her offering secures for her the merit she seeks while nourishing the Bodhisattva's body. Now he is able to undertake the arduous final steps on his journey to awakening.

Under the Bodhi Tree

Supported by the kindness and generosity of those around him, Gautama's body has become fully restored to health and wholeness. Whether by ordinary women, like the cowherd Sujata and the washerwoman Gava, or symbols of the feminine expressed through the animated spirits of the river and trees, he has been fed, clothed, bathed, and protected after emerging weak and vulnerable from his austerities. More than simple acts of nurturance, these elements mark Gautama's final preparations on his way to the tree of awakening and frame the beginning of his transformation from ordinary man to fully awakened Buddha. Sujata's rice milk will sustain him during this time, as that is the last food he will take for the next forty-nine days.

We'll resume our story at the river, where Gautama has just finished his meal and throws Sujata's golden bowl into the water. Caught by a whirlpool, it tumbles into the underworld, where it clangs loudly as it strikes against the bowls of three previous bodhisattvas. This incident sets off a cataclysmic earthquake, thunderous noise, and many miracles that all portend the dawning of a new buddha era.[60] The commotion awakes the slumbering king of the underworld, an old *naga* named Kala,* who is grumpy at being disturbed. He says,

----

* *Kala Nagaraja,* or Black Snake King.

> It was but yesterday that a royal Buddha assumed his dignity; today there is another. I never have time for a comfortable sleep.[61]

King Kala has prevailed over vast epochs comprising countless human generations and in his reign has witnessed the awakening of three buddhas.* Despite his initial irritation, he is elated to hear that a new buddha has arrived and quickly emerges from his lair to find the radiant Bodhisattva seated by the river "like lightning among the clouds." Recognizing the effulgent form from bygone eras, Kala is overwhelmed with happiness and sings praises to Gautama in lengthy, protracted verse. His words lovingly recall the Bodhisattva's predecessors while validating Gautama's presence in their continuum according to signs and miracles. He welcomes Gautama as savior of the world.

> Thou art like the great and glorious Saviours of the world whom I saw of yore. I have no doubt of this.
> . . .
> From the way this earth resounds like a beaten pan of metal, there is no doubt, Great Hero, that to-day thou wilt become Buddha.
> . . .
> From the way thou dost doff thy robe, and from the way thou goest down to the cool Nairanjana, to-day thou wilt become Buddha.
> From the way the Nairanjana is gaily covered with flowers, there is no doubt, Great Hero, that to-day thou wilt become Buddha.
> From the way flowers rain down and devas throw their garments, and from the way trees bow before thee, to-day thou wilt become Buddha.[62]

As Kala continues his reverent utterances, a multitude of creatures, gods, and celestial beings, male and female, converge around the Bodhisattva to honor him and rejoice that buddhahood is imminent. Also appearing at this moment is Kala's wife and queen with a retinue of *naga* maidens, who encircle the Bodhisattva and extend divine offerings of flowers, perfume,

---

* Krakucchanda, Konaka, and Kasyapa; as bodhisattvas these three were also named as recipients of Sujata's rice milk in her previous lives.

and ornaments. The *naga* women chant praises with words that encourage Gautama to fearlessness:

> Go forward! Lord of the World! firmly fixed in thy resolve,
> Without anxiety or fear, perfectly established;
> Rejoice and be very glad—thou who hast banished desire!
> Free from all doubt or anger . . . or covetousness.
> Thou art the Lord able to heal the world,
> And therefore we adore thee and we worship thee.[63]

On a clear full-moon night, with Kala acting as crier hailing the momentous occasion, the entire procession of divine and earthly beings departs from the river to accompany the Bodhisattva to the tree of awakening where all previous buddhas attained enlightenment.* Gautama himself is described as walking regally "with the bold bearing of the king of the lions" during this journey, his mind focused single-pointedly on buddhahood. Along the way, multitudes of *naga* maidens sprinkle the path with fragrant flowers while countless more sing, play joyous music, and beat their drums. In every direction, trees animated by goddesses bend in homage toward the *bodhi* tree, while spectacular miracles of healing and pacification take place throughout the realms of sentient beings. As described in the *Lalitavistara,*

> As the Bodhisattva was walking toward the seat of awakening, rays of light streamed forth from his body. The light pacified all the lower realms and caused all unfortunate states to cease. . . . Anyone who suffered from disease was healed. Anyone feeling discomfort attained happiness. All who were struck with fear found release. Anyone living in bondage was freed from his or her ties. Anyone suffering from poverty discovered wealth. . . . Those who were starving had their stomachs filled. All the ones who were parched were relieved of their thirst. Pregnant women gave birth easily. Those who were old and weak gained perfect strength. . . . At that moment everyone

---

* Calculated today as a distance of about two kilometers.

engendered love, altruism, and a feeling that all beings are each other's mothers and fathers.[64]

The rejoicing continues as the Bodhisattva spreads grass beneath the *bodhi* tree and prepares to take his seat. Recalling this moment from previous eons, the *naga* women further celebrate and encourage him:

> Approach the lord of trees and sit there without fear!
> Conquer Mara's army and become free from the web of disturbing
>   emotions!
> Just as the victorious lords of the past attained awakening,
> So you will attain supreme, sacred, and peaceful awakening!
> For many millions of eons you have aimed for this;
> For the sake of liberating beings you have gone through hardship.
> Now the time has come for your wishes to be fulfilled;
> So go to the lord of trees and connect with supreme awakening.[65]

Some legends describe how at first Gautama was unable to take his seat because the earth kept shifting beneath his feet. Not able to settle on one side of the tree, he tried another, but each time the earth rotated such that he still could not sit down. This was due to the intervention of the earth goddess, Prithivi, guardian of that seat, who demonstrates her powers of dominion by only allowing legitimate claimants access to the sacred spot beneath the *bodhi* tree, known as the *bodhimanda,* or "seat of awakening." Symbolically located at the center, or "navel," of her vast earth body, the *bodhimanda* represents the earth's supreme throne at the nexus of creation, accessible only to a *dharma raja,* or "righteous king," who is deemed worthy by virtue of lifetimes of accumulated good deeds and selfless acts of service to all creatures.[66] Like the hub of a spinning wheel, the *bodhimanda* is utterly still and stable. Only this sacred spot can bear the world-shaking force of a bodhisattva's dawning adamantine wisdom at the time of full enlightenment, and only a worthy bodhisattva is capable of being seated on it. According to the *Buddhacarita,*

> For this is the navel of earth's surface, entirely possessed of the highest power; for there is no other spot on earth which can bear the force of [the Buddha's] concentrated thought.[67]

After Gautama completes three circumambulations and faces east beneath the *bodhi* tree, the earth finally stops heaving—the sign that he has found Prithivi's sacred spot. By allowing him to scatter the grass and take his seat, she authenticates his worthiness to become the next buddha. Sitting in meditative posture, Gautama repeats for the last time his resolve to gain full awakening. In the *Mahavastu,* he addresses these words to the *naga* king:

> To-day, O Kala, thy word proves true. To-day I shall attain the supreme enlightenment.
>
> Even this great earth shall be mountainless, the moon shall fall from the sky, sooner than I shall fail to get there. Be joyful, O king of serpents.
>
> The wind shall cease to blow on Meru's summit,* earth and sky shall meet, sooner than one such as I, who have reached my throne, shall fail to attain immortality. . . .
>
> To-day, when the night passes away, I will destroy the root of all existence leaving not a trace behind.[68]

And thus the Bodhisattva becomes deeply immersed in meditation. What follows in the legends are dramatic portrayals of the struggles within his mind as illustrated by scenes of demons and battles, with particular focus on his protracted conflict with the evil demon king, Mara. In some of the legends, Mara has been appearing as a shadowy tempter since Siddhartha's youth, but now at the time of the Bodhisattva's full awakening he becomes a powerful, demonic presence. Dialogues with Mara and inspired descriptions of Gautama's brilliant, awakening wisdom predominate at this juncture in the narratives. These lengthy passages are complex and could well be a complete area of study by themselves. Here we will remain focused on the feminine presence in the Buddha's life as he is on the cusp of his awakening.

The divine entourage that has followed Gautama from the Nairanjana River continues to celebrate as he commences his meditation. The gods have festooned the *bodhi* tree with magnificent garlands and sparkling jewels, fragrant incense and banners of the finest silk. So resplendent is the display that some celestial observers perceive the sacred tree as luminous silver or gold, while others see it as made of crystal, emeralds, or precious sandalwood.

---

* A sacred mountain in the Himalayas.

The guardian goddess of the *bodhi* tree emerges, overjoyed that yet another bodhisattva has arrived at the seat of awakening. In devotion, she sprinkles incense and scatters her own precious ornaments as offerings before him. This catches the attention of the goddesses of all the surrounding trees, and they too shower the Bodhisattva with flowers, their palms pressed together above their heads in loving homage. Like the *naga* women, the goddess of the *bodhi* tree entreats the Bodhisattva to persevere in his purpose. Unfortunately we do not know exactly what she says because, according to the *Mahavastu,* her language is "the tongue of faery"![69]

Just as the *naga* king prepares to dance before the Bodhisattva, the jubilant gathering is interrupted by the appearance of evil Mara. In terror, Kala and his family abscond to the underworld, while the remaining celestial guests flee in all directions. Mara is outraged that Gautama would presume to the throne of awakening and has arrived to unseat him. This can only be achieved by disturbing the quietude of the Bodhisattva's fierce concentration, so Mara engages many different strategies, hoping that Gautama will become agitated and abandon his goal.

According to several Sanskrit legends, his first line of offense is to intimidate Gautama with frightening reports of his wives and family back home in Kapilavastu. Ever the trickster, Mara transforms into the figure of a disheveled messenger who arrives, out of breath, bearing a bundle of official notices appearing to be from the royal house of Shakya. "These letters are for you!" declares the "messenger," showing Gautama that each was signed by one of the Shakya princes. The false letters urge Gautama to return home immediately to help his kingdom avert further disaster, as his evil cousin Devadatta has staged a coup; taken over Gautama's palace; raped his three wives; and thrown Suddhodana, bound by chains, in prison. Just as cruelly, Mara magically live-streams a vivid apparition of Gautama's wives— Yashodhara, Mrigadja (Mrigi Gautami), and Gopa—in supposedly tearful, anguished states. "How can you stay here?" shouts the wicked "messenger," goading Gautama to leave his seat. Unbowed, Gautama reflects on the perilous state of the human condition. Mara's display only fortifies his determination to remain unmoved until achieving enlightenment.[70]

The Bodhisattva's cruel rival further uses women as bait to ensnare and destroy him, but it never works. In passages echoing earlier seduction scenes from Siddhartha's harem in Kapilavastu, Mara enlists scores of provocative demoness courtesans to lure the Bodhisattva away from his meditation into the trap of desire. When that fails, he manifests hideous, flesh-eating ogresses who converge upon the quiet saint, only to be deflected by the invincible aura surrounding him. As a final measure, the evil demon sends his own three daughters* to overcome Gautama with their feminine wiles. In one account, they even assume the guise of Yashodhara suckling Rahula.[71] Throughout these attempts and the additional assaults by Mara's vast armies which rock the earth and empty the oceans, the Bodhisattva sits unperturbed in concentration. At times he explains patiently to his assailants that he has severed all ties with sensual attachments and gives them what would later be described as a Buddhist teaching.

As the Bodhisattva is assaulted from all sides by multitudes of murderous demons, he reflects on his own solitary state. No longer is he surrounded by loving family and protected by regiments of Shakya princes. The *nagas* and celestial beings that recently surrounded him with devotion have all disbanded. Relationships, after all, are unreliable. Utterly alone, Gautama sits cross-legged, swathed in a simple robe, beneath the *bodhi* tree with no armies or weapons to protect him. Who can come to his defense? What can help him now? His meditative investigation brings him to an understanding of the strength of his own virtues such as generosity and selfless compassion that have accumulated over countless previous lifetimes. These gentle qualities, he realizes, are the forces that will decisively overturn the monstrous evil combatants that face him now. He reflects,

> [Mara's] great army comes to fight against me alone; my parents are not here; no brother is with me; nor is there anyone else to assist me; therefore the [virtue†] of truth that I have kept perfectly ... must be to me as a mother; the [virtue] of wisdom must be to me as a father; my knowledge of the [dharma] must be to me as an assisting brother; my [virtue] of kindness must be to me as most excellent friends, my firm faith must be to me as a beloved parent; my [virtue] of patient endurance must be to me as a helping son; these six relatives have

---

* Symbolically named for what in Buddhism are known as the three principal delusions: craving, ignorance, and aversion.

† *Paramita* (Sanskrit).

continually preserved me until now, not leaving me for a single day or hour; therefore my relatives that are as my life are here.[72]*

With this insight that his inner qualities are his only supreme protection, the Bodhisattva lets go of his remaining emotional ties to loved ones in Kapilavastu and rests in fearless ease "like a noble lion surrounded by deer, calm and unmoved by the army of Mara."[73]

The final battle comes down to one of words. Mara derides Gautama for being a puny weakling and challenges his right to be seated on the *bodhimanda*. Boastful of his powerful armies while falsely naming countless virtuous deeds, Mara claims universal sovereignty for himself and taunts the Bodhisattva to prove his own worthiness. With words that are both harmonious and firm, Gautama concedes his solitary status while declaring the inviolable nature of his mind:

> Oh Mara! Thou knowest not the . . . might of my army. Thou knowest not that my intellect is a piercing weapon against which no enemy can contend.[74]

Consumed with rage, Mara hurls his remaining insults. Above all, his ego is undone that a mere mortal could be defeating him, the mighty god Mara, who has prevailed for eons. However, nothing disquiets the Bodhisattva, who steadfastly retains his seat. In a final countering move that vanquishes his foe once and for all, he declares that Earth herself will testify to his worthiness:

> This earth supports all beings;
> She is impartial and unbiased toward all, whether moving or still.
> She is my witness that I speak no lies;
> So may she bear my witness.[75]

Reaching forward with his right hand, the Bodhisattva summons Prithivi. As he touches his fingers to the earth, the goddess thunders and quakes with such force that the reverberations are heard at the highest point of space.[76]

---

* The six relatives as virtues are suggestive of the six *paramitas,* or perfections, of Mahayana Buddhism.

Precisely what happens next varies in the legends. In the *Nidanakatha*, the earth bellows her affirmation of the Bodhisattva's sovereignty, while the *Lalitavistara* claims that Prithivi and one billion earth goddesses shake the earth.* In front of the seated Bodhisattva, she bursts through the earth's surface, revealing her upper torso. With jeweled ornaments draped across her voluptuous, motherly breasts, she bows to the Bodhisattva and validates his claim to the *bodhimanda* while praising his limitless virtues and insisting that he alone is the world's supreme authority. After rebuking Mara and displaying her great powers, she withdraws back beneath the surface.[77][†]

At this spectacle, the now enfeebled Mara collapses with fear, his body sweating, his mind disoriented. In the midst of this drama, a compassionate presence steps forward in the form of the goddess of the *bodhi* tree, who takes notice of his suffering. Reviving Mara by sprinkling water from her vase, she fiercely goads him with words of wisdom:

> Quick, get up! You must depart without delay!
> For this is what happens to those who pay no heed to the words
>   of the Master.
> . . .
> A fool who offends against those who are faultless
> Shall himself meet with many troubles.[78]

In the Thai tradition, the moment Gautama touches the earth, Prithivi springs forth in the form of a lovely goddess with long, flowing hair. Standing before the Bodhisattva, she validates his claim to the *bodhimanda* with the words,

> O Being more excellent than angels or men! it is true that when you performed your great works you ever poured water on my hair.[79]

The water she refers to represents the merit the Bodhisattva has accumulated over countless lifetimes. With each of his good deeds, another drop of water

---

* Here she is called Sthavara.

† Iconographically, Prithivi was frequently depicted in ancient Indian art and often shown only from the waist up (the earth itself being her lower body) supporting the Buddha's throne or supplicating him. Other images portray a warring Prithivi with her vast brigade of goddesses engaged in combat with Mara and his demon warriors.

was added to her tresses. Now on the day of his full awakening, the earth goddess's hair contains an inexhaustible ocean of virtue. In testimony to the Bodhisattva's supremacy, she raises her hands and wrings out her locks, thereby unleashing torrents of floodwaters that gush across the world, enveloping and destroying evil Mara and his armies.* A dramatic description appears in the text:

> Onwards against the host of Mara the mighty torrent rushed. His generals were overturned, his elephant swept away by the waters, his royal insignia destroyed, and his whole army fled in utter confusion, amid the roarings of a terrific earthquake, and peals of thunder crashing through the skies.[80]

As the demons are vanquished, Gautama's mind fully awakens and attains the state of utter, irreversible peace, or nirvana. His gesture of touching the earth was to become the symbol of this victory over inner struggle, conjoined with his unobstructed insight into the fathomless nature of reality. Now at long last, Gautama has become fully enlightened. The Bodhisattva has become the Buddha.†

The brilliance of this event has challenged generations of storytellers using imagination and metaphor to capture in words the transformation that took place that extraordinary night under the *bodhi* tree. The *Mahavastu* says,

> It would be easier for an infant to count the stars in the twinkling sky than it would be to tell in words the limit of this man's virtues.[81]

We're told that the clap of awakening simultaneously transformed the world, as if becoming a mirror of the Buddha's perfect mind—harmonious, compassionate, and wise. When dawn broke, people everywhere stood in awe of miracles: banners and lotus garlands hung from the sky; greenery burst forth with fruits and blossoms; the hell realms were flooded with

---

* The motif of Prithivi wringing out her hair is commonly found in Southeast Asian Buddhist art and water fountains.
† The "Awakened One."

light; ocean waters became sweet; the blind gained sight; the deaf could hear sounds; slaves were freed from bondage. All mental sufferings disappeared from the earth, and creatures everywhere became joyful and filled with love*:

> At this time there was no angry thought in the world;
> All sorrow disappeared, and there was great joy;
> The mad and drunken came to their right mind,
> And all who were in fear, were comforted.[82]

Women and men, girls and boys, even gods and mythical beasts, female and male, were all touched by the marvelous event. Wondrous portents blessed every living creature. What could they possibly foretell? The answer to that question has since revealed itself, as the Buddha's brilliant teachings continue as a living tradition engendering harmony, insight, and kindness throughout humanity.

As a postscript to our story, Gautama's parents, meanwhile, have been up all night. In Kapilavastu, Suddhodana is sleepless with anxiety. His heart ever tied to his beloved son, he feels the tumult of Siddhartha's fearsome battles with Mara as the earth shakes and roars beneath his bed. For her part, Maya has been anxiously watching her son's torrent of tribulations from her vantage point in heaven. Joyously, she beholds his consummate awakening under the *bodhi* tree. Swift as the wind, she brings the happy news to Suddhodana and Yashodhara in the palace. Taking the form of a servant girl, she gladly informs the king,

> Maharaja, be it known to you that on this night, your son, Siddhartha, has attained supreme wisdom, and on this account the earth shook.[83]

---

* Buddhist scholars and practitioners no doubt hear the similarity here with verses from Shantideva's *Bodhisattvacharyavatara*.

6

Return to Kapilavastu

*T*he Buddha's awakening marked the end of his life as an ordinary man caught in the web of worldly strife and the beginning of his forty-five-year ministry aimed at teaching others who wished to be free. That time frame and those teachings, of course, would form the foundation of the Buddhist faith. At first he was unsure how to proceed, struggling to articulate the ineffability of his realization even to himself, but soon, roused by compassion for humanity, he determined to return to public life to share what he now knew with seekers of the truth. Just as he had finally reached his goal after arduous commitment and inner struggle, so too could others. While lacking the power to single-handedly remove suffering in the world—after all, he was human, not divine—the Buddha saw that he could be as a lamp guiding individuals on their own paths to freedom. The potential he realized within himself is latent equally in all women and men. How could he not point the way? And so the fruition of his early labors, the purpose of his life, took form in helping others.

The First Female Disciples

After spending forty-nine days in meditation, the Buddha leaves his seat at the *bodhi* tree, but not before thanking the goddess of that tree who had so joyfully welcomed him. With nothing material such as flowers to offer, he gives her the gift of his gaze. Standing immobile and staring silently at the sacred tree for seven days, he offers her the "azure lotuses" of his eyes while generating thoughts of gratitude. He reflects,

Vast has been the kindness and the service which this great holy
Bo-tree has rendered to me. Trusting to its protecting shade have I
attained to omniscience.[1]

And the *Abhinishkramanasutra* says,

In this sacred arena I have got rid of every source of sorrow,
And seated here beholding that sacred throne on which I sat,
I remember it was there I fulfilled my vows, I arrived at the
   other shore,
In that place it was I reached the full enjoyment of Bodhi.[2]

Soon Gautama Buddha sets off, having decided to journey to present-day
Sarnath.* There he would find the five attendants who served him during
his six years of austerities only to abandon him in disappointment once
he fathomed the wisdom of the Middle Way. Despite their shortcomings,
the Buddha feels these adepts are best suited to hear—perhaps even
understand—the profound insights he now has to share. But first a pressing
need must be addressed: he is hungry. The body that has supported him well
throughout his grueling psychological transformation to buddhahood now
requires nourishment. Sustained by Sujata's superior rice milk, he has not
eaten in almost two months.

The theme of motherhood appears once again in the narrative, but
here indirectly as the Buddha takes his first meal as an enlightened being
from two brothers he meets along the road.† Wealthy merchants traveling a
regional trade route, they are driving a caravan of five hundred oxen whose
carts are heavily laden with goods. Unbeknownst to the men, their deceased
mother, now a goddess, is closely watching over them from heaven. As she
observes her sons coming upon the Buddha, she reflects,

Buddhas ought to be given food. Indeed, this one should not go
much farther without any. My two sons, who are now here in this
place, should be caused to make food offerings to the Buddha.[3]

---

*About two hundred kilometers.
† The following account weaves together variants of the episode from both Pali and
Sanskrit traditions.

She then causes the lumbering caravan to come to a sudden halt in a grove of blooming *shala* trees, the cartwheels bogged down in mud. Appearing in magical fashion before her sons, the goddess advises them of the supreme opportunity they now have to provide alms to the exalted saint, thereby attaining unsurpassed merit for themselves. In her motherly way, she is looking out for all three of the men's best interests, recognizing both the Buddha's hunger and the chance for her sons to benefit from an act of generosity. Greatly pleased and deeply reverential, the brothers offer the Buddha a meal of honey-sweetened gruel, for which, in return, he initiates them as his first disciples. Thus the new faith, which will come to be known as Buddhism, acquired its first converts. It should not be forgotten that this important event took place due to a mother's act of love.

Several Sanskrit variants of this episode bear noting. In the *Lalitavistara,* the merchants' offering to the Buddha is cream collected from one thousand cows, echoing the theme from Sujata's story.[4] Elsewhere, as recounted earlier, in a much more drastic turn, the Buddha becomes deathly ill shortly after eating the brothers' offering. In the *Abhinishkramanasutra,* the god Indra swiftly provides a cure in the form of a special fruit, and in gratitude, the Buddha initiates Indra's wife as his first female disciple. Nowhere else does this last detail occur, so perhaps it is safest to say that she was his first goddess disciple.[5]

The Kangyur story,* however, is much more significant for women. Having returned to the Nairanjana River, the Buddha eats the merchants' meal and is swiftly wracked with violent pain. Right on cue, ever wanting to thwart his opponent, evil Mara appears, crying out, "Blessed One, the time to die has come!" The Buddha's rebuttal makes it clear that Mara will be foiled once again. There is too much work to do, he says; dying at this time is not an option. Prophetically, the Buddha describes the blueprint for his upcoming ministry. He will not die until all believers in his faith—women and men, lay and ordained—have become accomplished through his teachings, and the dharma thereby flourishes in the world. In his own words:

----

* Fragments also appear in the *Lalitavistara* and Chinese sources.

Mara, as long as my disciples have not become wise and of quick understanding, as long as the [monks, the nuns] and the lay disciples
of either sex are not able to refute their adversaries according to the
Dharma, as long as my moral teaching has not been spread far and
wide among gods and men, so long will I not pass away.[6]

With this statement, the Buddha declares the four assemblies—nuns,
monks, laywomen, laymen—that he will be establishing over the next forty-
five years. Together, equally nurtured in the dharma, they form the body of
his life's work, his purpose in becoming an enlightened buddha.[7] It need
hardly be pointed out that women make up half of this equation.

And so the Buddha goes on to give his first teaching, or "turn the
Wheel of Dharma" in the Deer Park in Sarnath. While early Buddhist literature frequently uses feminine imagery to describe the natural world, the
following passage from the Sinhalese tradition is exceptional for its beauty.
Here a throne emerges spontaneously from the earth, and Buddha takes his
seat preparing to teach:

> The evening was like a lovely female; the stars were pearls upon her
> neck, the blue clouds were her braided hair, and the expanse was her
> flowing robe. As a crown she had the [heavens]; the three worlds
> were as her body; her eyes were like the white lotus . . . ; and her voice
> was like the humming of a bee. To worship [Buddha], and listen to
> the first proclaiming of the [dharma], this lovely female came.[8]

All humans and earthly creatures, female and male, come from the four
corners of the world to receive the Buddha's teachings. The celestial realms
empty as both goddesses and gods assemble, crowding so closely together
that one hundred thousand could fit on the point of a needle. Even Mount
Meru jumps for joy on the occasion of the Buddha's first teaching! Every
living being, including all species of animals, great and small, understand
the Buddha's words as if he were speaking directly to them in their own
language. It is noteworthy that in these scenes, the Buddha addresses his
teachings to both women and men and does not equivocate in avowing that
both sexes have equal potential in their pursuit of freedom. For example,
according to the *Abhinishkramanasutra,* he says in the Deer Park,

If a man or woman will leave the world, and follow me, desiring to find that highest condition of a true [Superior], to reach the fountain head of such a condition, then such an one shall surely find it, and arrive at the desired goal.[9]

The Buddha's noble first teaching and those that followed gave rise to an entirely new and prodigious body of literature, one spanning millennia and multiple cultures, its goal to record, systematize, and interpret the Buddha's profound message. The early biographical legends largely shift their focus at this point in the literature, turning to details of his ministry and away from his personal life. One can imagine there was little else to report, as the Buddha was now living as a simple monk, his life dedicated to teaching and ministering to his disciples. Contact with friends and family would resume, just as newfound relationships would form, but in an entirely different context now because he had extinguished all emotional ties and was unwavering as an ascetic and spiritual master.

Numerous conversions take place in the aftermath of the Buddha's first teachings. Of interest here is the conversion of a young man named Yasa, whose mother—Sujata of our earlier tale—is about to become Buddhism's first female disciple. In a story that echoes the Buddha's own youthful struggles, Yasa is disgruntled with ordinary life and leaves home secretly in the night to seek deeper meaning. Soon he takes ordination with the Buddha and becomes quite content. His parents, meanwhile, are distraught by his disappearance and search frantically for him. Yasa's father meets the Buddha and inquires after his son, but in short order he takes initiation himself as a lay disciple. The father then invites the Buddha to take a meal in their home, where the saint encounters Sujata and accords her the same teachings he has given her husband and son.* Joyfully fulfilling her earlier aspiration to become the Buddha's disciple, she takes refuge as the first laywoman convert to the new faith.†[10] Later the Buddha would describe her as "the foremost laywoman among those taking refuge."[11] Some ver-

---

* As often happens, the chronology appears convoluted. Only months before, Sujata appeared as a young mother making an offering on the occasion of the birth of her son. It could be argued that a different woman named Sujata is intended, but here it is suggested they are meant to be one and the same.

† Refuge in the three jewels of Buddha, dharma, and *sangha* constitutes a formal act

sions note that Yasa's wife also took refuge at this time. In a related note, it seems that Sujata's stated wish to attain enlightenment is on track. In a scene from the Pali canon that takes place after Sujata has died, Ananda asks the Buddha to comment on her future. With his divine eye that sees into the future, the Buddha replies,

> The female lay follower Sujata who has died had, with the utter destruction of three fetters, become a stream-enterer, no longer bound to the nether world, fixed in destiny, with enlightenment as her destination.[12]

The aspirations of the young girls Nanda and Bala, who previously fed him rice milk in the Tibetan tale, are also to be fulfilled. The Buddha returns to their village soon after leaving the Deer Park and gives them teachings after which they, too, become his disciples.[13]

Yashodhara's Pregnancy

In due course, after launching his ministry in the northeastern region of India, the itinerant Buddha returns to Kapilavastu where he sees his family again after many years. A lot has gone on in his absence, of course, especially in the lives of his wife, Yashodhara, and his parents. While we're told they've kept tabs on him during his absence, he has some major catching up to do. Nowhere is this more true than in matters concerning his young son, Rahula, who has never known his father and, according to tradition, is six or seven years old when the Buddha returns. Stories about this interim period are fragmentary at best, appearing almost entirely in the Sanskrit tradition, yet they are relevant for the glimpses they provide into some Gautama family drama that has been unfolding in the palace and Yashodhara's continuing travails since her husband, Siddhartha, left.

Before resuming our narrative, we must circle back to tie up some loose ends from the night of Siddhartha's departure from Kapilavastu. Recall that he entered the harem to bid a final farewell to Yashodhara, but when he saw that she was asleep holding the infant Rahula in her arms, the prince did

---

of initiation. It can be argued that there was as yet no sangha when Sujata took her vows, but the story is recounted according to the legends.

not wish to disturb her and slipped away silently. This traditional version of events is reported in Pali legends and widely portrayed in early Buddhist art, although it does not appear in the Pali canon or most Sanskrit sources. According to these Pali stories, Rahula was born earlier on the same day Siddhartha was out touring the pleasure park with his charioteer, and the prince heard about his son's birth from a messenger dispatched by his father.* If Suddhodana surmised that Siddhartha would share his joy over the birth of a male heir, he must have been very disappointed, because Siddhartha was utterly nonplussed: "That child," replied [Siddhartha] with great coolness, "is a new and strong tie that I will have to break."[14] The king is said to have been confused by his son's ambivalence and named the child Rahula, which Pali sources tell us means "fetter" or "bond." We also learn that Suddhodana—the infant's grandfather—attended to the proper birth and naming ceremonies, when normally this would be the function of the father, who was apparently not even present.

This episode and Siddhartha's subsequent peek at his sleeping wife and son would not be significant here except that the Sanskrit sources are consistent that Rahula had not yet been born when Siddhartha left home.† They relate that on the prince's last night at home, he made love to Yashodhara, thus engendering Rahula, but at the time of his Great Departure, he had no children. In the *Sanghabhedavastu,* he says,

> "Lest others say that the Prince Shakyamuni was not a man, and that he wandered forth without 'paying attention' to Yashodhara, Gopika and Mrgaja, and his other sixty thousand wives, let me now make love to Yashodhara." And he did so, and Yashodhara became pregnant.[15]

This variant would still not be especially significant except that the traditions diverge sharply when it comes to accounting for Rahula's age and the timeline of his father's ministry. The Pali accounts have the Buddha returning to Kapilavastu almost immediately following his enlightenment, or six or seven years after his Great Departure, whereas most Sanskrit legends maintain that he did not return home for twelve years, or six years

---

* The *Nidanakatha* says this took place seven days earlier.
† With the exception of the *Buddhacarita,* which follows the Pali tradition.

after awakening under the *bodhi* tree. Yet in both scenarios, Rahula is six or seven years old. While unreliable chronology is a signature of the early legends, and it is often impossible to reconcile conflicting details, these specific inconsistencies have caught the attention of generations of scholars. Sometimes the discrepancies are even pointed out by early editors within the legends themselves.[16] Specifically, these differences give rise to confusion about Rahula's birth, leading to questions surrounding his mother's pregnancy. At the center is the assertion in the Sanskrit tradition that Rahula was, in fact, born six years after Siddhartha left home, thereby creating an obvious conundrum regarding his conception, one that is explained by the claim in these stories that he remained in utero for the entire six years.

Thus, we have a curious mix of scenarios on our hands. While it's impossible to sort them out coherently, we'll turn to what's relevant here and embrace the elephant in the room—Rahula's paternity. With the exception of the Sinhalese sources, the Pali tradition is mostly silent on the subject, but little-known vignettes appear in the Sanskrit literature.

We first hear about Yashodhara's pregnancy at the time the Bodhisattva begins his austerities along the Nairanjana River. Recall that Suddhodana and Yashodhara's father, Suprabuddha, have kept track of the prince by sending out spies who bring back daily updates on his whereabouts and welfare. Upon learning that their beloved prince has begun to starve himself, the palace in Kapilavastu is thrown into a frenzy. "Alas! alas! for my poor child! how can he survive this penance of six years duration,"[17] laments Suddhodana. All the prince's wives, especially Yashodhara, are greatly distressed as well. Her face "wet with tears," she vows to emulate her beloved husband, so she casts off all her finery, sleeps on a bed of straw, and begins austerities in concert with Gautama by eating only a jujube fruit, grain of rice, or single sesame seed per day.* She says,

> How shall I enjoy the luxuries of a royal residence, and partake of delicate food, whilst my lord is thus enduring affliction and want. I will even share his self-privation and suffer the same pain.[18]

---

* This response is reminiscent of Suddhodana adopting asceticism in tandem with Maya while she remained secluded during her pregnancy.

As Yashodhara undertakes this campaign of deprivation, she becomes very thin. Her pregnancy dwindles and goes unnoticed. So severe is her penance that the viability of the fetus is threatened. This comes to the attention of Suddhodana, who is anticipating the birth of a grandson and potential heir. Fearing for the child, he isolates Yashodhara and the harem women from news of the prince and forbids anyone to speak to her about her husband. Thus sheltered, Yashodhara gradually begins to eat and regain her health. As it turns out, her course still mimics the Bodhisattva's actions because six years have passed, and he has simultaneously begun to eat and resume alms rounds in the village. We have already seen how Sujata followed a parallel course with the Bodhisattva when she fed the mendicants daily for six years, dedicating the merit of her generosity to the fulfillment of the Bodhisattva's awakening. Even the gods followed a six-year course during that time, watching over the Bodhisattva day and night while making offerings and maturing in their own mission to awaken. As John S. Strong has noted, in Yashodhara's parallel program, her pregnancy mimics the "gestation" of her husband's spiritual quest, both of them lasting six years.[19]

The couple's parallel efforts further coincide as Yashodhara gives birth to Rahula at the exact moment the Buddha becomes enlightened. The Sanskrit sources explain that their son was so named because an eclipse (*rahu*) of the moon took place that night. With the birth of his grandson, Suddhodana is overjoyed and sets about arranging celebrations in his kingdom. Of note is that this passage also asserts the conatal birth of Ananda in Kapilavastu that night, and his birth gives the populace further reason for joy (*ananda*) and celebration.[20]

Once Rahula is born, an entirely new sentiment surfaces in these Sanskrit legends, one that appears almost jarring alongside the previous, mostly happy, accounts. No longer is Suddhodana cast as the protective patriarch showering concern on his daughter-in-law and grandchild. Rather, the king is outraged because he believes that Yashodhara has been unfaithful to the prince and that his "grandson" is actually a bastard. How else can one explain the belated birth? He no longer appears to subscribe to the theory of a six-year pregnancy. According to the Kangyur, Yashodhara is extremely distressed that her honor would be in question. Left alone to defend herself, she publicly appears before a jury of Shakya princes. Placing the infant Rahula on a stone that is thrown into a nearby pond, she says,

If the child be the Bodhisattva's, may it and the stone float; if it is not, may it sink![21]

When the stone floats, she performs the additional miracle of having it cross from one shore to the other. Her honor thus confirmed, she declares,

Sirs, I have demonstrated to you that this is the child of the Bodhisattva; I have not gone astray.[22]

Another version found in a collection of Chinese stories has the Shakyas throwing Yashodhara into a fire, whereupon she calls out her innocence. Her claim is corroborated as the fire transforms into a cool lake, and she is found seated in the center on a large lotus blossom holding Rahula on her lap.*[23] As we shall see, however, these measures do not entirely allay the Shakyas' or Suddhodana's doubts. Yashodhara will have more answering to do when the Buddha comes home in six years' time.

The *Abhinishkramanasutra* adds a graphic detail to the six-year pregnancy episode, which is framed as being told by the Buddha himself to his disciples in later years. Here Suddhodana is so angry with Yashodhara for (seemingly) dishonoring both his son and his royal house, that he calls an assembly of Shakya princes to decide her punishment. The all-male council comes up with horrendous suggestions, which include that she be, "whipped, burned, mutilated, blinded, impaled, buried alive."[24] We know this meeting takes place six years after her husband left because the Buddha explains that Rahula was born at the moment of his enlightenment. He clears up any confusion about Yashodhara's extended pregnancy, however, by saying that it was her profound grief over his absence that caused her to carry Rahula in her womb for six years. Only upon the joyous occasion of his awakening did she again experience joy herself, thereby inducing their son's delivery. Delighted by the birth, she duly clothed and adorned the baby according to his birthright as a prince. The Buddha goes on to express

---

* This story is reminiscent of the Tibetan tale of Padmasambhava and Mandarava, whose purity was tested by a flaming pyre that transformed into a lake with both of them seated on a lotus in the center.

confidence in Yashodhara's conduct by relating the following *Jataka* tale, which comes across as a love story.

Long ago, a mighty deer king (a previous incarnation of the Buddha) lived in contentment with his herd on beautiful pastureland, until one day he was caught in a hunter's snare. All the deer fled except his wife, the deer queen (Yashodhara), who was pregnant. Desperately but unsuccessfully, she tried to free him. Soon the hunter approached, and knowing that he intended to kill her husband, the deer queen offered herself instead:

> He is my husband. I love and revere him with all my heart, and therefore I am determined to share his fate; kill me first, hunter![25]

The story concludes as the hunter is swayed by her devotion, releases them both, and grants amnesty to the herd.[26]

While the dots don't particularly connect to her current predicament, the point is that Yashodhara has been steadfast in her faithfulness to her husband over their lifetimes together. It's out of the question that she would break that causal chain now by being unfaithful. The Bodhisattva is also loyal (or simply kind) to her in this story, as we see when he defends her honor from afar. Although he is practicing austerities by the Nairanjana River, he knows of her distress and his father's harsh accusations via his mystical powers. He immediately sends a message to the king saying, "This child is my child." As a result the charges are withdrawn and "all honor was done to both mother and child."[27] In this way, he averts Yashodhara's certain execution and, for the record, affirms Rahula's paternity. In this era before DNA testing, a father's word was apparently all that was required.

Unfortunately we don't hear anything from Yashodhara herself concerning these difficult circumstances, and no accused suitor is named or brought forward as a villain. However, two more *Jataka* tales provide a quick backstory on the karma that gave rise to her unusual pregnancy in the first place. It turns out that in a previous life Yashodhara was a young milkmaid who, along with her mother, tended to her father's large herd of cows. One day, she and her mother were returning home with pails of milk. The mother made her daughter carry the heavier pail and only urged her to go faster when the girl complained. At last, the girl became angry and put down the pail, telling her mother to carry it while she stepped aside to relieve herself. Dawdling deliberately, the girl waited until her mother carried the heavy load for six *krosas* (a distance of about twenty kilometers). This negativity toward her mother was paid forward, and Yashodhara must now suffer a six-year pregnancy.[28]

But why must Rahula bear the travails of gestation for so long? This unfortunate occurrence also arose from past actions. In this story, there were two brothers, Surya (the Buddha) and Chandra (Rahula), whose father, the king, had just died without naming a successor. Rather than fight for the crown, neither prince wanted it. Finally, to settle the matter, Surya as the eldest son briefly assumed the royal title, then ordered his younger brother to succeed him. Now Surya was free to go forth and happily pursue the spiritual life of a mendicant. After many years as a hermit practicing austerities, he attracted a large following and became a religious teacher. At this time, he made a vow that he would rely entirely on charitable offerings for his support, not taking food, water, or even a tooth cleaner,* unless it had been given to him freely. This worked out well until one day Surya forgot his vow and, being very thirsty, took a drink of water from a disciple's pitcher. When the owner arrived and called for the thief to confess, Surya was inconsolable with remorse. Though the disciple instantly forgave him, the hermit could not endure the weight of his transgression. He finally resolved to appear before the king—his brother—to request due punishment. Now Chandra was not the slightest bit interested in prosecuting his brother for such a trivial offense. Surya, however, would not be dissuaded. In frustration, Chandra suggested that his brother sit in the palace garden and consider himself a prisoner. This Surya gladly did, and because his brother forgot about him, the hermit sat there patiently for six days. The transgression of forgetfulness was one for which Chandra had to pay later, leading to his six-year sojourn in utero as Rahula. There was also unfinished business with his former brother, as he must now wait six more years to meet his present father, the Buddha.[29]

An abundance of *Jataka* literature addresses the complicated relationship between the Buddha, Yashodhara, and Rahula, an area of study that invites deeper inquiry. Unlike the more stock female figures—such as Maya, who is almost invariably cast as virtuous and pure in her previous lives—

---

* A willow twig.

Yashodhara's persona takes on a range of emotions and characterizations in the *Jatakas*. While many of these past-life tales are love stories, Yashodhara may take the lead as a seductress or clever heroine who saves the Buddha's life rather than playing a powerless damsel. Other stories illustrate the Buddha's ambivalence toward her; for example, in a villainous account in the *Mahavastu* called the *Syama Jataka,* she is cast as cunning courtesan murderess that the Buddha then attempts to murder.[30] Tales of her alleged infidelity are also found couched within these tales. In one story fragment, the Buddha as a former king spares his queen's life just as she is about to be executed for infidelity. He says to her,

> The executioner could make his steel pierce [your] body, which is as soft as a vessel of unbaked clay. But I spare your life and restore you to your former position.[31]

Much more detailed is the following *Jataka* story, which explains the karmic precedent for Suddhodana presuming Yashodhara's infidelity and unjustly ordering her execution. A hermit (the Buddha) dwelling deep within the forest of the Himalayas caused a doe to give birth to a human daughter (Yashodhara). He loved the child dearly, and while he raised her as a human, she suckled at the teats of her doe mother and roamed the forest with fawns as her playmates. Because of her exceeding virtue in a previous life, lotus blossoms magically sprang up in her footsteps wherever she went; hence her name was Padumavati.* Never meeting another human being besides the hermit, the girl grew up tending the sacred fire, fetching water, and gathering wild fruits and roots for her father's hermitage, always accompanied by deer and birds. One day, the local king (Suddhodana) was out hunting and came across Padumavati in a glade. Instantly smitten by her beauty and magical power, he resolved to marry her. The hermit acceded to the king's request for his daughter's hand, but with the divine eye of a seer expressed concern for her fate:

> Your majesty, let her be your wife. Let her be considered worthy of your majesty, and do not put her away on the mere accusation of another and without trial.[32]

---

* Meaning "possessing lotuses."

With great fanfare, Padumavati became queen and soon after was pregnant. So far, so good, except now the king's other wives became jealous. He had not paid them any attention since meeting this miserable forest waif dressed in animal skins. All day long he cavorted with her instead of them. If he favored her now, how much worse would it be once she gave birth to his child in a palace that had so far been childless? The wicked ladies decided on a scheme that exploited Padumavati's innocence. Convincing her that women must be blindfolded during childbirth, they delivered her of two beautiful sons, quickly locked them in a chest marked with the royal seal, and tossed it in the river. The jealous wives then smeared Padumavati's face with the bloody afterbirth and reported to the king that she had devoured her own newborn sons. "She must be an ogress!" they reported. Dismayed by this gory turn of events, the king ordered Padumavati put to death, just as Suddhodana would later unjustly order Yashodhara's execution. Luckily for Padumavati, the king's counselors knew the wicked ways of the harem women and hid her, while a goddess appeared before the king and exposed the evil plot. She said,

> Your majesty, it was on a false report, without true knowledge and understanding, that you sent the innocent Padumavati away to be killed without examination or trial, and you forgot the words of the blessed seer.[33]

After a few more twists, which include Padumavati's brief return to the forest as a wandering nun, her honor and rightful status as queen were fully restored. As we shall see, Yashodhara did not herself share this happy outcome.

While uncertainty surrounding Rahula's paternity does not arise in the early Pali legends, it shows up later in the Southeast Asian Buddhist folk tradition. In a Thai text entitled *Yashodhara's Lament*—from the eighteenth or nineteenth century, but likely based on earlier accounts—we witness Yashodhara's despair over accusations of infidelity. In this story, she sobs uncontrollably when asked to appear before the Buddha in Kapilavastu after his six-year absence:

> Oh my beloved Rahula, You were a misfortune for your father from the very beginning. . . . Everyone accuses you of being illegitimate;

and people look down on me as a widow. My suffering brings only tears. How can I continue to live? I am ashamed before everyone. It is better for me to take poison and die or to put a rope around my neck and hang myself from the palace.[34]

The Rape of Yashodhara

Unfortunately, there may be more to the story of Yashodhara's troubles than we have addressed so far. Even more fragmentary than evidence of her deferred pregnancy are intimations in some Sanskrit sources that she was raped—or at least there was an attempted rape—while her husband was absent. Either way, the storytellers are unanimous in casting her as a powerful heroine in these scenarios rather than a hapless victim. The ubiquitous theme of Suddhodana as the family protector or avenger is absent here, as Yashodhara appears in these scenes without support or friendship. Her pregnancy and rape are not linked in the stories and are treated as separate incidents here.

We've already seen that at the time of the enlightenment, the evil demon Mara taunted the Bodhisattva with an apparition of Yashodhara and two more wives being raped by the similarly evil Devadatta, who was attempting to overthrow Suddhodana and seize the royal house of Shakya.* In two more related stories, Devadatta is again the lecherous villain, although contradictory details make it impossible to sort out just where they are meant to fit in the overall timeline. In the first, Devadatta is cast as an unwilling member of the new monastic order, having been ordained during the Buddha's first visit home in the sixth year of his ministry. After the Buddha has gone to teach in Shravasti, Devadatta secretly absconds to Kapilavastu with the intention of abducting Yashodhara.† He sneaks into the harem with the intention of raping her, but she squeezes his hand so hard that blood spurts out, whereupon she throws him from the terrace into a nearby pond. Summoned by the noise, the Shakyas are appalled that Devadatta would breach their prince's harem, especially with such evil intentions, and want him put to

* In some Pali sources, Devadatta is said to be Yashodhara's brother, but that is not the case in any of the Sanskrit sources.
† In this instance, she is identified as Gopa.

death. In the end, they let him go because they remember that the Buddha once predicted that Devadatta would inevitably be going to hell anyway.[35]

In the second account, Devadatta aspires to become the king of Kapilavastu. Upon learning that the Shakyas are considering offering the throne to Yashodhara, he goes to her palace to seduce her. Taking her hand, he proposes that she be his wife and they rule the kingdom together. Horrified, she hurls him to the ground and responds,

> Thou shameless fool! . . . I cannot bear thy touch. My husband must be the one who will become an universal monarch or a bodhisattva.[36]

This time, the Shakyas tell him to ask forgiveness of the Buddha and, if he receives it, they will permit him to be king. Nothing more is said on the matter. It should be noted that these stories of Yashodhara and the harem display typical examples of narrative inconsistencies and skewed chronology.

A related story is noteworthy for Yashodhara's palpable hatred of Devadatta. It is found in the *Mahavastu* under the guise of a thinly veiled *Jataka* tale. In a past life, she was a queen who was sought after by the wicked king (Devadatta) of a nearby region. He threatened to take her by force if her husband (the Buddha) would not give her up. Shedding a flood of tears, she made clear her intention to kill the evil king if he carried out his threat. Rather than asking her husband for help, she graphically described her own murderous plan:

> My lord, I am adept whether the need be for stabbing or thrusting with the sword, and so expert that not even you surpass me in the use of arms.
>
> O king, you shall see [his] proud head cut off by me and rolling all gory at your feet.
>
> Woman though I am, I'll shoot an arrow that will pierce [his] body, nay go through it and pierce the ground where it lies food for dogs.
>
> Whether he be on horseback, in chariot, or riding an elephant, or at the head of a brave army, I will make an end of [him].[37]

After tricking the evil king into entering her private apartment, she overpowered him. Standing across his body with one foot on his heart and the other on his ankles,* she prepared to kill him, but first taunted him with the words,

> You have not heard it said, O wretched man, that the lotus which a wild elephant in rut has once uprooted, trampling it in mud and water, still preserves its virgin freshness. Other elephants do not wanton there.
>
> You have set your heart on winning this graceful woman of faultless body, who, when she lies at night like a necklace of pearls in the arms of an honoured king, trembles with joy. You are like a man who standing on earth, would fain win the moon.[38]

Only due to the intervention of her husband does she spare the would-be rapist. In all these stories, we find Yashodhara enraged by Devadatta's advances and remarkably empowered to defend herself.

Reunion of Suddhodana and His Son

The time has come for the Buddha to return home. His family and the Shakya people have heard all about their beloved Siddhartha's successful spiritual quest, his enlightenment, and his ever-expanding religious ministry, but to them, he is still their son, husband, and prince. Despite the benefits to humankind already spawned by his many accomplishments, Siddhartha's departure years earlier has left a painful void in their hearts, and they long for his return.

Suddhodana launches this process by sending messengers to his son in Rajagriha, where the Buddha and his followers are sojourning at a secluded monastery donated by King Bimbisara. Employing a timeless stratagem known as the parent guilt-trip, Suddhodana's missive points out to his son that since he is now the Buddha, showing compassion to gods and humans, perhaps it is time to show compassion to his family as well. But the message is never delivered. No sooner do the king's scouts meet the Buddha than, one after another, they become captivated by his teachings and take ordination

---

* In the familiar stance of the prototantric Kali and later Buddhist tantric goddesses.

as his disciples. Frustrated, Suddhodana entrusts his favorite messengers—none other than Siddhartha's beloved childhood companions, Chandaka and Kalodayin—with the mission. When they finally come upon the Buddha, Kalodayin's words beautifully convey the loving anticipation with which Suddhodana and Mahaprajapati await their son's return:

> Your father looks out for your coming as the lily looks out for the rising of the sun; and the queen as the night-blowing lily looks out for the rays of the moon.[39]

Chandaka and Kalodayin take ordination as well, but Kalodayin continues to broker the king's purpose by shuttling information back and forth (now airborne) between the palace and the Buddha, who has begun the sixty-day journey on foot to Kapilavastu with his entourage. Suddhodana uses this opportunity to nurture his son by sending the aerial messenger back every day with an alms bowl filled with delicious palace cuisine. He further makes preparations by building a monastic compound known as the Nigrodha grove* in the woodland environs of Kapilavastu, where he and the citizenry will receive his son and his disciples when they eventually arrive.

Yet the stories are mixed on just what sort of reception the Buddha receives upon returning home. As much as his people love him, they are still ambivalent about the choices he has made and, understandably, feel some uncertainty as to how they should now regard him. The Pali sources describe a joyous procession greeting the Buddha when he arrives in Kapilavastu, as the entire town turns out led by the Shakya children, an equal number of girls and boys of all ages bearing garlands of fragrant flowers. However, as the Buddha takes his seat in the Nigrodha grove, a conundrum arises that is similar to the one we saw earlier when the infant Bodhisattva was presented to the goddess Abhayadevi in her temple. Not only is it improper not to prostrate to a buddha, but one runs the risk of having one's head split in seven pieces by failing to do so. Now the elder Shakya princes were very proud and had no intention of prostrating to the Buddha, who in their minds was still their impudent upstart nephew. What's more, their expectation was that Siddhartha would pay homage to his father, the king, not the other way around. Out of compassion and to remedy matters quickly, the Buddha

---

*Named after a type of fig tree.

rises into the air and walks above them so that his relatives appear below his feet—in a sense, doing their prostrations for them. Then, lest there be any lingering doubts about his attainment, he performs a few more miracles for their benefit. So in awe is Suddhodana that he now gladly prostrates to his son, recalling how he did so twice before—once at his birth and again under the rose-apple tree. All the Shakyas follow suit.

Significant variants of this episode are found in the Sanskrit sources, which give a darker, more sorrowful side to the stories. Perhaps inevitably, the Buddha's return to Kapilavastu meets with emotional rough spots. Suddhodana, for one, always loves his son but continues to struggle with the loss of his heir and is baffled by the austere life his son has chosen over royal privilege. Twelve years may have passed, but like so many parents, this father clings to the notion of what he wanted for his son without understanding the choices his son has made for himself.

A lengthy story in the *Mahavastu* begins with the king eagerly setting off in a horse-drawn chariot to welcome the prince followed by a grand procession of Shakyas, including all the women of his court, headed by Yashodhara. However, just as the entourage arrives at the city gates, a company of bedraggled, barefoot monks comes in begging for alms. Suddhodana has never seen such a decrepit sight. Who are these bald, skinny beggars? Upon hearing that they are none other than his son's disciples, the king is overcome with aversion. Ordering the mendicants expelled from the city, Suddhodana returns to the palace.[40] Poetic lines go on to describe his depression:

> The lord of the Sakyas is sorely stricken in mind and disturbed of thought. He stands dejected like an elephant which has fallen over a mountain cliff.
>
> Like a strong man in the grip of a demon that saps his strength, he, supreme lord of the earth though he is, no longer knows either his own self nor his son.[41]

News of his father's intransigence reaches the Buddha and his assembly in the Nigrodha grove. After some debate, the worthy Kalodayin is once again chosen for the role of go-between. While he is game for the challenge of approaching the king, Kalodayin admits to some misgivings about his chances for success in persuading the king to change his mind, saying,

> Just as . . . it is difficult to approach a sixty-year-old elephant, so is it
> difficult to approach kings who are anointed nobles enjoying security
> in their empire.[42]

However, Kalodayin prevails again. The king is overjoyed to see him
and listens with an open heart to the beloved messenger's praises for
the Buddha's accomplishments and the many reasons why Suddhodana
should be proud and accepting of his son's new way of life. Affectionately
saying to Kalodayin, "since you are a son to him, so you are a son to
me,"[43] the king has a public proclamation made at the crossroads and
marketplaces of Kapilavastu lauding the prince's supreme awakening
and ordering all Shakyas of every age, class, and guild to proceed to the
Nigrodha grove to meet the Buddha. It is now that the miracle of the
Buddha's walking through the air takes place, followed by a lengthy,
endearing conversation between father and son in which Suddhodana
candidly expresses worry for his son's new lifestyle only to be reassured
on each point that the Buddha feels entirely fulfilled and satisfied with
the choices he has made.

A related story in the *Abhinishkramanasutra* describes Suddhodana's
unhappy shock upon seeing his son's austere appearance after twelve years.
As the king's procession arrives at the Nigrodha grove,

> Then the Raja beholding his son's appearance, that he wore no royal
> headdress, but was close shaved, and clad in a poor . . . robe, was, for a
> moment transfixed to the earth; but recovering himself after a while,
> he found relief in tears and sad lamentations.[44]

Next, an argument breaks out between father and son. The final straw comes
when the Buddha introduces his disciples one by one to his father, and Suddhodana realizes with dismay that they are all from the brahman caste. From
the viewpoint of his proud *kshatriya* lineage, it is entirely unacceptable that
his royal son would associate with such ignoble company. With sorrow and
disdain, the king turns away and returns to the palace.[45]

The Pali sources add another story that underscores the family's royal
pride. Upon awaking the first morning in the Nigrodha grove, the Buddha
and his disciples set out to seek alms in typical fashion in the town. Soon
rumors are flying, and the citizens of Kapilavastu are gawking out their

windows to see their royal heir behaving like an indigent beggar. In the Burmese account, they say,

> How is this? . . . We see Prince [Rahula] and his mother [Yashodhara] going out attired in the richest dresses, sitting in the most elegant conveyance, and now Prince [Siddhartha] is appearing in the streets with his hair and beard shaved, and his body covered with a yellow dress befitting a mendicant. Such a thing is unbecoming indeed.[46]

Alerted to his son's embarrassing conduct, Suddhodana swiftly shows up and is outraged:

> Illustrious Buddha, why do you expose us to such shame? Is it necessary to go from door to door to beg your food? Could not a better and more decent mode be resorted to for supplying your wants? . . . There is not a single person in our illustrious race that has ever acted in such an indecorous manner.[47]

A pivotal conversation ensues wherein the Buddha disavows his Shakya ancestry, proclaiming instead his loyalty to the traditions and lineage of enlightened buddhas.

Mahaprajapati's Tears

Stories of the Buddha's mother, Mahaprajapati, are few and precious in his biographical legends, but she appears again in this story in Sanskrit narratives when he returns to Kapilavastu. When last we saw her, she was caught in the struggles of mothering an obdurate young son as he rocked kingdom and family with his resolve to leave home for the spiritual life. Now we learn that Mahaprajapati's grief was so profound and her tears so endless after Siddhartha's departure that she went blind from weeping. Twelve years have passed, and she is joyfully riding out with Suddhodana in the grand procession to greet her son. They arrive in the Nigrodha grove just as the Buddha is performing his miracles. As he performs one miracle after another, the gleeful crowd of thousands loudly claps and cheers, "Bravo! Bravo!" Due to her blindness, Mahaprajapati is unable to see the cause of the celebration and asks her daughter-in-law, Yashodhara, to explain what is going on. In a rare account that portrays the two women together, Yashodhara tenderly explains to Mahaprajapati that the Buddha is demonstrating many miracles, including walking on air and causing jets of water to stream from his body. She says, "Come, I shall contrive that you see them!" Cupping her hands together, Yashodhara captures water flowing from the Buddha's body. With this blessed substance, she gently rinses Mahaprajapati's eyes, and lo, the queen's sight is restored, becoming as clear and faultless as before.[48]

A beautiful *Jataka* tale adds depth to this story, citing a past-life example of the loving bond between Mahaprajapati and her son. It takes place on the slopes of the Himalayas in a thick forest filled with an abundance of flowering, fruit-bearing trees; wild beasts; lotus ponds; and secluded retreats harboring spiritual adepts. Here also dwells a large herd of elephants. Among them is a mighty young male (the Buddha), his body white like a lotus, with six tusks and a scarlet head.* This young elephant is utterly devoted to caring for his elephant mother (Mahaprajapati), who is blind, aged, and weak:

> When he grew up he looked after his mother with reverence and affection. He gave her food and drink before eating and drinking himself. He duly groomed and cleaned his mother's tall body with a creeper that grew in the forest. And so this young elephant carefully looked after his mother at all times with kindness, affection and reverence.[49]

One day, while his mother was resting, the young elephant went off briefly in the company of other elephants. A party of hunters saw him and suggested to the king that this jewel among beasts would be an exceptional royal mount. The king himself captured the young bull elephant and took him back to the royal stables, where he showered him with affection and delicious food. But the young elephant was despondent and refused to eat. He wept, languished, and wasted away from worry about his mother. The

---

* This description is identical to the white elephant that appears in Maya's conception dream.

king, a kind man, did not understand and beseeched the young elephant to explain the cause of his sadness. With the heart of the Buddha, the young elephant replied,

> My mother is past her prime, old, advanced in years, and blind. Without my company, O King, she will die. That is why I grieve.
>
> To her who cannot see I used to give the lily's stalk and root, and then I would feed myself. Today she has no food, and that is why I grieve.
>
> And when her body was scorched by the summer's heat I would bring cool water from the shady forest and bathe her. But today there is none to ward her. And for this I grieve.
>
> Sightless she now roams the wood, her body covered with dust, crying, "Where is my son?" This is the greater sorrow I am this day afflicted with.[50]

The king was very touched by this son's devotion to his mother and freed the young elephant to reunite with her. However, the young elephant searched high and low and could not find her. Finally, standing on top of a large hill, he trumpeted loudly so she could hear his voice. Caught in brambles, mired in filth, and weeping from grief, his blind mother joyfully trumpeted in response. Her son went to her immediately and, filling his trunk with cool water, gladly bathed her in the soothing stream. Then he cut down jungle vines to groom and feed her. Now nourished and clean, she miraculously regained her sight. Overjoyed, she lovingly declared, "So, my son, may the king . . . and his people rejoice as I rejoice today at the sight of my son." As the Buddha tells this story to his disciples, he explains that he was then the young elephant and Mahaprajapati, then as now, was his beloved mother. He identifies the compassionate king as Nanda, Mahaprajapati's other son, the Buddha's half-brother.[51]

One other short episode of note concerning Mahaprajapati during this time appears in the *Mahavastu*. After the Buddha is welcomed in the Nigrodha grove, members of his family invite him to meals in the palace. First he dines in Suddhodana's palace, after which Mahaprajapati invites him to dine separately as her guest in the women's quarters. Bowing at his feet, she says, "Let the Exalted One consent to eat tomorrow at my house."[52] With his assent, she joyously proceeds to make elaborate preparations,

> [She] prepared a plentiful supply of solid and soft food. She had her house sprinkled and swept, hung with festoons of fine cloth, strewn with heaps of flowers and made fragrant with incense. She assigned a very costly seat for the Exalted One and seats according to their rank for the company of his monks.[53]

The Buddha arrives with his retinue. No longer dressed as a prince, of course, he wears a mendicant's robe and carries an alms bowl. Despite her many servants and rank as queen, Mahaprajapati reverentially serves her son herself. At the conclusion of the meal, the Buddha proceeds to give his mother and the women of the harem a dharma teaching, referred to as a "graduated discourse on dharma." What does this mean?

> Now this is what the graduated discourse of exalted Buddhas is, namely a discourse on charity, a discourse on morality, a discourse on heaven, a discourse on merit and a discourse on the fruition of merit.[54]

Mahaprajapati readily understands her son's meaning on these topics, so the Buddha goes on to teach her the Four Noble Truths.* By the conclusion of the evening, she has attained "clear dharma-insight, pure and unsullied" into the nature of reality. Of significance here is not just that we learn of Mahaprajapati's first dharma teaching, but we're told what that teaching consisted of and how adeptly she grasped it. Certainly this story deserves a place in her own biography since she goes on to become first and foremost of the early Buddhist nuns. The episode is also noteworthy because, in addition to Mahaprajapati, the Buddha's teaching audience is entirely an assembly of laywomen, perhaps those who later followed their queen in taking ordination.

---

* Suffering, the cause of suffering, the cessation of suffering, and the path of freedom from suffering.

Rahula Meets His Father

Tension is mounting in the palace. After twelve years, Yashodhara and her husband will soon meet again.* Their lives could not be more different now, as he has attained his goal of awakening and is content with the religious path, while she continues to struggle as an abandoned wife living under the protection of her father-in-law, raising her six-year-old son alone. She was angry, shattered, when Siddhartha left, and added to that she now faces the humiliation of scrutiny surrounding her pregnancy and her son's paternity. How will the Buddha receive her and Rahula? Not only Yashodhara, but her in-laws and the Shakya people† are anxious to see how this drama will play out.

The Pali sources describe the couple's first encounter taking place after the Buddha and his disciples take a meal with Suddhodana in the palace. The ladies of the court arrive afterward to pay their respects—all of them that is, except Yashodhara. Refusing to attend, she passes along the message, "If I have virtue in my eyes, my lord will come to me."[55] While this could have been viewed as an affront, the Buddha kindly goes to her apartments accompanied by his two chief disciples. On the way, he prepares them for her emotional distress and asks them not to intervene in any way. She is understandably upset, he says, and explains that their imminent reunion is a necessary karmic step before she and the other harem wives will take ordination:

> From not having seen me for so long a time, she is exceedingly sorrowful; unless this sorrow be allowed its course, her breast will cleave; she will take hold of my feet, but as the result will be that she and the other queens will embrace the priesthood, you must not prevent her.[56]

Indeed, Yashodhara is overcome with emotion upon seeing her husband,

---

*Based on these stories, the Sanskrit timeline of a twelve-year absence is adopted in this section.
† Forty thousand, according to the Singhalese account.

From the abundance of her affection, she was like an overflowing vessel, unable to contain herself; and forgetting that she was a mere woman, and that [Buddha] was the lord of the world, she held him by the feet and wept.[57]

Now, not even a god may touch a buddha's body, but under the circumstances, her infraction of grasping his feet was overlooked. In these accounts, Suddhodana apologizes to the Buddha for Yashodhara's emotional behavior and launches into a lengthy testimonial lauding her faithful devotion to him, while describing her austerities and self-denial in his absence. Calling Yashodhara his "daughter," the king recounts that she has refused suitors and an offer to return to her own father's household to await her husband's return. The Buddha takes this news in stride and proceeds to tell a *Jataka* tale about Yashodhara's devotion to him in a previous life.[58] This story is characteristic of the Pali tradition where Yashodhara is uniformly portrayed as a faithful wife with no suggestion of an ill-timed pregnancy or sexual adversity during her husband's absence. However, the Sanskrit sources provide an entirely different spin.

In the *Abhinishkramanasutra,* Yashodhara hears that her husband is in town and invites him to a meal as her guest in the palace. Pained from her life as a scorned woman, she wishes to confront the accusations against her and see the matter of her son's paternity settled once and for all. The passage reads,

> Now at this time Rahula began to be about six years of age, having been born six years after his father had left his home. His mother, therefore, seeing Buddha had returned to Kapilavastu, and in recollection of all the charges which had been made against her, resolved to set the matter clear, and to vindicate both her own and her son's character.[59]

The Buddha arrives with his retinue and takes his seat, at which time Yashodhara instructs Rahula to greet their guest, identifying him as the boy's father. With Rahula now standing before the Buddha, Suddhodana asks his son plainly, "Is it true or not that this is your son?" To the relief of everyone present, the Buddha replies, "Yashodhara is perfectly pure and innocent. This is my son." As the company celebrates the good news, the Buddha launches into the *Jataka* stories, recounted earlier, explaining the karmic history of Yashodhara's six-year pregnancy and the reason it was Rahula's fate to spend so much time in his mother's womb.

The *Abhinishkramanasutra* offers an additional account that focuses sweetly on Rahula as a little boy. Here, when Suddhodana prepares a feast for the Buddha and his disciples, he gives strict orders that no one in the palace may tell Rahula that the Buddha is his father. Surrounded by other noble children, the little prince is sent to the Nigrodha grove to advise the saint that the meal is ready. Rahula watches in awe as the Buddha and his retinue of twelve hundred monks comport themselves with great dignity in a stately procession toward the palace. He marvels at their decorum in contrast to the boisterous disorder of his playmates. Returning to the palace, the boy goes in search of his mother, who has watched the approaching procession from a balcony. Upon seeing her husband with his shaven head and the hempen robes of a mendicant, Yashodhara dissolves into tears: "Her heart was grieved, and her tears flowed fast." Naturally worried about his mother, Rahula asks why she weeps, to which she responds, "My child, yonder [mendicant] whose skin is bright as gold, is your father." Rahula is overjoyed by this news. In a delightful scene, he dashes into the assembly hall, plops down by the Buddha, and impishly pulls his father's robe over his head. The monks are horrified by his perceived impudence and try to drive him off, but the Buddha gently intercedes, saying, "Let him stay, and let him hide himself in my robes."[60]

A related story appears in the *Mahavastu*, but here Suddhodana proclaims that anyone telling Rahula that the Buddha is his father will be put to death. At the dinner gathering in the palace, the little prince is said to be spellbound by the Buddha's presence:

> Then the shadow of the Exalted One happened to fall on Rahula. And all the hair on Rahula's body bristled, all his limbs perspired, and his whole frame thrilled.[61]

After staring intently at the saint, the boy turns to Yashodhara and begins a lengthy interrogation about the identity of his father. However, Yashodhara prevaricates, fearing reprisal from her father-in-law if she tells the truth.

In the following dialogue between Rahula and Yashodhara we hear the universal longing of a fatherless child:

> [Rahula:] Where is my father gone, mother?
> [Yashodhara:] My son, he has gone to the south country.
> [R:] What has he gone to the south country for?
> [Y:] He has gone there to trade.
> [R:] But why does not my father send me a nice present?
> [Y:] The way is stopped by the nobles. When it is possible for him to come, he will come himself.[62]

Rahula goes on to insist that the magnificent sage has "taken possession of [his] . . . heart" and must be his father. Yashodhara continues to deny it but is troubled that she is keeping the truth from her son. Finally, she decides that she would rather face Suddhodana's death sentence than continue to lie. Invoking vivid, violent imagery, she says,

> Come what may, I will tell him. I would rather that the Sakyans stab and hack me limb by limb with a sharp knife than that I should not tell my own son, the noble Rahula. I would rather that the Sakyans cut my body into strips with a sharp knife than that I should not tell my own son, the noble Rahula. . . . I would rather that the Sakyans cut up my body into a hundred pieces than that I should not tell my own son, Rahula.[63]

At last Yashodhara tells Rahula that the Buddha is his father and continues to praise the sage's greatness at length, while recounting the story of his Great Departure from Kapilavastu. We hear her abiding reverence for him in the following verses:

> He, my son, whom you see yonder in golden beauty, rising up amid his noble company like a golden elephant, is your father.
> He, my son, whom you see yonder in golden beauty like a fanged and powerful lion surveying all around him, is your father.
> He, my son, whom you see yonder in golden beauty attended by his noble company, like a bull among the herd, is your father. . . .

> He, my son, whom you see yonder in golden beauty, like the flowering *shala* tree, his body resplendent with the thirty-two marks of excellence, is your father.[64]

When little Rahula hears confirmation that the wondrous sage is his father, he clings to the Buddha's robe and will not leave him, saying,

> Mother, if he is my father, I will go forth from home to the homeless state and follow the way of my father.[65]

So it came to pass that Rahula was allowed to ordain, even at the young age of six. The account of his ordination as a novice monk will be continued later.

In the Kangyur, Rahula meets his father for the first time under more magical circumstances. Here Yashodhara is still very much in love with her husband. Determined to win him back, she gives five hundred coins to a sorcerer who devises an aphrodisiac that should do the trick. She gives the magic confection to Rahula and tells him to take it to his father. Aware that her honor is under scrutiny, the Buddha kindly devises a plan to vindicate her. Since a true son knows his own father, the sage creates an apparition of five hundred illusory replicas of himself. As Rahula arrives, the boy readily recognizes his father among them and carries out his mother's instructions. However, the Buddha hands the aphrodisiac right back, and Rahula ends up eating it himself. Thus charmed, the little boy becomes smitten with his father and cannot leave his side. Yashodhara is apparently exonerated but loses her son since this attachment to his father leads to his ordination even though he is only six. But the story is not over. In a sad turn of events, Yashodhara employs further methods of seduction and, when all fails, attempts to commit suicide by jumping off the palace roof. The Buddha intervenes and saves her, but clearly she is very unhappy. The theme of Yashodhara as a seductress is continued in this sequence as the Buddha launches into a related *Jataka* story.[66]

As intriguing as these stories are, the ambiguity surrounding Rahula's paternity isn't exactly cleared up now that he and the Buddha have met. The Pali sources, which don't address the issue, transfer the literal notion of paternity onto one of inheritance. After all, Prince Siddhartha abdicated his right to succession, and a legal heir to King Suddhodana's throne still has not been designated. Rahula would be the obvious choice, but the royal family is waiting for validation from the Buddha before making this official. Will the Buddha accept Rahula as his heir? This can be viewed as an indirect method of legitimizing him as his biological son. Once again, the onus is on Yashodhara to clear things up. From an upper-story window in the palace, she points out the Buddha to her son, saying,

> Look, dear, at that monk, attended by twenty thousand monks, and beautiful in appearance as [a god]! That is your father. He had certain great treasures, which we have not seen since he abandoned his home. Go now, and ask for your inheritance, saying, "Father, I am the prince. When I am crowned, I shall become a king over all the earth. I have need of treasure. Give me the treasure; for a son is heir to his father's property."[67]

Dressed in his finest princely attire, little Rahula approaches the Buddha and, affectionately calling him "father,"* demands his inheritance. The Buddha pays no attention even as Rahula doggedly follows him around repeating his request. Finally, without ever acknowledging the boy, the Buddha reflects on the transient nature of the wealth Rahula is seeking. Better to give him the treasure of spiritual inheritance, he decides, and directs his chief disciple, Shariputra, to ordain the little boy immediately. In this way, the Buddha skillfully sidesteps issues of paternity and inheritance altogether. He also saves his father embarrassment by removing a possibly illegitimate contender from the line of royal succession (only he and Yashodhara know for sure). While the child is very pleased at becoming a monk, his mother and the rest of his family are despondent at the news.[68]

Rahula's ordination is treated at length in the stories and is noteworthy for the emotions it evokes, which are reminiscent of those associated with Siddhartha's Great Departure. Here we continue the earlier story where Rahula grasps the Buddha's robe and cries out that he will follow the way of his father. On hearing this news, the women of Suddhodana's harem burst into wails of grief. The king hears the cries and is terrified. The uproar

---

* In the *Nidanakatha,* he uses the term "monk."

sounds just like the lamentations that rang out when Siddhartha left home twelve years earlier. "What is this dreadful noise?" he asks. The people explain that Rahula has renounced his princely life and intends to go forth as the Buddha's disciple. This is the king's worst nightmare. As he weeps, so do all the Shakyas. Not only has the kingdom lost Siddhartha and now Rahula, but Suddhodana's son Nanda had taken ordination several days earlier. The Pali sources relate that now Suddhodana makes his way to the Nigrodha grove and, kneeling down before the Buddha, speaks of his heart-wrenching grief at losing not just his two sons, but now also his grandson to the monastic life. Not wishing other parents to suffer, he beseeches the Buddha to adopt a rule that would require the permission of both mother and father before the ordination of a boy. His description of the depths of parental love is timeless:

> Love for our children, Lord, cuts into the outer skin; having cut into the outer skin, it cuts into the inner skin; having cut into the inner skin, it cuts into the flesh; having cut into the flesh, it cuts into the sinews; having cut into the sinews, it cuts into the bones; having cut into the bones, it reaches the marrow and stays there. Lord, it would be good if the venerable ones did not give the going forth without the parents' consent.[69]

The Buddha agrees, and this rule was adopted as part of the monastic code still in use today.

The *Mahavastu* tells the story of Rahula's ordination with an entirely different twist. In this account, Suddhodana sounds exasperated, even bitter, as he approaches the Buddha and asks him to refrain from ordaining Rahula lest the Shakya royal line become extinct. Clearly he considers Rahula the rightful heir to the throne:

> It is enough that the Exalted One should have renounced his great universal sovereignty and left his family and gone forth from home. Well would it be, therefore, if the Exalted One should order Prince Rahula not to go forth so that the royal family be not made extinct.[70]

The Buddha refuses, owing to Rahula's karmic readiness to be ordained. He says it is impossible that the boy should live the life of a householder, even a princely one. In a curious passage that once again points to questions surrounding Rahula's birth, Suddhodana then asks for seven days to prepare Rahula for ordination. Due to the Buddha's absence, the boy was never accorded the proper ceremonies suitable to his rank, such as the braiding of his hair and the gifting of special earrings. Perhaps most unusual for a royal heir, his horoscope had never been cast. The Buddha agrees to wait seven days and directs Rahula to return to the palace with his grandfather.[71]

Now Yashodhara becomes the central figure as she desperately tries to dissuade her son from becoming a monk. Holding the little boy on her lap, she admonishes him at length:

> Rahula, my son, do not go forth to the religious life. What you have in mind, my son, is hard to achieve. Here in the royal palace you have fine garments ... to wear. You have magnificent beds to lie on, and delicate food to eat. But Rahula, my son, when you have gone forth, you will have to lie on a spreading of straw on the ground. Your seat will be at the foot of a tree; you will have to go begging for alms among the low caste ... you will have to look at the snorting mouths of angry men, and eat cast-off morsels of food. You will have to collect the discarded rags of a slave-girl from the cemetery, and you will have to dwell in forest tracts. There you will hear dreadful noises, such as the cries of lions, tigers and jackals. But you, Rahula, my son, grew up in the royal palace delicately nurtured and used to comfort. You, Rahula, my son, were bathed while listening to the sweet strains of lute and fife and cymbal. How will you have any joy? Surely you will overcome this delusion. It were well for you, Rahula, my son, to divert and amuse yourself with ... sensual pleasures here in the inner apartment. Why should we have another one going forth?[72]

Displaying a precociousness far beyond his age, Rahula refutes her arguments, essentially saying, "If my father can do it, so can I!" As Yashodhara woefully accepts his decision, she proceeds to give him motherly advice on how to conduct himself as a renunciate. Of interest is her counsel regarding women:

> You must, my son, have good self-control. And why? Women will come, my son, who are venerable, gracious and beautiful to make

obeisance to the Exalted One, and these, my son, you must regard as you would your mother. Women will come, my son, who are young, gracious, beautiful and bedecked with jewels. But for these, my son, you must not have any desire, and on such occasions you must abide having an insight into what is ill and what is transient.[73]

This story concludes as Rahula is taken to the Nigrodha grove with great fanfare to receive his ordination. Dancers, drummers, acrobats, and musicians accompany the procession as it makes its way through the streets of Kapilavastu, a city festooned with flowers and colorful banners. With cries of loving farewell, the Shakyas have accepted Rahula's decision and wish him well. Yashodhara, too, lets him go, although tears pour from her eyes when she sees her six-year-old son with his head shaved and wearing the simple cotton robe of an ascetic. The spiritual path first claimed her husband, and now it has taken her son.

Women during the Buddha's Ministry

*T*he Buddha's sojourn in Kapilavastu proved to be a critical step in settling matters with his family. No longer was there confusion in anyone's mind that he might still return as husband to Yashodhara and his harem wives or as the heir to the kingdom. The Shakyas' beloved Prince Siddhartha, who had departed in turmoil twelve years earlier, was truly and forever gone. Lingering doubt about his son, Rahula, was also more or less dispelled now that the little boy had been removed from the line of succession and was ordained as a novice monk. That step left Suddhodana with his persistent problem, however, as many more Shakya princes also converted during this time and took themselves out of the line of succession for the throne. In fact, conversions to the Buddha's ministry became so widespread that the king had to restrict ordination to one son per family in order to keep his kingdom intact.

While the Buddha established his ministry mostly in the region of India to the south and west of his hometown, it appears from the records that he returned to Kapilavastu at least a few more times during the remaining forty years of his life. The Pali canon names two discourses he gave in nearby Devadaha, his mother Maya's birthplace and home to the Koliyan side of his family. He is also said to have returned to mediate a dispute over water rights between his clan members. A Nepali recension of the *Buddhacarita* describes the Buddha's return to his birthplace, Lumbini's grove, followed by a large assembly of monks and Shakya citizens. There, under the sacred *shala* tree where Maya had grasped the branch and given birth to him tenderly supported by Mahaprajapati, he gave a teaching to Abhayadevi, the goddess who had presided over that sacred event. He further gave the crowd a discourse honoring Maya at the nearby bathing tank where he and his mother had been washed following the birth.[1]

Suddhodana's Death

One detail of family business that remained on the Buddha's plate, however, concerned his obligations as the eldest son upon the death of his father.* As much as he had severed all personal emotional ties, he averted further pain to his family by fully executing his filial responsibilities when the time came. As with most of the chronology during the Buddha's ministry, it is impossible to say where this event fits in the overall timeline. The Burmese legend treats this portion of the Buddha's biography in poignant detail and it is told as follows.

Word reaches the Buddha that his father is desperately ill and wishes to see him one last time. Although far away, the saint can confirm via his divine eye (which instantly knows the condition of beings) that his father is racked with physical pain and extremely sad. Filled with compassion, the Buddha quickly summons Ananda and a select band of disciples. Flying through the air, they arrive at the palace and go directly to Suddhodana's bedside. In this touching account, the disciples gather around the dying king as the Buddha meditates. Then, placing his hands on his father's head, the Buddha says,

> By the virtue of the merits I have acquired during countless existences, by the power of the fruits gathered during forty-nine days round the tree Bodi let this head be forthwith relieved from all pain.[2]

And "in the twinkling of an eye," Suddhodana's head is free of pain. Next Suddhodana's son Nanda, the Buddha's half-brother, takes the king's right hand, saying,

> By the merits that I have obtained at the feet of the Buddha, let this right hand be freed from all pain.[3]

---

* His half-brother, Nanda, is not mentioned as a contender for this filial task.

Once again Suddhodana's pain vanishes. This healing ritual is repeated, as Ananda takes the king's left hand, Shariputra touches his back, and Maudgalyayana* grasps his feet, each in turn uttering a similar prayer.

Happily the king is soon delivered from all bodily pain, although he remains very weak. Now the Buddha informs his father that he has exactly seven days to live and prepares him for death by giving him teachings and practice instructions on the impermanence of all phenomena, including the human body. Suddhodana's realizations advance rapidly, and soon he is cheerfully consoling his weeping wife, Mahaprajapati, and the women of his harem with his own teachings on impermanence. When the moment of death arrives, Suddhodana is utterly peaceful and free of attachments.[†] The Buddha's bedside ministry is not done, however, as now he gives the same instruction on transience to comfort his grieving mother and the harem wives who, "with disheveled hair, were wailing aloud and striking their breasts." In performance of his filial duties, he washes the corpse and arranges the funeral procession that will carry the king's body through the streets of Kapilavastu accompanied by music and the cadence of drums. At the funeral pyre, he personally places the body and sets the fire that cremates his father's remains. As the Shakyas loudly lament their king's passing, the Buddha again teaches impermanence, this time to the grieving public assembly.

The significance of Suddhodana's death to the Shakyas cannot be overstated. It augured the end of life in their kingdom as they knew it. Their world would never be the same. The question of who succeeded the king is never clearly answered in the legends, and it would be only a short time—before the Buddha's own death—when the clan would be laid to waste by war with the Kosalas, and the city of Kapilavastu would be destroyed. Before this happens, however, the steady stream of Shakyas seeking ordination in the Buddha's ministry—which began with the Buddha's first visit to Kapilavastu—becomes a torrent after Suddhodana's death. A big difference is that those vast numbers now include women as well as men. According to the Sinhalese text,

---

* Shariputra and Maudgalyayana are the Buddha's two chief disciples.
† According to the Pali commentaries, Suddhodana achieved arhatship at death.

The number of females who were admitted to the profession after this period cannot be computed, but the chapters, both of the priests and the priestesses, increased so greatly, that in all Jambudvipa it was scarcely possible to find a suitable place for the exercise of . . . solitary meditation.[4]

Taking Ordination: Mahaprajapati, Yashodhara, and the Five Hundred Women

With so many men departing to join the Buddha's ministry, it naturally follows that family life in Kapilavastu was torn asunder. The men, as patriarchs, were the glue that held the social system together, and the Shakyas had no plan B for women and children bereft of their husbands, sons, brothers, and fathers. We've already seen the pain and disruption wrought by Siddhartha's departure years before (complicated, of course, by his being the heir apparent), but at least the king could and did step in as patriarch and protector of his son's family. Yashodhara had the choice to return to her own father's home but chose to remain behind with her son as Suddhodana's "daughter" in his palace. Not knowing otherwise, Rahula grew up thinking that Suddhodana was his father.[5] It is not immediately stated what happened to Siddhartha's other wives and harem consorts, although some evidence (arguably) points to Mrigi Gautami returning to her family home under the protection of Amritodana (possibly her father), who was Suddhodana's brother. Other Shakyas did not have the resources of the royal family, however, and turmoil ensued once the men began to leave Kapilavastu and widespread "widowhood" set in. Apparently a similar effect was being felt in Magadha, where inhabitants resented the growing population of monks. According to the Burmese text,

> Behold how the [Buddha] by his preachings, causes the depopulation of the country, and forces countless wives to the unwished-for state of widowhood. . . . What will become of our country?[6]

Some stories mention that among the Shakyas there was such a rush for young men to become monks that a backlash took place, where many later regretted the decision, which was often forced on them by their parents. Hearing news from unhappy wives at home, they struggled with second thoughts, reportedly allayed, however, by further teachings from the Buddha:

> Though they had become priests, it was not from their own choice, but from the wish of their parents; and they became additionally dissatisfied when their wives sent to inform them how much pain had been caused by their separation.[7]

One reason allegiance flowed to the Buddha so readily was that in the Shakyas' eyes, he was still their prince. The Shakya men would have pledged their loyalty to him anyway, had he remained home and become their king. As related in the Sinhalese text,

> If [Siddhartha] had become [king] the princes would have become his personal attendants; and they concluded that it was therefore right that they should still pay the same respect to him, as he was the supreme [Buddha].[8]

There is no question that immense social upheaval was brought about by the founding of the Buddhist ministry and, indeed, by the emergence of Buddhism itself. This provokes fair questions that are still asked today: Isn't it hypocritical that the Buddha taught the way out of suffering yet was himself, wittingly, the cause of suffering? Perhaps more to the point, what kind of role model is a man who abandons his wife and child? Easier asked than answered, these valid questions have a rightful place in a larger dialogue, especially among contemporary Buddhist women and men, students and teachers.

While both women and men had been converting to the Buddha's teachings as lay disciples (it would still be too early to call it "Buddhism") from the beginning, only men had so far taken the further step of ordination as celibate monks. Soon enough and perhaps inevitably, the notion of ordination, or "going forth into homelessness," became attractive to women as well. One can imagine a combination of reasons. No doubt women too were drawn to the Buddha's powerful soteriological teachings on emancipation from suffering. For lay disciples, both female and male, this new path could be fulfilling while posing little or no disruption to family life. However, as the men began to ordain and leave their families behind, women were faced with the unprecedented dilemma of fending for themselves. This would have posed huge emotional as well as practical challenges. With the loss of the traditional patriarchal social structure women were not only without identity, but their safety—if not survival—was at stake. Where lay participation in the Buddha's new faith may have been their first choice, the absence of husbands would have made ordaining as nuns increasingly attractive.* Practically speaking, life in Kapilavastu had nothing to offer "widows" on this scale. It would have been only natural for women to turn to the Buddha and his ministry as a surrogate patriarchal system. As much as this notion may chafe against modern feminist values, it would have been a woman's reality circa 400 B.C.E.

The stories further suggest that, mingled with their own spiritual aspirations, Shakya women wished to follow their loved ones—husbands and sons—however separated the families would now be by the conventions of monasticism. Bereft of family, the Buddha's own sister is said to have become a nun, "not at all because of faith, but solely because of love for her kinsfolk."[9] Further, the Shakyas retained a very insular sense of clan. Especially now that Suddhodana was dead, whether as prince or priest, it made sense that the women and men together would turn to Gautama Buddha as their leader. In short, entering into formal discipleship with him would have appealed to women, not only as an expression of their spiritual aspirations, but also as an attempted means of retaining protection, familial connections, and a coherent though altered sense of community with their clan. Each woman would have had her unique story about how elements such as these came into play in making her personal decision to request ordination. It is curious that virtually nothing is said in the legends about the fate of children during this time of upheaval.

It is widely known that the Buddha's mother, Mahaprajapati, became the first Buddhist nun. The story of her ordination is most frequently cited from the Pali canon. Particularly nowadays, this passage is closely scrutinized and widely debated because it has proved problematic to varying degrees in the evolution of women's monasticism in Buddhist history. At issue in this record is the Buddha's apparent reluctance toward ordaining women

---

* There was a precedent for women ordaining as nuns in the contemporaneous Jain religion.

in the first place, and according to this passage, when he finally agrees, his imposition of eight additional rules—all of them misogynist to varying degrees—that apply only to nuns. Adding to the confusion is his assertion in the same passage that women and men have the same potential to attain enlightenment.

More questions arise: Did the Buddha ever really say any or all of this? Was he indeed a misogynist? If not (and supposing these are his words), why would he add the eight extra rules? Alternatively—and this view is commonly held today—was this passage added or altered by misogynist monk editors later, vastly misrepresenting the Buddha's own sentiments? The field is divided on this topic, yet the implications are huge for Buddhist women, especially nuns, today. Here we will look at stories about Mahaprajapati and the early ordination of women that appear outside of the Pali canon from both Pali and Sanskrit sources. Perhaps they will shed some light on the larger discussion.

The notion of women joining the ministry comes up during the Buddha's first visit to Kapilavastu, but according to some accounts, it is Yashodhara and not her mother-in-law who requests ordination. In the Tibetan Kangyur, the Buddha's three wives—Yashodhara, Gopa,* and Mrigadja†—along with sixty thousand women of the harem all lavishly adorn themselves with the intention of seducing the saint when he arrives at the palace seeking alms. However, they are instantly chastened in his presence and convert to his new faith; all except Yashodhara, who, "blinded by love," stubbornly holds out hope that her husband will return to her. Soon, however, she converts as a lay disciple, followed by her ordination as a nun. Here the Buddha says, "Yashodhara, the mother of Rahula, is the most modest of all my female disciples."[10] The duration of this sequence is not made clear in the text.

The Sinhalese story says explicitly that Yashodhara was the first woman to request ordination, although not necessarily the first to receive it. Here we return to the episode where she adopts ascetic practices in the palace in tandem with the Bodhisattva's austerities during his six-year retreat in the forest. When he finally returns to Kapilavastu as the Buddha, she requests ordination at their first meeting. He refuses, however, claiming that the

---

* Here Gopa and Yashodhara are two different wives.
† Mrigi Gautami.

right of women entering the order belongs first to Mahaprajapati. As the story continues, Rahula is ordained, and Suddhodana tries to cheer up the unhappy Yashodhara:

> Bye and bye you also will become an ascetic; but it will be better to delay now, as people would say you have renounced the world on account of your sorrow.[11]

She then resolves to wait and become a nun after Suddhodana has died. When the story picks up again, his death has taken place and, in a detail not recounted in any other legend surveyed here, Yashodhara has succeeded Suddhodana as queen of the Shakyas. Everyone else who might be the rightful sovereign—Maya, Mahaprajapati, Nanda, Rahula, Devadatta, and Suprabuddha*—has either died or joined the Buddha's ministry. Yashodhara has no interest in remaining as queen, however, and is repulsed by the role "as if a dead [snake] were tied around her neck."[12] Instead, she longs to find Mahaprajapati and join the ordained community of women that has already established itself in Vaishali. The entire Shakya population tries to dissuade her, no doubt stricken that yet another member of their beloved royal family wishes to depart. But she will not be stopped. Accompanied by one thousand women, Yashodhara sets forth on the journey in much the same way her mother-in-law did previously. Soon she is ordained and happily so, especially now that she can hear teachings and from time to time see her beloved Rahula. Apparently she becomes acclaimed as the former wife of the Buddha because citizens everywhere shower her with more gifts than she ever received as queen.† Finally Yashodhara moves to Rajagriha to escape her fame.

This story is noteworthy not just because it suggests that she was the first woman to request ordination, but also because she briefly succeeded Suddhodana as regent of the Shakyas. In her hagiography, discussed at length below, she is said to have been the leader of eighteen thousand nuns. Despite what is stated in the Pali canon, Horner speculates that Yashodhara

---

* The last two in this tradition being her brother and father, respectively.

† In the stories there is never mention of divorce or official change in status when couples separate due to ordination, so technically Yashodhara is still the Buddha's wife.

may have played a larger role than her mother-in-law in founding the order of nuns:

> A good deal of uncertainty surrounds the actual foundation of the Buddhist Order of Almswomen, and its beginnings are wrapped in mists. It is possible that Mahaprajapati came late into the Order, after her husband had died, and that the woman really to make the Order open for women was Yasodhara.[13]

A passage in the Nepali *Buddhacarita* has Yashodhara (Gopika) leading Rahula, Gautami,* and other women "with staves in their hands, as shaven ascetics," in the practice of fasting. Further along, she and Gautami are described as coleaders of the nuns.[14]

An exceptional story in the Kangyur addresses women's early participation in the Buddha's ministry. It opens with comments that the Shakya men, including Suddhodana, are all delighted by the Buddha's teachings during his first visit to Kapilavastu. Many men have already ordained as monks. One of Suddhodana's chief ministers, Mahanaman, is so pleased after a dharma teaching in the Nigrodha grove that he goes home and enthusiastically raves about it to his wife. After telling her that the Buddha is their "saviour," the following dialogue ensues:

> "He is the saviour of men, but not of women," she exclaimed.
> "Say not so," her husband replied; "his mercy extends to all creation. Go seek him and you will hear the truth from his mouth."[15]

Apparently women had not yet been allowed to attend dharma teachings because Mahanaman now asks the king's permission for women to be included in the assemblies at the Nigrodha grove. Suddhodana refuses. Undeterred, Mahanaman then asks Mahaprajapati to make the same request to the king, and she succeeds in getting the necessary permission. Five hundred† Shakya women now accompany Mahaprajapati to the grove, but when they arrive, a monk bars entrance to Mahanaman's wife because she is wearing too much jewelry. Not wanting to miss the teaching, she

---

* Mahaprajapati.

† Five hundred is a conventional number used to represent "many."

sends her servant girl back to town with her jewels, but the servant girl is so heartbroken at missing the Buddha's teaching that she dies along the way. This story is noteworthy because it is a man, Mahanaman, who initiates permission for women to attend the Buddha's teachings, presumably out of love for his wife. We also see that this permission, when granted, extends to women of all castes and that a servant girl shares equally the other women's passion for dharma teachings.

Mahaprajapati's leadership is a key theme in these stories. Once the king dies and "widowhood" is on the increase, women in Kapilavastu found strength in each other's company and turned to her for direction. After all, her struggles were no different from their own. She was the clear candidate to make the case for ordination, not just as their queen, but also as a widow and the Buddha's mother. The Sinhalese text says that after Suddhodana died, the women went together to the Nigrodha grove to beseech the Buddha for ordination. Mahaprajapati made their case three times, but three times the Buddha refused, and soon after he left Kapilavastu to resume his itinerant ministry. Passionate in their resolve, Mahaprajapati and five hundred Shakya women decided to follow him.

So much change was taking place in Kapilavastu! First there was a mass exodus of men, and now the women were leaving too. So determined were these five hundred women to become nuns that they took measures as if they had already been ordained—exchanging their fine clothes for simple robes, shaving their heads, and taking up alms bowls in the tradition of mendicants. A beautiful passage from the Sinhalese tradition paints a stark contrast between the austere life the women chose over the "delicate" life they gave up:

> Previously [the women] had thought it a great thing to have to descend from the upper to the lower story of the palace; they were only accustomed to walk in places so smooth that they were like mirrors that reflected the image of all things near them; for the fuel in the palace, when fires were required on account of cold, they had only burnt cotton and silk cloth smeared with oil, as common wood would have caused too much heat, and sandal wood too much smoke; even when they went to the bath they were protected by curtains and canopies; and in every respect they were brought up in the most delicate manner.[16]

It took Mahaprajapati and her company several months to walk the more than four hundred kilometers to Vaishali where the Buddha was residing. Needless to say, they became exhausted and filthy, their bare feet swollen and blistered. Kindhearted villagers along the way offered them food, litters for transport, and other means of assistance, but the women resolutely refused.

What follows when they finally catch up with the Buddha goes to the crux of the confusion around the early ordination of women. In addition to the story in the Pali canon, two similar accounts are examined here, one from the Kangyur and the other from the Sinhalese record. In all these accounts, Mahaprajapati arrives in Vaishali overwhelmed with emotion and fatigue. Not allowed entrance to the all-male cloister where the Buddha stays, she slumps in the doorway awash in tears. Here Ananda finds her. Of course he is shocked not only to see his queen and a multitude of bedraggled Shakya clanswomen, but also to find his family's beloved matriarch (and perhaps his own grandmother) in this desperate state. The Sinhalese text reads,

> When Ananda saw them, with bleeding feet, covered with dust, and half dead, his breast was full of sorrow, and his eyes filled with tears, and he said, "Why have you come? For what reason have you endured these hardships? Have the Sakyas been driven from their city by the enemy? Why does the mother of [Buddha] remain in such a place?"[17]

Mahaprajapati repeats her original request for the ordination of women, which Ananda relays immediately to the Buddha. Vigorously taking the women's side, Ananda petitions the Buddha three times on her behalf, and three times the Buddha demurs, not exactly saying no, but showing reluctance. In the Pali canon, three times he replies, "Be careful, Ananda, of the going forth of women,"[18] leaving his answer ambiguous. In the Sinhalese text, he repeats, "Ananda, seek not to have females admitted to the profession"[19]—also ambiguous. Now an event occurs that truly demonstrates the intimate bond between Ananda and his mentor, one not seen in the relationships between the Buddha and his other disciples. Just as his childhood friends Chandaka and Kalodayin earlier challenged Gautama's logic in rendering a decision, so now Ananda intensifies his case, respectfully but boldly reasoning that the Buddha should reconsider

Mahaprajapati's request. In the Sinhalese variant, Ananda points out that there is precedent to ordain women from the Buddha's previous lifetimes:

> My lord, it is right that women should be admitted to profession; when you delivered the [*Buddhavamsa*] discourse, you made known that this was one of the institutions of the twenty-four [Buddhas] who have preceded you.[20]

The Buddha is described as pleased by Ananda's argument. Ananda now skillfully changes the subject, asking if women who enter into the path of dharma are capable of attaining the same states of mental freedom or "perfection" as men.[21] When the Buddha says yes, Ananda takes an entirely personal tack and argues that Mahaprajapati is the Buddha's own beloved adoptive mother, who took him to her breast and nursed him when Maya died, who raised him selflessly with the utmost tenderness and care. How could he, the Buddha, possibly refuse her request now? At this point, the Buddha assents to the ordination of women, with the condition that Mahaprajapati agree to the eight extra rules for nuns, as mentioned earlier. Hearing this news from Ananda, Mahaprajapati is overjoyed and accepts the Buddha's conditions. Her assent constitutes tacit acceptance on behalf of her followers and her formal ordination as a nun. The Buddha appoints her "chief of all the nuns" with responsibility for the discipline and instruction of the other women.[22]

There are several key elements surrounding the Buddha's ambivalence in ordaining women: his initial hesitation, his declaration that women and men are equally capable of achieving complete realization, and the eight extra rules. Taken together, these appear inconsistent and suggest a conflation of narratives or significant editorial redrafting. We'll look at them separately in reverse order. Of all the elements here, the eight extra rules smack of monk-editor interpolation seeking to codify the subjugation of women within the monastic order. For example, one rule is that any nun, regardless of seniority, must join palms and bow down to even the most novice monk, thereby acknowledging her inferior status. These rules remain in effect today and are the subject of extensive controversy in the Buddhist world, especially (of course) among nuns. Evidence found in this book's investigation of the early biographies finds them completely out of character for the Buddha, and supports the view that they are not genuine.

Many authoritative resources address this debate, and it won't be discussed further here.

In another detail arising from this contested passage, the Buddha is reported to have described numerous ill effects that would result in the future from establishing an order of nuns, including that the dharma would last only five hundred rather than one thousand years. While the entire passage is problematic, we know for sure that this prediction did not pan out. Twenty-five hundred years later, the dharma is not only flourishing worldwide, but more women than ever—ordained and lay—are not only Buddhists, but Buddhist leaders, scholars, and teachers.

The Sinhalese variant sheds light on the Buddha's assertion that women and men have equal potential to attain nirvana. Referencing precedent in his previous births, the Buddha says,

> Are the [Buddhas] born in the world only for the sake of men? Assuredly it is for the benefit of females, as well. When I delivered the Tirokudha-sutra, many women entered the paths, as did also many [goddesses] when I delivered the Abhidharmma in [Tryastrimsha heaven]. Have not [Visakha] and many other [laywomen], entered the paths? The entrance is open for women as well as men.[23]

While this is a very positive statement regarding women, his mention of Visakha (who is discussed at length later) and other laywomen seems to suggest that the Buddha still favors the lay faith option over monastic ordination for women. This is similarly reflected an earlier admonition to Mahaprajapati:

> Gautami, wear the pure white dress of lay-women; seek to attain perfection; be pure, chaste, and live virtuously, and you will find a lasting reward and happiness.[24]*

In these passages, the Buddha is not discouraging women from the path per se, but he is encouraging them to pursue his teachings as lay practitioners. These remarks may provide some context for his apparent reluctance

---

*From the stories, it seems that laywomen practitioners wore white dresses to signify their status.

to found an order of nuns. While we can't know for sure what the Buddha did and did not say, if he really was reluctant to ordain women, it does not necessarily follow that he was biased. The following passage suggests that the problem was perhaps one of timing:

> It was clearly perceived by the sage that if these females were admitted to [the order], they would derive therefrom immense advantages; and he saw also that it was the practice of former [Buddhas] to admit them; but he reflected that if they were admitted, it would perplex the minds of those who had not yet entered into the paths, and cause others to speak against his institutions. He therefore, thought it would not be right to accede to their request at once, and said, "Women, seek not to enter my immaculate order."[25]

From this we learn that the Buddha always intended to ordain women, just not so soon because of potential social backlash within a culture that was already undergoing radical change. His misgivings may also have arisen because establishing a separate order of nuns at that time appeared as a logistical challenge, one for which he was yet unprepared. In this scenario, his hesitation would have arisen out of concern for his charges, not bias. Creating and managing a monastic community of men was one thing, but now hundreds of women were also asking to put their future in his hands. Too much, too soon. It would have been reasonable for the Buddha to doubt the efficacy of undertaking an entirely separate monastic community for women at this early stage in his ministry. Requiring more than just a system of religious guidance and discipline, his suppliants all needed food, clothing, and shelter. Now living outside the patriarchal social structure, the women would also require a measure of protection. The cultural mores were such that in a sense the Buddha was being positioned to resume the patriarch's role for vast numbers of women, including, once again, his relatives. From his position as an ascetic, this was no doubt more than he had bargained for, and as a leader it simply could have been more than he felt he could responsibly handle. It's only human that the Buddha may have balked at such a daunting undertaking at that time. His ministry was growing rapidly, and the entire weight of the movement was on his shoulders. Not long before, he had been a lone ascetic sitting under the *bodhi* tree, unsure if he should even teach. Now he had burgeoning responsibility for hundreds, if not thousands, of homeless women and men.

Visakha, Chief among Laywomen

All of the Buddha's immediate female relatives became nuns, after which we learn little more about them. Yashodhara disappears almost entirely from the records, while Mahaprajapati, appointed by the Buddha to head up the order of nuns, holds a mostly silent presence, occasionally mentioned in the literature in the context of formal interactions with other nuns or the Buddha himself. The stories tell us that later in her life, Sujata also ordained as a nun. However, as the women we have come to know in the Buddha's biography drop from view, new laywomen disciples emerge in the stories. These women warrant a more extensive study than is offered here, but one of them in particular—Visakha—must be mentioned.

Almost entirely forgotten today, Visakha was a devoted and influential lay disciple whose generous patronage helped shape the formation of the Buddha's early ministry. Accomplished in the dharma, she was one of his trusted advisors, weighing in on matters concerning the clergy, and was an advocate for the nuns. As a householder (wife, mother, grandmother, great-grandmother), Visakha dedicated her life to the dharma, juggling faith and family with joyful ease. Her stories are told in delightful detail in the Pali tradition and are summarized in a biographical sketch that follows.

Born to one of the richest families in King Bimbisara's realm, Visakha was remarkably precocious from a very young age. One day, her grandfather learns that the Buddha and his retinue of monks are approaching their city. Immediately he sends for Visakha and affectionately says,

> Dear girl, this is a happy day for you and a happy day for me. Summon the five hundred maidens who are your attendants, mount five hundred chariots, and accompanied by your five hundred slave-maidens, go forth to meet the [Buddha]. [26]

Although just seven years old, Visakha readily agrees and sets out with her cortege to the outskirts of town to meet the Buddha. When the road becomes impassable, she and the other girls dismount and proceed on foot, finally finding the great teacher, to whom they pay proper respect. Pleased with their conduct, the Buddha gives them a discourse on dharma, after which Visakha and the five hundred girls are converted to the faith. The Sinhalese text adds that it was at this time the Buddha recognized Visakha's superior merit and knew that she would become either the mother of his lay disciples or his principal female disciple.[27] Thereafter, her grandfather also converts and invites the Buddha and his monks to be his honored guests, providing for them all manner of abundant food during the fortnight they remain in town.

The story now skips ahead some years, and Visakha's family has moved near Shravasti in the kingdom of Kosala, where their holdings of goods, animals, and servants are so vast that they establish a city of their own. At this time, a wealthy family is in search of a suitable daughter for their eldest son and dispatches a party of eight brahmans to scour the region on their behalf. It so happens that their search coincides with an annual public holiday where highborn maidens, normally cloistered at home, sally forth together on foot with their female attendants to bathe in the river. As one can imagine, highborn young men are not far behind. Lining the roads, the suitors show admiration for the maiden of their choice by throwing a garland of flowers over her head. On this particular holiday, Visakha, now sixteen years old, is making her way to the river with her attendants when suddenly the skies break open, and the crowd is pelted with rain. Everyone scurries to a nearby hall to take cover except Visakha, who remains composed and does not alter her gait. By the time she gets to the hall, she is soaked. The brahmans happen to be there and are drawn to her because she appears to possess the "five beauties" they were assigned to find for their client. First they ask Visakha why she took her time walking through the rain. The answer she gives is astonishing for its insightful assessment of how girls were valued in her culture. The context is certainly sexist, but the answer coming from this young woman demonstrates her keen awareness of the reality of her social situation and marks her cleverness because she is turning it to her advantage:

> Dear friends, mothers and fathers bring up their daughter seeking to preserve intact the greater and lesser members of her body. For we are goods for sale, and they bring us up with the intention of marrying us off into some other family. The result is that were we, while running, to trip over the hem of our skirt, or on the ground, and fall and break either a hand or a foot, we should be a burden on our family. But if the clothes we wear get wet, they will dry. Bearing this consideration in mind, dear friends, I did not run.[28]

The brahmans are very impressed and, as surrogates for their client, throw a garland over her head to signify they have chosen her to be his bride. After questioning them carefully regarding the groom's family, Visakha determines that their client is of suitable standing and agrees to the marriage. She then sends a message to her father asking him to dispatch a chariot to pick her up since, according to custom, a noble maiden who has gained a marriage garland must leave the festivities by chariot, not by foot. How exceptional that Visakha chooses a husband of her own will without her father or family even knowing about it!

Visakha continues to be characterized as extremely competent and in charge of her life. She is described as having wisdom and "intelligence ... as keen as the edge of a diamond."[29] When the groom's family travels to her home for the marriage, Visakha's father puts her in charge of the hospitality details. This is no mean feat since the arriving caravan comprises most of the citizens of Shravasti, their servants, chariots, horses, elephants, and handlers. Further, King Prasenajit has a political stake in the marriage and shows up with his entire royal household and a massive retinue. With cheerful ease, Visakha generously arranges superior lodging, food, and entertainment for everyone.

As it turns out, what was originally intended to be a visit of several days becomes the duration of the rainy season, or four months. This is because Visakha's father has commissioned a marriage parure* for his daughter that requires the participation of expert guildsmen from across the land. No lavish detail has been spared, so everyone must wait while it is being completed. Needless to say the price tag breaks all records, but that is only the trousseau. Visakha's dowry is equally unmatched, consisting of a twelve-mile caravan of costly items and a vast herd of cattle. In a final flourish, her father invites anyone from his fourteen tenant villages to follow his daughter into married life as her servant. As Visakha is dearly beloved by all, men and women vacate the fourteen villages to join the caravan returning to Shravasti. However, Visakha's new father-in-law, Migara, now shows his miserly colors. The lavish dowry is welcome, but how is he going to feed and house all these servants? Cruelly, he has them driven back with sticks and clods of dirt. Only those who stand their ground are allowed to continue.

---

* Head-to-toe suite of matching jewelry customary for royal or wealthy families.

Trouble lies ahead, but Visakha, as usual, is adept at strategizing what she wants as she steers her life toward the Buddha and his teachings.[30]

That Visakha is going to be no ordinary wealthy wife becomes obvious from the outset. In gratitude for her father's hospitality, all the citizens of Shravasti lavish her with gifts according to their means and rank. These she immediately redistributes to families throughout the city with kind personal notes designating them for her "mother," "father," "brother," and so forth, as if each citizen were her own kin. Another story has Visakha stealing out to the stables at night with servants bearing torches to help her mare give birth to a foal. Only after ensuring that both animals are resting safely, washed with warm water and anointed with oils, does she return to her quarters.

Visakha's husband is barely mentioned in her biography, but her stingy father-in-law plays a significant role. Unlike Visakha, he has not converted to Buddhism; rather, he adheres to the customs of the "naked ascetic" sect.* For that reason, he does not invite the Buddha to the marriage festivities, even though the saint and his assembly are staying nearby. Instead, Migara invites a company of five hundred naked ascetics to his house for a celebratory feast and asks his daughter-in-law to attend and pay proper homage. Hearing that she would be dining with holy men, Visakha is delighted and looks forward to the occasion. However, upon arriving at the hall and beholding a sea of naked men, she is utterly repulsed. Furious with her father-in-law for subjecting her to this indecency, she reproaches him in front of the guests and departs. As might be expected, her outburst enlivens the dinner conversation. The naked ascetics say,

> Householder, why did you not seek some other maiden to be the wife of your son? In admitting a female disciple of the monk Gotama to your house, you have admitted [bad luck]. Expel her from this house immediately.[31]

Migara does not disagree but is reluctant to jeopardize such an asset to his fortune. He assures his guests that his obstreperous daughter-in-law is simply young and immature.

Family tension over religion soon flares up again. This time Visakha is

---

* Most likely referring to early Jainism.

fanning her father-in-law as he takes his midday meal. A monk from the Buddha's assembly comes to the door seeking alms. Migara can see him but completely ignores him and continues to eat. Embarrassed, Visakha says apologetically to the monk, "Pass on Reverend Sir. My father-in-law is eating stale food,"[32] which is to imply that his food was not fit for the monk. With this perceived insult, Migara has had enough of his daughter-in-law and angrily orders the servants to throw her out of the house. However, all the servants are her own and, having loved her since childhood, will not budge. Visakha also stands her ground, pointing out to Migara that she comes from an honorable family, and he cannot throw her out as if she were a "common wench." In the end, a lengthy tribunal tries her on numerous infractions, but Visakha is found innocent of all of them and allowed to stay. Having cleared her name as she intended, Visakha announces she wishes to leave anyway and instructs her servants to load her carts and carriages for departure.

This episode marks a turning point where Visakha finally takes full charge of her life and directs it toward her faith. As Migara begs her forgiveness and cajoles her to remain in his household, she counters with her terms:

> Dear father-in-law, I pardon you freely so far as in me lies. But I am the daughter of a house which has firm faith in the Religion of the Buddha, and we cannot exist without the Congregation of the Monks. If I may be permitted to minister to the Congregation of Monks, according to my inclination, I will remain.[33]

Migara agrees, and from this point on, Visakha calls the shots. Without delay, she extends an invitation to the Buddha and his disciples to dine in her house the following day. She also invites Migara, but he is dissuaded by the naked ascetics who tell him, "Do not think of going to the monk Gotama."[34] After the meal, Visakha once again sends an invitation to her father-in-law, this time to hear the teaching. Now Migara is curious and, in consultation with the naked ascetics, agrees to listen to the teaching from behind a screen. Fully aware of all that is going on, the Buddha directs his teaching so that everyone in attendance, including Migara, understands its meaning. Migara is overwhelmed by the truth of the dharma and converts on the spot. In gratitude, he dubs Visakha his "mother" and pays reverential homage to the Buddha. The following day, Visakha entertains the Buddha again, and her mother-in-law also converts.[35]

After these events, Visakha redirects her life to support the Buddha and the flourishing of his ministry. Her tremendous wealth becomes quite serviceable now, as she uses it to provide for the needs of the nuns and monks, ensuring that they have the "four requisites" of food, clothing, housing, and medical care. It is noteworthy that she had full control, independent of any man, over her own wealth. The Pali commentary says,

> No other woman in the world gave away so much money as this woman who lived in the house of a heretic.[36]*

The Buddha's modified form of asceticism—one that endorses a simple life rather than mortification—allowed for Visakha's creativity in devising ways to relieve physical hardships, which, as the Buddha himself discovered during the period of his austerities, are an obstruction rather than a boon to spiritual attainment.[37] One way Visakha funds her prodigious philanthropy is through her aforementioned marriage parure, which she sells (since no one in the land can afford it, she buys it herself) and asks the Buddha on which of the four requisites she should spend the money. When he suggests she build a new dwelling place for his ever-expanding community of monks, "her heart filled with delight."[38] Known as Pubbarma (Eastern) monastery, Visakha sees to its completion by the following rainy season when the Buddha returns. On the day of its consecration, she dances joyously surrounded by the children of her vast family, rejoicing that the prayers of her previous lives have been fulfilled. On this occasion, the Buddha refers to her as his "daughter" and praises her with the words,

> The mind of Visakha inclines to the doing of all manner of good deeds.[39]

---

*While Visakha is very wealthy, the measure of "merit" or spiritual benefit wrought by a gift stems from intention rather than material value, according to the Buddhist faith. A pauper kindly sharing a mango with a hungry stranger, for example, could gain more merit than a rich person lavishing gifts of gold as a show of ego or with the expectation of something in return.

The laity lived in close proximity to the ordained clergy in Shravasti, so it was not difficult for Visakha to observe the living conditions of the nuns and monks. Especially with so few resources at this early time in the ministry they were often hungry, ragged, cold, and sick. Prior to the building of monasteries, however, conditions had been much worse. Early nuns lived as itinerant forest dwellers and, without male "protectors," were subjected to widespread violence and rape from marauding men. Drawing from the Pali canon on this, Horner says,

> Crimes of violence are mentioned so often in some parts of the Vinaya that an impression is created of a land infested by thieves and brutal men constantly on the lookout for the violation or molestation of unprotected women.[40]

According to stories found in both the Pali and Sanskrit sources, a turning point for women occurred following the rape of the nun Utpalavarna.* Here she lives alone in the forest in a small hut she has built for herself. Returning home one day from collecting alms in the village, she goes to sleep only to find that a man has hidden under her bed. Despite her screams, he ruthlessly rapes her. She tells the other nuns, who tell the monks, who tell the Buddha (this was apparently the usual sequence for communicating with their teacher unless Mahaprajapati was present to be the nuns' spokesperson). The Buddha is quite concerned and summons King Prasenajit of Kosala. In the following words, the Buddha asks the king to build a monastery for the nuns within the city walls of Shravasti so they would be protected:

> Your Majesty, in this religion young women of family, as well as young men of family, renounce many kinsfolk, and much wealth, and retire from the world, and take up residence in the forest. In case women reside in the forest, it is possible that evil-minded men inflamed by lust may conduct themselves towards them with disrespect and arrogance, do them violence and bring their religious life to naught. Therefore a religious place of residence for the Community of Almswomen should be erected within the City.[41]

---

* In the Kangyur, Utpalavarna is named as one of Siddhartha's three wives.

Prasenajit agrees to this request and subsequently builds a monastery for them. Regulations aimed at protecting nuns were also added to the monastic code at this time, for example nuns could not travel alone in dangerous places or sleep alone at night.[42]

Returning to Visakha, she is said to have fed two thousand monastics per day and also freely distributed medicines. She came and went frequently from the monastic quarters, attending teachings and seeing to the needs of the clergy. As she became aware of pervasive problems in their living conditions, she determined to remedy them. However, changes on a large scale required the Buddha's permission. The story on this follows.

Over a meal in her home, Visakha asks the Buddha if he would grant her eight "favors." While he counters that he doesn't grant favors, he agrees to hear her out. Visakha proceeds to enumerate eight specific areas of need within the monastic community that she wishes to fund for the rest of her life. We gain a window into her kindness and generosity of heart by learning what she observed and subsequently requested to benefit the clergy.

1. Robes for the rainy season. Visakha observed that monks removed their robes when they went outdoors in the rainy season to avoid getting them wet. This gave rise to nakedness, which was improper. By providing special robes for the rainy season, monks would always have dry robes to wear indoors.

2. Food for visiting monks. Visakha observed that newcomers did not know the streets of the town, thus they became weary searching for alms and would often go hungry. She wanted to provide food for visiting monks until they learned their way around.

3. Food for monks setting out on a journey. Visakha observed that travelers missed their caravans because they were struggling to procure alms before leaving. She wanted to guarantee food for traveling monks to ensure they were fed before departure.

4. Food for the sick. Visakha observed that sick monks were unable to beg for alms and were left with unsuitable food—or none at all. This made them sicker or led to their deaths. She wished to guarantee wholesome food for the sick.

5. Food for those who nurse the sick. Visakha observed that those who

cared for the sick did not have enough time to search for alms for themselves, especially because of the rule that monastics could not eat after midday. She wished to guarantee all caregivers their timely meal.

6. Medicine for the sick. Visakha observed that monks were dying from lack of medicine. She wanted to provide all the needed medicines.

7. Wholesome food. Visakha observed that monks were eating unwholesome food. She wished to provide rice porridge as a staple for those who needed it.

8. Bathing garments for the nuns. Visakha observed that the nuns were bathing naked in the river, often side by side with prostitutes, who made fun of them. Nakedness was improper in any case. She wished to provide special bathing garments for all the nuns.[43]*

The Buddha is very pleased with her eight requests and grants them all. He then asks her to account for the benefit of this gift to herself. In her response, we hear the joy that infuses Visakha's generosity, as well as her practical insight into how the method of giving advances her personal spiritual goals:

> When I remember [my gifts], I shall be glad. When I am glad, I shall be happy. When my mind is happy, my body will be tranquil. When my body is tranquil, I shall feel pleasure. When I feel pleasure, my mind will become concentrated. That will maintain the spiritual factors in being in me and also the spiritual powers and also the enlightenment factors.[44]

Visakha's tireless generosity nurtured the Buddha's mission in more ways than providing for the physical needs of the clergy. Devotion to him and his teachings combined with her own sensitive wisdom earned her a

---

* Although the texts record that rules 1 through 7 were stipulated for "monks" there is no reason to believe that Visakha's generous donations would not have extended equally to the nuns, as she was both their champion and their advocate.

unique role as one of the Buddha's closest lay advisors. That he took her advice and granted the eight favors is just one example of monastic changes for which she is credited. Positioned as she was between the laity and the clergy, she knew both worlds well and no doubt had many insights to share with the Buddha in helping him construct his early ministry. Only a few of their conversations have been preserved, yet we can imagine that her counsel as a woman would have been of particular value to him as he sorted out how to manage the separate community of nuns. Mahaprajapati would have provided similar support in Vaishali, but that was a long way from Shravasti.

A touching story comes to us of a young nun who turned up pregnant, and there was no precedent on how to handle the situation. First the case is brought to Devadatta, now a monk, who cruelly orders her expelled from the order. As the nun insists she must have conceived before taking ordination, the matter is brought to the Buddha, who turns it over to Visakha. Drawing a curtain for privacy, Visakha kindly interviews and examines the young woman before affirming her story. Soon a healthy baby boy is born in the monastery and is later adopted by King Prasenajit himself.[45]

Visakha's close proximity to the Buddha allowed her access to personal teachings and spiritual guidance as well. In one story, she hurries to him unannounced, grief stricken, and drenched with rain to seek his solace on the sudden death of her granddaughter.[46] In another, the Buddha gives her a private teaching on the eight requisites for a laywoman to advance on the spiritual path. Among these, the first four deal with practical matters of living in the world, while the remaining qualities are faith, moral discipline, generosity, and wisdom—all of which Visakha cultivated and exemplified throughout her life.[47]

An important story from the Pali canon demonstrates the Buddha's confidence in Visakha's knowledge of the dharma and places her as an equal with Mahaprajapati. Here he requires a representative from each of the four assemblies (laywomen, laymen, nuns, and monks) to help resolve a dispute among quarreling monks. Visakha is selected to represent the laywomen, and Mahaprajapati is selected to represent the nuns, while two men are designated to represent the remaining cohorts. The four judges are to hear the dispute separately and rule, not according to any subjective measures, but according to the veracity of the dharma espoused by the disputants.

Note that women and men, lay and ordained, were equally entrusted with this task. Horner remarks,

> Both Mahaprajapati and Visakha were considered to be endowed with as reliable powers of discretion as the men, and to possess as thorough a knowledge of the Dhamma as the men. That their mental stature was estimated to be of equal growth is evident from the fact that it was not suggested to either of the women that she should consult with the almsmen as to which of the disputants was right according to the Dhamma.[48]

She further comments on Buddhism's egalitarianism as demonstrated by this account:

> A religion which allows this amount of independence of judgment to its women members, and does not differentiate between the capacity of the two sexes, is ennobled, for the women rise and justify the faith which is placed in them.[49]

While Visakha's life was deeply committed to supporting Buddhist monasticism, she never showed interest in taking ordination herself, nor does it appear the Buddha ever suggested such a thing.* No doubt he realized that her spiritual life as a laywoman dedicated to the dharma was equally fulfilling and that joyful generosity was her path. Like Sujata, Visakha's goal for many lifetimes had been to attain the opportunity to serve a buddha. Finally, in this lifetime, she had achieved the optimal birth for doing so. Practicing the faith as a laywoman was a boon, not an obstacle, and a powerful means for her to advance on her personal soteriological path. Because of her exceptional generosity, the Buddha declared her "chief female lay benefactor." More than that, Visakha was in every way a loving mother to her vast family, to an enormous community of nuns and monks, and to early Buddhism itself. As Horner says,

---

* She is likely not the same Visakha named in the *Therigatha*.

Visakha, by her constant gifts of alms, clothes and dwellings, and also by her criticism, was an unflagging help in the process of binding the almspeople together and to the laity. She may indeed be regarded as a true and faithful mother to the religion.[50]

In her unique way, Visakha has earned her seat at the table with the mothers of early Buddhism: Maya, Mahaprajapati, Mrigi Gautami, and Sujata.

The Deaths of Buddhism's First Nuns

We now return to stories of Mahaprajapati and Yashodhara. While little more is said about them in the legends after they become nuns, we learn about their deaths from several hagiographic accounts from the Pali tradition.

In separate stories, both Mahaprajapati* and Yashodhara are elderly nuns and the leaders of large assemblies of nuns (five hundred and forty-six thousand, respectively). In contemplation, they each perceive that their lives are complete and have come to a natural end. Due to the power of their spiritual attainments, they have control over their destinies and now choose to seek death—for them, nirvana—on their own terms. But first they must get the Buddha's permission. Their death stories are very similar, both taking place over the course of one day with flashbacks to earlier lifetimes. As we shall see, the differences are also significant.

Both hagiographies, called *apadanas,* are recorded in the *Khuddhaka Nikaya* of the Pali canon as well as in variants that appear in Sinhalese sources. Like the poems in the *Therigatha,* the women's *apadanas* were likely composed by women several centuries after the death of the Buddha.[51] In this genre, the women speak in the first person about their current and past lives, the point of the autohagiography being to provide self-laudatory testimony before witnesses of their accomplishments that justify their arhatship, or final freedom from rebirth. In turn, the Buddha praises them for their lifetimes of accumulated merit and validates their claim to arhatship. In a larger context, these stories also provide religious paradigms for laywomen, since all nuns were laywomen once, particularly in past lives, and it is eons of merit accumulated over their entire karmic trajectory that brought them

---

*As a nun she is commonly called Gautami.

to this day of departure from the cycle of rebirth and their final reward of nirvana.[52]

The following discussions of Mahaprajapati and Yashodhara draw from their *apadanas* in the Pali canon, which were translated with a commentary by Jonathan Walters,* and R. Spence Hardy's translations of Sinhalese accounts of the same stories.[53]

MAHAPRAJAPATI

Mahaprajapati returns from a meeting with the Buddha that has stirred thoughts of death in her mind. Dropping deeply into contemplation, she sees via her superior powers that the Buddha's senior disciples will soon pass into the state of nirvana, after which her exalted son will also depart earthly existence. She reflects,

> I am now 120 years of age, though in appearance I am as young as when I was a maiden of sixteen ... it is meet that the child should see the departure of the parent, and not the parent the departure of the child.[54]

As much as Mahaprajapati is a nun and the Buddha is her teacher, her reflection poignantly returns her to her identity as his mother. Expressing a deep-seated sentiment of motherhood, she does not want to outlive her child. She thus determines to pass out of existence before he does and makes a plan to request the Buddha's permission to die. As she makes her decision, the earth shakes, alerting the monastery's resident goddesses who weep and wail with grief, begging her not to depart. Also distressed are the laywomen, who lament that she will leave them destitute. With kindness, Mahaprajapati addresses them all:

> This is the time for drums of joy!
> Why are you crying, children?

---

* The *apadanas* comprise an entire text of the Pali canon that remains untranslated. Walters has translated portions that appear in various publications (see the general bibliography).

If you have love for me,
and if you all appreciate
the dharma's great stability
then strong and fervent you should be.

The great Buddha made women nuns
only at my beseeching.
So if you love me, be like me,
and follow after him.[55]

Her five hundred women disciples decide to follow her into nirvana. After all, these women have been together virtually their entire lives: from long-ago days as Shakya girls, wives, and widows in Kapilavastu; as weary renunciates trudging to Vaishali to beseech the Buddha for ordination; and as nuns surviving under difficult conditions in a disciplined community as religious practitioners. Mother, queen, mentor, and dharma teacher, Mahaprajapati has always been their beloved leader—the lamp that guides them.

Soon after, the women all assemble before the Buddha. Mahaprajapati addresses him with tender words that express the unique bond of mother and son. She claims that just as she has nurtured his body as his mother, so he has nurtured her "dharma-body" as her spiritual father:

Well-gone one, I am your mother;
you're my father, O wise one.
Lord, you give the truth's pure pleasure!
Gotama, I'm born from you!

It was I, O well-gone one,
who reared you, flesh and bones.
But by your nurturing was reared
my flawless dharma-body.

I suckled you with mother's milk
which quenched thirst for a moment.
From you I drank the dharma-milk,
perpetually tranquil.[56]

And similarly, from the Sinhalese legend,

> You have repaid me in a way that no other son can assist his parent;
> I have sheltered you from the sun and the storm, and you have
> protected me from the perils of existence; the mothers of [universal
> kings] are yet enduring the pains of existence . . . but I have been the
> foster-mother of a Buddha, and I am therefore saved from future
> birth.[57]

She goes on,

> I am the chief of women; and I have to request that before any other
> of your disciples I may be permitted to attain nirvana.[58]

As is the custom in taking leave of a buddha for the last time, Mahaprajapati
asks his forgiveness for any transgressions committed during this or past
lifetimes. The Buddha's response reveals that he regards her as an equal:

> The queen mother need [not] be forgiven as there is nothing to
> forgive. It is not requisite that those who have seen [nirvana] should
> forgive each other.[59]

With this statement, he grants her wish to enter nirvana first among all his
disciples, male and female, thereby establishing her preeminence.* Among
the large assembly witnessing this exchange are her remaining Shakya family
members, including her son, Nanda, and her grandson, Rahula. Ananda
is the only one who dissolves in tears, and for this, Mahaprajapati gently
chides him. It is not a time to indulge in grief, she says, as she is about to
obtain the longed-for freedom of eternal release from suffering.

Before her departure, the Buddha requests that she perform miracles to
remove any doubt from the minds of witnesses that women, too, can attain
nirvana. In the Pali canon, he says,

---

* While establishing her preeminence in this story, it should not be taken literally
that Mahaprajapati was the first of the Buddha's disciples to die.

> Yet still there are these fools who doubt
> that women too can grasp the truth.
> Gotami, show miracles,
> that they might give up their false views.[60]

In a display of spiritual prowess, Mahaprajapati rises repeatedly into the air, ascending to the god realms and back, proclaiming to all who will hear her devotion to the Buddha. She fills the sky with images of herself repeating his praises. The five hundred nuns also take their turn, filling the sky like stars as they perform miracles demonstrating their spiritual attainments.

In the Sinhalese account, we find a passage that echoes the final verse of Mahaprajapati's poem in the *Therigatha*. Here she bestows blessings on her son, while tenderly remembering his mother, her sister, Maya:

> May your glory increase continually. By means of your mother, Mahamaya, who brought you into the world, blessings without number have been conferred. . . . May you live long; may you never decay or die; may you exist a whole [eon] that you may continue to bless the world.[61]

Finally, after paying final homage to her beloved son and teacher, Mahaprajapati departs, that night attaining nirvana simultaneously with her company of nuns. Miracles continue to occur in heaven and on earth. The Buddha announces her cremation, and by his power which requires no effort, all who wish to attend are immediately transported, resulting in the largest assembly ever gathered during the time of his ministry, larger even than at his own cremation. The gods bring 501 golden litters upon which the corpses of Mahaprajapati and the nuns are borne through the sky to the burning site—a supreme honor, the chronicler notes, one that was not accorded either the Buddha or any other disciples. A separate funeral pyre, built of sandalwood and saturated with perfumed oils, is made for each of the bodies. All corporeal remains are consumed by fire except Mahaprajapati's body, which remains like a heap of precious pearls, a testament to her supreme sainthood. In his eulogy, the Buddha says,

> Know this, O monks, she was most wise,
> with wisdom vast and wide.

She was a nun of great renown,
a master of great powers.
She cultivated "divine ear"
and knew what others thought.

In former births, before this one,
she mastered "divine eye."
All imperfections were destroyed;
she'll have no more rebirths.[62]

Mahaprajapati's *apadana* is exceptionally important early literary evidence in support of Buddhist women. Walters points out that she is portrayed not only as preeminent among the Buddha's female disciples, but as a female buddha she is the Buddha's counterpart.

> She is the female counterpart of the Buddha, the founder and leader of the nuns' order who parallels (though does not supersede) Gotama, the founder and leader of the monk's order. Gotami is represented as the Buddha for women.[63]

He cites as an example that the use of her clan name, Gautami, sets her up in apposition to him (Gautama), as his counterpart.[64] Walters further points out that her death narrative mimics stages in the Buddha's own *parinirvana* as recorded in the *Mahaparinibbanasutta* of the Pali canon, illustrating that "what Gotama was for men, Gotami was for women."[65] Mahaprajapati similarly seeks liberation not just for herself, but for her disciples. As their beloved leader and role model, she opens the door for the nuns to follow her. As we see, Mahaprajapati's *apadana* ratifies women's soteriological potential, taking aim at the ignorance that would construe enlightenment as a genderized state.[66] In this vein, the Buddha's remark about "fools" not believing in women's attainments speaks to his egalitarianism and calls out the misogyny within his own ranks. On this point, Walters says,

> It is worth noting that *Gotami-apadana* also addresses a male audience, namely the androcentric ecclesiastical hierarchy of early Buddhism. The vindication of woman's spirituality does not only encourage women; it also serves as a corrective to men who belittle

women's spiritual potential. Misogynist attitudes, explicitly and implicitly, are countered by the example of Gotami.[67]

Mahaprajapati's story of leadership and liberation is as needed and relevant today as it was twenty-five hundred years ago. With Buddhist women continuing to struggle for gender equality in a faith system that continues to be broken by androcentrism, her spirit persists as a steady, guiding light. Yet while she is remembered as a role model for religious women, especially Buddhist nuns, she must also be remembered for the pivotal role she played earlier in life as a wise laywoman and loving mother. The woman who nursed the infant Buddha at birth and—like her sister, Maya—never wavered in her devotion to him, Mahaprajapati commands an incomparable place of honor not just in the Buddha's life story, but in the story of Buddhism.

YASHODHARA

We turn now to Yashodhara's *apadana.* Sitting quietly in contemplation, she determines that the time has come for her to enter nirvana. She is seventy-eight years old, and her family members Rahula, Suddhodana, Mahaprajapati, and Nanda have already died, not to mention numerous members of the clergy she has known her whole life. She reflects that she was born at the same moment as her husband, and in the natural order of things, they should also die at the same moment. With special insight, she sees that he will pass into nirvana in two years. However, because now he is the Buddha, it would be improper for her to leave at the same time.

The earth quakes as Yashodhara makes the resolution to pass into nirvana that very day. Surrounded by the retinue of women who followed her into the monastic life, she seeks out the Buddha to request his permission. By now monks and townsfolk have assembled, fearing that the former queen's arrival bodes that their beloved teacher will soon be passing away. Calling her "the most virtuous of women," the Buddha assents to Yashodhara's request to die but with a caveat. While it is clear to him that she has fulfilled the goal of becoming an arhat—thus, she will be fully liberated at the time of death—others may have doubts. Before passing into nirvana, it would behoove her to display miraculous powers that demonstrate her superior level of attainment.* This Yashodhara does before the vast audience after paying homage to the Buddha and publicly recounting her past lives. In a final flourish, she rises into the air and gives a teaching on "seven kinds of wives there are in the world of men," before returning to her residence and passing into nirvana that night.[†68]

Yashodhara directs her testimony to the Buddha and her case centers on their marriage, which has been ongoing for "tens of billions of lives."[69] She asserts that despite her manifold sufferings as his wife (which she lists in great detail), she has dutifully obliged his needs throughout the eons by serving him in all ways. She gives examples:

> Waiting upon him, cooking for him, dressing and undressing for him, giving up everything for him to acquire merit (including money, treasure, villages, small town, fields, sons, daughters, elephants, horses, cows, slaves, slave girls, and all the wealth he gave her).[70‡]

While this report may appear offensive to women in a modern-day feminist context, we further learn that being wife to buddhas past and present has been Yashodhara's mission all along. The role of wife has been the worldly means to her soteriological ends. In what Walters has dubbed "the feminist edge," she has intentionally chosen to align herself with men on the path to enlightenment in order to further herself spiritually.[71] Just as over the eons Sujata's soteriological path had been to be the Buddha's mother, and Visakha's path had been to be his benefactress, Yashodhara's this-life relationship with the Buddha comes at the end of manifold repetitions of intentionally being his wife. Indeed, these women have skillfully made the best of a man's world by leveraging the opportunities available to them in order to further their own ends. As testimony to the merit she gained

---

* Normally, it is forbidden for saints to perform miracles unless there is a soteriological purpose.

† The text does not elaborate this list, although the Buddha is said to have given a teaching on the same topic to Sujata elsewhere in the Pali canon. The content is painfully misogynist and suggests the attitudes of husbands at that time.

‡ The stories hold that the Buddha made similar sacrifices for her toward the same ends.

by serving her husband, Yashodhara makes the following claim before the Buddha and surrounding witnesses:

> The waters of the ocean, 84,000 leagues deep, would not be sufficient for dissolving the salt I used for the gruel I prepared. So it was with the salt, water, molasses, oil, and lemon that I used. Therefore . . . know that it was no small Act of Merit that I performed.[72]

However, more than her own advancement is in play here. Implied in Yashodhara's testimony is the contention that as his wife and primary support from the very beginning, she has also been the primary enabler of the Buddha's achievements. In other words, the cause of the Buddha's buddhahood traces back not just to his own good acts, but also to hers. To couch a timeless theme: he wouldn't be where he is today without her. In a sort of community property argument, her point is not just that she has served him selflessly, but that in so doing she rightfully shares his vast merit generated over the countless eons. Therefore, she would argue, her own religious rewards, which warrant certain nirvana upon death, flow from their long-standing relationship.

With her speech, Yashodhara is marking closure to their karmic bond, severing their tie of marriage forever. No longer is her existence interdependent with his; she is taking leave of her husband and teacher for the last time to embark solo on her intended final journey. She says,

> Lord, just as the water that reaches the sea does not flow back into the river and as the water that goes into the mouth of a . . . [sea monster] does not return to the sea, so I who never left you over an infinite period of time, will now go away and not be seen again.[73]

Hearing her out, the Buddha upholds her claims of supreme merit and praises her accomplishments:

> There is no woman comparable to Yasodhara in this entire Buddha era.[74]

Further, he confirms that she has attained arhatship and will reach nirvana upon death:

This Queen Yasodhara together with me in *samsara* fulfilled the requirements needed for Enlightenment, and over a long period of time practiced the Ten Perfections such as Generosity and Moral practices.[75]

The story concludes as the Buddha presides over Yashodhara's funeral rites. He directs that a huge stupa be erected over her relics that it might endure as a place of worship and pilgrimage.[76]*

Adding to the richness of Yashodhara's hagiography in the *Khudda-kanikaya* are three additional hagiographies that immediately follow. These recount the collective achievements of Yashodhara's company of nuns, all of whom followed her in taking ordination and, upon the day in question, chose to follow her into nirvana. These unnamed nuns—forty-six thousand women—are identified as the Buddha's harem wives from this and countless previous lifetimes. Like Yashodhara, they intentionally shaped their spiritual destinies by aligning themselves with him, in their case by taking cobirths as beautiful women serving him in the palace's upper chambers. Like Yashodhara, the consorts lay claim to a share of his success (or merit), which warrants their nirvana. After all, how could Siddhartha have come to the limits of sensual desire without first traveling its path? Clearly they had done their job. Looking more deeply into this detail, we realize that just as the Buddha extinguished his passions, so have the ladies extinguished theirs. In a sense, no one more closely paralleled his journey than the harem wives.

While this line of reasoning may appear particularly specious, sexist, or just funny, it should be remembered that women likely wrote these stories. We cannot know the world they lived in, but we can try to imagine what these authors aimed to accomplish. Perhaps this passage is a corrective to disparaging characterizations of women, especially harem women, in their androcentric culture and religion (recall the night of Siddhartha's Great Departure where the consorts are dehumanized as vile and disgusting). In these *apadanas,* not only are the women not maligned, they are recognized for their potential to awaken in female bodies. Like nuns from all walks of life, they have shed their pasts and are now simply religious women, equally

---

* The site of Yashodhara's stupa remains unknown today.

worthy of nirvana due to their diligent practice and past merit. Taking another view of this passage, while obviously Siddhartha did not have forty-six thousand consorts, we could see this number as a literary device, typical of the tradition, whereby all the nuns in the Buddha's early ministry are lumped together into one story that aims to honor their religiosity. Leaving none of the earliest nuns behind, the authors were acknowledging the sacredness of their religious purpose and authenticating their claims to nirvana. In contrast, imagine what the monks might have come up with had they written the consorts' end-of-life stories. No doubt details would have been recorded quite differently, the women castigated for their passions, perhaps, and relegated to countless rebirths in the hell realms.

Returning to these elderly nuns, their abiding mission is complete, and they ask the Buddha's permission for the "privilege" of death, mostly reiterating verbatim Yashodhara's words. Cast as her mirror image, forever nameless, the forty-six thousand nuns declare themselves as the Buddha's wives, saying, "We are Yashodharas." Like Yashodhara, they are ultimately leaving their husband behind to realize their own awakening.

Overall these *apadanas* deeply valorize the early nuns, conveying the message that lots of women attained arhatship—the highest goal in early Buddhism. Walters points out that although there are far more hagiographic accounts of men than women attaining nirvana in the early Buddhist community (550 versus 40), women have the men far outnumbered if one factors in the forty-six thousand followers of Yashodhara who were previously the Buddha's harem wives.[77]

Maya's Conversion, the Demise of the Shakyas, and Amrapali

We return to the Buddha's biography as he, too, has reached the end of his life. For forty-five years he roamed northeast India, teaching his disciples and converting an ever-growing number of women and men to the new Buddhist faith. At the core of his ministry's purpose lay his simple altruistic wish—shared by all previous buddhas—to be a lamp on the path for those seeking freedom from the throes of worldly suffering. Among the Buddha's early converts were his family members, all of whom (except Suddhodana) took ordination and became part of his monastic order.

However, on the family side, one loose end still needed the Buddha's attention. In the tradition of buddhas, the conversion of one's parents is the supreme act of gratitude for their loving gifts of life and nurturance. It is also an item on every buddha's bucket list—to convert one's parents before passing into *parinirvana*. The Buddha's father and Mahaprajapati, as we know, had converted to the new faith. However, the Buddha's mother, Maya, abiding in heaven as a goddess, had not yet converted. She died well before she could benefit from his salvific teachings. With her welfare in mind, the Buddha determined to travel to the heavenly realms to find her. The stories about this significant event typically focus on the important teachings the Buddha reputedly gave while abiding three months in Trayastrimsha heaven. However a few narrative fragments center on the interactions between mother and son that took place at that time.

The Buddha ascends to heaven without difficulty because immense mountains lower their summits and lift him up, taking him to the sacred teaching spot at the nexus of the celestial realms.[78] The Kangyur describes this seat as a gleaming white stone surrounded by a beautiful grove of trees.[79] Multitudes of goddesses and gods gather around, including the Buddha's mother, to whom his subsequent teachings are directed. In some traditions, Maya has become male; for example, in the Sinhalese story, she appears as the male leader of the entire celestial assembly but is still conspicuously named Matru, or "mother."[80] In the Burmese tradition, she remains female and appears as the daughter of an unnamed god.[81] The *Lalitavistara* concludes before this event takes place, but we know from earlier accounts that Maya in heaven retained her femaleness both as a goddess and as an emotionally engaged mother. Now the Buddha's profound teachings convert not only her, but everyone within earshot. Due to her exceptional merit, Maya attains arhatship on the spot. As other women in the Buddha's life have expressed, she states that her goal over countless lifetimes has now been fulfilled. Her son's karmic debt to her has been repaid. She says,

> You who have been born from my womb so many times, have now rendered me a recompense. In one birth, from being a slave I became the wife of the king of Benares, but that exaltation was not equal to the privilege I now receive. From the time of Piyumatura [Buddha], during an [eon], you sought no other mother and I sought no other son. Now, my reward is received.[82]

Soon after this, the Buddha descends to earth on a resplendent staircase surrounded by rainbows and retinues of newly converted celestial devotees.*

A much more complete story of mother and son reuniting in heaven appears in the *Mahamayasutra,* originally composed in Sanskrit but now extant only in Chinese.† This account opens with the Buddha already in Trayastrimsha heaven, seated under a tree in meditation and surrounded by a vast assembly of disciples. In lengthy verse, he opines to a messenger stories of his birth and his long-held wish to see again the sublime face of his mother and preach to her the dharma as an act of gratitude for giving him life. The messenger swiftly conveys this message to Maya some distance away. Upon hearing the words of her son, milk streams from her breasts. If the Buddha is indeed Siddhartha, she says, then her milk will reach his mouth directly. So, miraculously, her milk enters his mouth from afar. As miracles attend this event, she declares that she has not experienced such joy since the moment of his birth. Thus, mother and son are reunited. Maya greets him ceremoniously by taking refuge, with the stated purpose of realizing the fruits of awakening. For innumerable eons, as his mother nourishing him at her breast, her motivation has been to cut the bonds of rebirth and enter the stream of arhatship.‡ The Buddha demonstrates his gratitude by giving her a teaching that notes the inevitability of separation and his impending nirvana. When the time comes for him to depart, Maya is beset with sorrow.

There are two details of special note for women in this sutra. First, before the Buddha delivers his homily, Maya herself gives extensive teachings to the assembled disciples. In fact, most of the dharma passages are delivered in her voice. Further, in a departure from the convention that only deities can appear in the celestial realms, the seated assembly witnessing the reunion of Maya and her son numbers both human and nonhuman living beings, including a host of earthly laywomen, laymen, nuns, and monks. Together, they accompany the Buddha on his return to earth via the magical staircase. Greeting them below is King Prasenajit, similarly surrounded by a throng

---

* This famous scene is commonly depicted in Buddhist art.
† The sutra does not appear in an English translation at this time. What follows is summarized from an article by Hubert Durt.
‡ We find clear parallels between Maya and Sujata in this story.

of the fourfold community, which has been clamoring to see their beloved teacher again.[83]

Toward the end of his life, another family matter draws the Buddha's attention: the impending war between his Shakya clan and the neighboring Kosalas. Enraged by a perceived insult, the Kosalan king* vows to utterly wipe out the Shakyas, a peaceful people who have no particular defenses, especially after the exodus of countless men to follow the Buddha. While the Buddha himself has severed all emotional ties to his clan, he is saddened by the imminent suffering of all those concerned, driven inexorably (as he can see with his divine eye) by negative karmic behaviors on both sides from the past. His immediate family members have long since left Kapilavastu, yet the Shakyas are still his kin.

As told in the Kangyur, his compassion aroused, the Buddha makes his way on foot to his hometown, where he stays once again in the Nigrodha grove. Although he cannot avert the impending disaster, he offers his people teachings to free them from the pangs of rebirth. Overjoyed by his return, citizens flock to hear him, and many more convert to the Buddhist faith as lay or ordained disciples. Soon the Kosalas surround the city, preparing to attack. Upholding their belief in nonviolence, the Shakyas issue a proclamation forbidding anyone to kill lest they be expelled from the clan. Seeing this as their advantage, the Kosalans observe,

> The Sakyas are Buddhists ... they would not kill anything that has life; no, not even a black beetle.[84]

Slaughter ensues. Blood runs through the streets of Kapilavastu as more than seventy-seven thousand Shakya citizens are massacred. His mission accomplished, the king returns to Shravasti with five hundred captive Shakya maidens—the spoils of war—whom he intends to add to his harem as concubines. However, he is disappointed because once he arrives home, the proud young women mock him and refuse his advances. Enraged, the cruel king orders that their hands and feet be cut off, which is carried out along the banks of a nearby pond, later known as "the pool of the severed hand." Here the Buddha finds the young women suffering terribly and dying. Ministering to them with great love, he has their wounds dressed,

---

* The son of King Prasenajit.

which brings them relief just long enough to hear a final teaching before they die. The five hundred young women are reborn in the celestial realms but return each night to hear more of the Buddha's teachings. Soon their minds become free, and they are no longer bound to the cycle of rebirth.[85]

By the end of the Buddha's ministry, many wealthy patrons like Visakha had donated land and resources such that monasteries and dedicated parklands dotted the landscape in northeast India as teaching centers and sanctuaries—especially during the three-month rainy season—for an ever-growing number of monastics. One such benefactor was Amrapali, the beautiful courtesan of Vaishali.* Her story, told in all the legends, is significant for the view it presents of the Buddha's unbiased regard, not just for women generally, but in this case, for an independent and powerful woman working in the world's oldest profession. An exception to the norm that all women needed a patriarch to survive, Amrapali owned her own land, managed her own money, and ran a business that counted among its clients the most powerful nobles in the land, including King Bimbisara. So considerable were her nightly revenues that the entire town of Vaishali flourished as a result, having plentiful food, as well as beautiful buildings, parks, and lotus tanks.[86] While famous for her charms and "clever at dancing . . . singing and lute-playing,"[87] Amrapali is portrayed as modest and deeply reverential in the presence of the Buddha. She was a generous supporter of his ministry and later a nun, as told in the following tale.

One day Amrapali learns that the Buddha will be teaching in a nearby grove and sets out with her women attendants in a procession of chariots to see him. After hearing one of his sermons for the first time, she is deeply moved and invites him to her home for dinner the following day, along with his assembly of monks. By his silence, the Buddha assents. In her haste to leave, Amrapali's chariot collides with chariots belonging to richly dressed young nobles who, it turns out, also plan to invite the Buddha to dine the next day. Rudely berating the courtesan, the princes order her out of their way. However, elated by her own news, Amrapali reveals that the Buddha has accepted her dinner invitation. The princes are furious that they have been outdone by a "mango-girl" and loudly bemoan, "Oh, the mango girl has beaten us, the mango-girl has outwitted us!"[88]

---

* Sanskrit *amra* means "mango."

The men now attempt to bribe her with a hundred thousand pieces of gold, but no amount of money can tempt the jubilant Amrapali to forfeit the honor she has just procured. Now the princes make their case to the Buddha himself. How could he possibly choose her invitation over theirs? However, the Buddha quite properly declines their request due to his prior commitment with Amrapali. The meal takes place as planned, after which he gives her and her invited guests a dharma teaching. In return, she makes him a gift of her vast mango grove and a monastery. It truly speaks to the Buddha's egalitarianism that a courtesan's heartfelt entreaty would trump male aristocratic power and privilege, as told in this remarkable story. Amrapali would later abandon her trade to join the order as a nun. Her poem about the loss of youth and beauty counts among the most beautiful verses in the *Therigatha*.[89]

Amrapali's meal is among the last noted in the records of the Buddha's life. Now eighty years old, he was to spend his final rainy season in the vicinity of Vaishali. Already there were reports of him having some kind of severe digestive ailment,[90] and while no one can be certain, it appears that three months later he may have been on his way home to Kapilavastu where he planned to die. As it turned out, he took what was to be his final meal in the home of a metalworker named Chunda. History has been unkind to Chunda, telling us that he fed the Buddha spoiled pork or even that the Buddha may have been poisoned. In any case, after Chunda's meal, the Buddha is wracked with pain and clearly does not have much longer to live. Despite his bodily anguish, he expresses concern that Chunda may suffer remorse or later be accused of causing the sage's demise. To the contrary, the Buddha says, by feeding him his last meal, Chunda has garnered a blessing tantamount to Sujata's offering of rice milk before his enlightenment. These two meals are the greatest possible offerings that can be made to a buddha because they are the two sacred events that bookend the state of buddhahood. In the Sinhalese legend, the Buddha says,

> Before the [Buddha] received the incomparable wisdom, an offering was presented to him by ... Sujata; and now before he attains to the final rest of nirvana, another offering has been made by Chunda. These are the two most estimable gifts. Their merit acquired by the illustrious Chunda, will endure long, and be exceedingly great.[91]

According to some accounts, the gods also want to participate in this event. Knowing that Chunda's meal would be the Buddha's last, they add divine flavors to the preparation just as they did when Sujata was boiling her porridge. Observing that a rare buddha cycle is coming to an end, the gods remark,

> From the time that the rice-mixture presented by Sujata was eaten by the lord of the world, for the space of forty-five years, he has preached to us: now he will eat of the pork to be presented by Chunda, and enter nirvana: even in many millions of years the acquisition of [Buddha]ship is accomplished with difficulty.[92]

Women at the Buddha's Parinirvana

The Buddha's final days, death, and the immediate aftermath are recorded in the *Mahaparinibbanasutta* of the Pali canon in a lengthy section often said to be the most complete account of that period. Yet other than the story of Amrapali, this source includes almost no mention of women. Other Pali biographies, as well as Sanskrit sources, have preserved story fragments in equivalent sections that tell us a little more, particularly about laywomen who were present at the time of the Buddha's death, not only as mourners, but as participants in the funeral rituals. It only makes sense that women were there and were as deeply affected as men by the passing of their beloved teacher and leader. Further, the Buddha died outdoors in a public area near a village, not in a monks-only monastery, so there would be no reason to believe that women were not present. While we'll never know the actual events that transpired, what's of interest is some traditions appear to have embraced both feminine and masculine elements in the final narrative and others did not.

Exhausted and dying, the Buddha can make it no farther than the hamlet of Kushinagara before telling Ananda to lay out his robes as a resting place in a grove between two large *shala* trees. There he spends his final hours, tying up some loose ends with Ananda and allowing visitors from his order and the surrounding communities to say their good-byes. Once again we see that a momentous event in the Buddha's life story takes place under trees. Just as earlier goddesses animated the trees to harbor him protectively, here the *shalas* sheltered him and burst into magnificent blossoms in a display of devotion and reverence. Similar expressions of beauty and fecundity took place throughout all realms, as if Nature herself were paying homage to the saint on the occasion of his imminent passing into *parinirvana*:

> When the Buddha was reclining on the couch, the two [*shala*] trees became suddenly loaded with fragrant blossoms, which gently dropped above and all around his person, so as almost to cover it. Not only these two trees, but all those of that forest, and also those in ten thousand worlds, exhibited the same wonderful and graceful appearance. All the fruit-trees yielded out of season the best fruits they had ever produced; their beauty and flavor exceeded all that had ever been seen. The five kinds of lilies shot forth from the bosom of the earth, and from every plant and tree; they displayed to the astonished eyes the most ravishing sight. The mighty [Himalaya mountains] shone with all the richness of the colors of the peacock's tail.[93]

This episode from the Burmese tradition goes on to relate that all manner of gods, *nagas,* and magical beasts show up in a vast array resembling the time of enlightenment, showering the Buddha with pure offerings of flowers, perfumes, and incense. To the sweet sounds of celestial instruments, they lovingly sing praises, extolling his great gifts that have benefited gods and humans alike. While the Buddha appreciates their intentions, he turns to Ananda and refutes the notion that this "vain and outward" display is proper homage to one who has fully realized the dharma. It's fine for gods, but not for buddhas. The only proper homage, he says, is for every believer, woman and man, to practice the wisdom he has taught. Only those who practice his teachings can deservedly be called Buddhists. In his words,

> Every believer, man or woman, who practises the excellent works leading to perfect happiness, these are the persons that render me a true homage, and present to me a most agreeable offering. The observance of the [dharma] alone entitles to the right of belonging to my religion. Ever remember this, O Ananda, and let every believer in my religion act upon it.[94]

Among other final admonishments, the Buddha stipulates that laywomen and laymen "endowed with faith" should seek out as pilgrimage sites Lumbini, his birthplace; Sarnath, where he first taught the dharma; Bodh Gaya, where he gained enlightenment; and Kushinagara, where he would attain *parinirvana*.[95]

The Buddha instructs Ananda to advise the nearby officials that he has arrived in their town and will be passing away in the morning. It would bring much grief and embarrassment to the community were he to attain *parinirvana* among them without their knowledge. On delivery of the message, sixty thousand princes together with "as many princesses, nobles and eminent ladies" are all overcome with sorrow:

> Some tore their hair; others struck their heads with their hands; they bowed this way and that, as the tree that had been cut nods to its fall; they threw themselves down, and rolled upon the ground in every direction; they cried aloud; and there was grievous mourning.[96]

Still weeping, the townsfolk make their way to the *shala* grove, where they throw themselves into prostrations before the Buddha. To appease their grief, he gives them a final public teaching.

An odd deathbed episode involving a monk appears in the Pali canon and is mentioned here because evidence in the Burmese text indicates that the character originally may have been a nun. This is a scene where the monk Upavana is fanning the Buddha as he rests under the *shala* trees. Quite abruptly, the Buddha tells him to move aside. Ananda is surprised at this and reflects how unusual it is that the Buddha would rebuke someone who has served him faithfully for so many years. (The Buddha explains that the gods were complaining the monk had been blocking their view of him.) In the Burmese text, the scene is almost identical, but the disciple in question is a woman—Utpalavarna, the nun mentioned earlier who was raped and who is named in Sanskrit sources as one of Siddhartha's junior wives. In a footnote, the translator of the Burmese text addresses possible gender confusion by confirming that his palm leaf manuscript identifies the character in this scene as the well-known nun.[97]

With the Buddha's passing into *parinirvana*, the citizens of Kushinagara attend to funeral arrangements, which per his earlier instructions are to be carried out according to standards for a *chakravartin* king. For seven days there is music, song, and dance in the *shala* grove, together with abundant offerings to the body of the finest perfumes, incense, and flowers. Ananda is in attendance, keeping an eye on things and making sure that everyone has an opportunity to venerate the corpse. On one occasion, he notices that some women at the back of the crowd have not had a chance to come forward, and he kindly summons them. Breaking into loud lamentations, they make their offerings, all except one poor woman who has no offering to give. Overwhelmed with grief, her tears fall on the Buddha's feet, permanently discoloring them. Later the monks reprimand Ananda for allowing the Buddha's feet to be stained. They also rebuke him for apparently allowing women to see the holy one naked. In the Kangyur, however, it was the Buddha himself who uncovered his body to illustrate his final teaching that all component phenomena are subject to decay. It is possible, too, that the allusion to nakedness stems from women having washed his body in preparation for cremation, a funeral rite in India typically carried out by women relatives.[98]

On the seventh day, the body is to be transported in a procession from the *shala* grove into the city for cremation, and according to the Kangyur, this task is accorded the town women and girls. In an announcement, the male chieftain of Kushinagara says,

> Let the … women and maidens make a canopy of their garments over the Blessed One; then when we have honoured his remains with perfumes and garlands, they will carry his body to the western gate of the city, which we will traverse and leave by the eastern gate; then after having crossed the [river], we will go to the [prayer hall] and there we will burn the body.[99]

In an unexplained twist, the women are unable to move the body, so it is carried by the men (in some versions, the men can't move it either, so it is carried by the gods). Once the cortege arrives in the center of the town, according to the Burmese legend, it is spotted by a devout laywoman named Mallika, the widow of a great general.* In her possession is a magnificent

---

* Not to be confused with Mallika, the wife of King Prasenajit.

ceremonial cloth that she has not worn since her husband's death. Immediately she is moved to offer it to the Buddha's body, as described here:

> She perfumed it with the choicest essences, and holding it in her hands until the procession reached the front of her house, she desired the bearers to wait for awhile, that she might offer to the body her beautiful piece of cloth, and extend it over it. Her request was granted. By a very happy chance, the cloth had the desired dimensions in breadth and length. Nothing could equal the magnificent sight of the body; it looked beautiful like a statue of gold, when covered with that splendid cloth, finely worked and adorned with the richest embroidery.[100]

Thus, covered by Mallika's splendid cloth, the body is taken for cremation.

There are differing accounts of the final episode before the corpse caught fire. Most commonly, the elder monk Mahakasyapa makes a last moment appearance at which time the Buddha's feet spontaneously emerge from beneath the cloth so that this disciple can venerate them. The *Mahamayasutra,* however, claims that Maya is the last to pay homage to the Buddha.* From heaven, she hears of her son's death and, arriving at his coffin, faints from emotion. Revived by her celestial maiden attendants, she approaches the coffin lamenting sorrowfully, tenderly touching his robe, bowl, and staff which are lying nearby. At that moment, the lid miraculously opens and light bursts forth as the Buddha sits up. Maya and her son are reunited briefly for the last time. The Buddha praises her as a woman and a mother, then comforts her with a teaching that his passing away is in harmony with the natural law. And so Maya is the last among all the Buddha's disciples to receive his earthly blessing.[101]

Followers of the Buddhist faith can rest assured that the Buddha's mission to bring dharma to the world was complete. He himself made this clear

---

* That this story was known in early Buddhist India is evidenced in the record of the seventh-century Chinese pilgrim Xuanzang who observed a stupa in Kushinagara near the Buddha's cremation site that commemorated Maya's mournful final visit with her son.

three months prior to his death in a conversation with evil Mara. Just as the demon had appeared to him after his enlightenment when he was deathly ill from the merchants' offering of gruel sweetened with honey, so Mara appeared again when the eighty-year-old Buddha became stricken with deathly intestinal pains in Vaishali. For the second time, Mara exhorted the Buddha to die. He reminded the saint of his previous words that he would be ready to die when his four assemblies—laywomen, laymen, nuns, and monks—were equally well established in wisdom and discipline, that all four were engaged in teaching dharma to others, and that the dharma itself was esteemed, widespread and flourishing. Well, that time had come, Mara insisted. The Buddha's mission had been accomplished. This time the Buddha did not disagree and conceded that in three months time he would pass into *parinirvana*. In the forty-five years since his enlightenment, he had laid a firm foundation for women and men to seek liberation for themselves. Now it was up to them.

NOTES

All quotations from the *Lalitavistara* in this book are translations from the Tibetan by the Dharmachakra Translation Committee (DTC), published as *The Play in Full* by the nonprofit organization 84000: Translating the Words of the Buddha, online at http://84000.co/. Citations to the DTC translation are to the text at http://read.84000.co/browser/released/UT22084/046/UT22084-046-001.pdf, accessed November 2, 2015. Citations refer to this *Lalitavistara* translation by chapter number rather than page number, to make it possible to locate text in forthcoming editions of *The Play in Full* on the 84000 website, in which pagination may change significantly.

Introduction

1. J. J. Jones, trans., *The Mahāvastu* (London: Luzac, 1949–56), 2:261–62.
2. I. B. Horner, *Women under Primitive Buddhism: Laywomen and Almswomen* (New York: E. P. Dutton, 1930; facsimile reprint, New York: Gutenberg, 2011), 308.
3. Ibid., xx–xxi.
4. Dharmachakra Translation Committee, trans., *The Play in Full* (84000, 2013), chap. 21, http://read.84000.co/browser/released/UT22084/046/UT22084-046-001.pdf. (Translation hereafter referred to as DTC, *Lalitavistara*.)
5. Miranda Shaw, *Buddhist Goddesses of India* (Princeton, NJ: Princeton University Press, 2006), 63.
6. Maurice Winternitz, *A History of Indian Literature*, trans. S. Ketkar and H. Kohn (New Delhi: Oriental Books Reprint Corporation, 1977), 2:247.
7. Ibid., 2:251
8. Bhikkhu Bodhi, in an e-mail message to the author on September 22, 2015; Winternitz, *A History of Indian Literature*, 2:260

Chapter 1. Maya, Mother of the Buddha

1. Bhikkhu Nanamoli, ed. and trans., *The Life of the Buddha According to the Pali Canon* (Onalaska, WA: BPS Pariyatti Editions, 1992), 3–4.
2. Hermann Oldenberg, *Buddha: His Life, His Doctrine, His Order,* trans.

William Hoey (London: Williams and Norgate, 1882; reprint, London: Forgotten Books, 2012), 97–99; Sarla Khosla, *The Historical Evolution of the Buddha Legend* (New Delhi: Intellectual Publishing House, 1989), 25.

3. Edward J. Thomas, *The Life of Buddha as Legend and History* (Delhi: Motilal Banarsidass, 1997), 5.

4. Samuel Beal, trans., *Romantic Legend of Sakya Buddha: From the Chinese-Sanscrit* (London: Trübner, 1875), 21–22.

5. W. Woodville Rockhill, trans., *The Life of the Buddha and the Early History of His Order* (London: Trübner, 1884), 12.

6. Jones, *Mahāvastu,* 1:297.

7. Rockhill, *Life of the Buddha,* 12.

8. Jones, *Mahāvastu,* 1:298–301.

9. Henry Alabaster, trans., *The Wheel of the Law: Buddhism Illustrated from Siamese Sources* (London: Trübner, 1871), 85.

10. Rockhill, *Life of the Buddha,* 14. See also John S. Strong, *The Buddha: A Short Biography* (Oxford: Oneworld, 2002), 39; Bhuwan Lal Pradhan, *Lumbini-Kapilavastu-Dewadaha* (Kathmandu: Tribhuvan University, 1979), 12.

11. See note to "Hymn CLXXVII" in Ralph T. H. Griffith, trans., *The Hymns of the Ṛg Veda* (Delhi: Motilal Banarsidass, 1976), 648.

12. Monier Monier-Williams, *A Sanskrit-English Dictionary* (Delhi: Motilal Banarsidass, 1974), 811.

13. K. R. Norman, *A Philological Approach to Buddhism: The Bukkyb Dendo Kybkai Lectures 1994* (London: School of Oriental and African Studies, University of London, 1997), 5:66.

14. Oldenberg, *Buddha,* 94.

15. Jones, *Mahāvastu,* 1:301–2.

16. Beal, *Romantic Legend,* 23.

17. R. Spence Hardy, trans., *A Manual of Budhism in Its Modern Development* (London: Partridge and Oakey, 1853), 137.

18. Paul Bigandet, trans., *The Life or Legend of Gaudama, the Buddha of the Burmese* (London: Kegan Paul, Trench, Trübner, 1911–12), 1:15.

19. Alabaster, *Wheel of the Law,* 80.

20. Ibid., 83.

21. Ibid., 83–84.

22. Ibid., 84.

23. Charles Willemen, trans., *Buddhacarita: In Praise of Buddha's Acts* (Berkeley, CA: Numata Center for Buddhist Translation and Research, 2009), 3. http://www.bdk.or.jp/pdf/bdk/digitaldl/dBET_T0192_Buddhacarita_2009.pdf.

24. Jones, *Mahāvastu,* 2:4.

25. Beal, *Romantic Legend,* 26–35.

26. Jones, *Mahāvastu,* 2:1.

27. DTC, *Lalitavistara,* chap. 3.

28. Ibid.

29. Beal, *Romantic Legend,* 31.

30. DTC, *Lalitavistara,* chap. 3.

31. Bigandet, *Legend of Gaudama,* 1:25.

32. Jones, *Mahāvastu,* 1:113.

33. Ibid.

34. DTC, *Lalitavistara,* chap. 3.

35. Ibid., chap. 5.

36. Jones, *Mahāvastu,* 1:115.

37. DTC, *Lalitavistara,* chap. 5.

38. Jones, *Mahāvastu,* 1:115.

39. Beal, *Romantic Legend,* 36.

40. Jones, *Mahāvastu,* 1:115.

41. DTC, *Lalitavistara,* chap. 5.

42. DTC, *Lalitavistara,* chap. 6. See also A. Foucher, *The Life of the Buddha, According to the Ancient Texts and Monuments of India,* trans. Simone Brangier Boas (Middletown, CT: Wesleyan University Press, 1963), 26.

43. Bigandet, *Legend of Gaudama,* 1:28.

44. Ibid., 1:29.

45. DTC, *Lalitavistara,* chap. 6.

46. Jones, *Mahāvastu,* 1:116.

47. DTC, *Lalitavistara,* chap. 6.

48. Ibid.

49. DTC, *Lalitavistara,* chap. 5.

50. Jones, *Mahāvastu,* 2:12.

51. DTC, *Lalitavistara,* chap. 3.

52. Rockhill, *Life of the Buddha,* 15.

53. Johnston, E. H., trans. *The Buddhacarita; or, Acts of the Buddha,* by Aśvaghoṣa (Delhi: Motilal Banarsidas, 1977), 2.

54. Beal, *Romantic Legend,* 36.

55. Thomas, *Life of Buddha,* 36.

56. Jones, *Mahāvastu,* 1:114–15.

57. Ibid., 1:134.

58. Foucher, *Life of the Buddha,* 26; Thomas, *Life of Buddha,* 36; John S. Strong, personal communication with the author, September 4, 2014.

59. Alabaster, *Wheel of the Law,* 99.

60. DTC, *Lalitavistara,* chap. 6.

61. Alabaster, *Wheel of the Law,* 100.

62. Jones, *Mahāvastu,* 1:114.

63. Ibid., 2:14.

64. Beal, *Romantic Legend,* 41; Foucher, *Life of the Buddha,* 27.

65. DTC, *Lalitavistara,* chap. 6.

66. Foucher, *Life of the Buddha,* 27; DTC, *Lalitavistara,* chap. 6.

67. Jones, *Mahāvastu,* 2:14.

68. Hardy, *Manual of Budhism,* 141.

69. DTC, *Lalitavistara,* chap. 6.

70. Ibid.

71. Liz Wilson, *Charming Cadavers: Horrific Figurations of the Feminine in Indian Buddhist Hagiographic Literature* (Chicago: University of Chicago Press, 1996), 8.

72. Bhikkhu Bodhi, ed., *In the Buddha's Words, An Anthology of Discourses from the Pali Canon* (Boston, MA: Wisdom Publications, 2005), 283.

73. Bhikkhu Bodhi, e-mail message to the author, February 9, 2015.

74. Charles Hallisey, trans., *Therigatha, Poems of the First Buddhist Women,* Murty Classical Library of India Volume 3 (Cambridge, MA: Harvard University Press, 2015), 55.

75. DTC, *Lalitavistara,* chap. 6.

76. Foucher, *Life of the Buddha,* 27.

77. DTC, *Lalitavistara,* chap. 6.

78. Alabaster, *Wheel of the Law,* 100.

79. Jones, *Mahāvastu,* 2:13.

80. DTC, *Lalitavistara,* chap. 6.

81. Jones, *Mahāvastu,* 1:114.

82. DTC, *Lalitavistara,* chap. 6.

83. Ibid.

84. Beal, *Romantic Legend,* 41.

85. Hardy, *Manual of Budhism,* 144.

86. DTC, *Lalitavistara,* chap. 6.

87. Jones, *Mahāvastu,* 1:116–17.

88. DTC, *Lalitavistara,* chap. 6.

89. T. W. Rhys Davids, trans., *Buddhist Birth-Stories (Jataka Tales): The Commentarial Introduction Entitled "Nidānakathā, The Story of the Lineage,"* rev. ed. (London: George Routledge & Sons, 1908), 153; Hardy, *Manual of Budhism,* 144; Pradhan, *Lumbini-Kapilavastu-Dewadaha,* 15–16.

90. Alabaster, *Wheel of the Law,* 100–1.

91. Jones, *Mahāvastu,* 1:117.

92. Ibid., 1:117–18.

93. Beal, *Romantic Legend,* 42.

94. Ibid.

95. Elinor Gadon, personal communication with the author, November 8, 2013.

96. D. D. Kosambi, *Myth and Reality: Studies in the Formation of Indian Culture* (Bombay: Popular Prakashan, 2013), 100–1, 106; Miranda Shaw, *Buddhist Goddesses of India* (Princeton, NJ: Princeton University Press, 2006), 54–59.

97. Pradhan, *Lumbini-Kapilawastu-Dewadaha,* 42–43, 57. See also *National Geographic* online, "Archaeological Discoveries Confirm Early Date of Buddha's Life," November 25, 2013, http://press.nationalgeographic. com/2013/11/25/birth_of_buddha/.

98. Kosambi, *Myth and Reality,* 101, 106, 108.

99. Jones, *Mahāvastu,* 1:177, 2:22, 2:139. See also Strong, *The Buddha,* 39, 43; Beal, *Romantic Legend,* 52; Shaw, *Buddhist Goddesses,* 57.

100. Julia Aditi Jean, personal communication with the author, September 20, 2013.

101. Beal, *Romantic Legend,* 42.

102. DTC, *Lalitavistara,* chap. 7.

103. Ibid.

104. Jones, *Mahāvastu,* 2:17.

105. Bigandet, *Legend of Gaudama,* 1:35.

106. Pradhan, *Lumbini-Kapilawastu-Dewadaha,* 42; Patricia Eichenbaum Karetzky, *The Life of the Buddha: Ancient Scriptural and Pictorial Traditions* (Lanham, MD: University Press of America, 1992), 18.

107. Bigandet, *Legend of Gaudama,* 1:35.

108. Bigandet, *Legend of Gaudama,* 1:36; Rockhill, *Life of the Buddha,* 16; Rhys Davids, *Nidānakathā,* 154; Hardy, *Manual of Budhism,* 145; Jones, *Mahāvastu,* 1:118, 2:17; DTC, *Lalitavistara,* chap. 7.

109. Beal, *Romantic Legend,* 43.

110. Jones, *Mahāvastu,* 1:118.

111. Johnston, *Buddhacarita,* 7.

112. Beal, *Romantic Legend,* 46.

113. Griffith, *Rg Veda,* 212; Foucher, *Life of the Buddha,* 30.

114. Strong, *The Buddha,* 38.

115. Johnston, *Buddhacarita,* 3.

116. DTC, *Lalitavistara,* chap. 7.

117. Jones, *Mahāvastu,* 2:21.

118. Rhys Davids, *Nidānakathā,* 154.

119. DTC, *Lalitavistara,* chap. 7.

120. Bigandet, *Legend of Gaudama,* 1:37.

121. Jones, *Mahāvastu,* 2:18.

122. Ibid., 2:20.

123. DTC, *Lalitavistara,* chap. 7.

124. Johnston, *Buddhacarita,* 23.

125. Rhys Davids, *Nidānakathā*, 152.
126. Jones, *Mahāvastu,* 2:3.
127. Johnston, *Buddhacarita,* 21.
128. Beal, *Romantic Legend,* 63.
129. R. L. Mitra, trans., *The Lalita-Vistara: Memoirs of the Early Life of Sakya Sinha (Chs. 1–15)* (Delhi: Sri Satguru Publications, 1998), 150n 34; S. Lurie. "The Changing Motives of Caesarean Section: From the Ancient World to the Twenty-First Century," *Archives of Gynaecology and Obstetrics* 271, no. 4 (2005): 281.
130. Hardy, *Manual of Budhism,* 306.
131. Karetzky, *Life of the Buddha,* 22.
132. Beal, *Romantic Legend,* 63.

Chapter 2. Mahaprajapati, Goddesses, and Growing Up in the Harem

1. Johnston, *Buddhacarita,* 23.
2. Beal, *Romantic Legend,* 63.
3. DTC, *Lalitavistara,* chap. 7.
4. Beal, *Romantic Legend,* 64.
5. Ibid.
6. Ibid.
7. Bigandet, *Legend of Gaudama,* 1:49.
8. Hardy, *Manual of Budhism,* 149–50.
9. Jones, *Mahāvastu,* 2:22.
10. Ibid., 2:22–23.
11. John Strong, *The Legend of King Aśoka: A Study and Translation of the Aśokāvadāna* (Princeton, NJ: Princeton University Press, 1983), 245.
12. Purna Chandra Mukherji, "A Report on a Tour of Exploration of the Antiquities in the Tarai, Nepal, the Region of Kapilavastu," *Archaeological Survey of India* (1899), 29.
13. Beal, *Romantic Legend,* 58–59.
14. Jones, *Mahāvastu,* 2:35n1.
15. Hardy, *Manual of Budhism,* 147.
16. DTC, *Lalitavistara,* chap. 8.
17. Beal, *Romantic Legend,* 65.
18. DTC, *Lalitavistara,* chap. 9.
19. DTC, *Lalitavistara,* chap. 9; Beal, *Romantic Legend,* 64–66.
20. Bigandet, *Legend of Gaudama,* 1:50–51; Hardy, *Manual of Budhism,* 150–51; Alabaster, *Wheel of the Law,* 118; Rhys Davids, *Nidānakathā,* 163–65.
21. Hardy, *Manual of Budhism,* 151.
22. Rockhill, *Life of the Buddha,* 23.

23. DTC, *Lalitavistara,* chap. 11.

24. DTC, *Lalitavistara,* chap. 11; Beal, *Romantic Legend,* 73–78; Jones, *Mahāvastu,* 2:42–45.

25. Johnston, *Buddhacarita,* 62–63.

26. Jones, *Mahāvastu,* 3:94.

27. Johnston, *Buddhacarita,* 45–47; Beal, *Romantic Legend,* 123–25.

Chapter 3. Yashodhara, Mrigi Gautami, and the Harem Wives

1. Hardy, *Manual of Budhism,* 151.

2. DTC, *Lalitavistara,* chap. 11.

3. Jones, *Mahāvastu,* 2:113.

4. Beal, *Romantic Legend,* 79.

5. Ibid.

6. Ibid., 101–2.

7. Alabaster, *Wheel of the Law,* 120.

8. Hardy, *Manual of Budhism,* 152.

9. DTC, *Lalitavistara,* chap. 13.

10. Jones, *Mahāvastu,* 1:121.

11. Beal, *Romantic Legend,* 79–80.

12. Ibid., 80.

13. Ibid., 81.

14. Ibid., 92.

15. Ibid.

16. DTC, *Lalitavistara,* chap. 12.

17. Ibid.

18. Ibid.

19. Ibid.

20. Ibid.

21. Ibid.

22. Ibid.

23. Ibid.

24. Hardy, *Manual of Budhism,* 152.

25. Bigandet, *Legend of Gaudama,* 1:52; Alabaster, *Wheel of the Law,* 120, 211n111.

26. Jones, *Mahāvastu,* 2:90.

27. Ibid., 2:87–91.

28. Ibid., 2:61–64.

29. Hardy, *Manual of Budhism,* 153n2; Rockhill, *Life of the Buddha,* 24; Rhys Davids, *Nidānakathā,* 165.

30. M. Srinivasachariar, *History of Classical Sanskrit Literature: Being an Elaborate Account of All Branches of Classical Sanskrit Literature, with*

Full Epigraphical and Archaeological Notes and References, an Introduction Dealing with Language, Philology, and Chronology, and Index of Authors and Works (Delhi: Motilal Barnarsidass, 1974), 47.

31. Vatsyayana, *Kama Sutra: A Guide to the Art of Pleasure*, trans. A. N. D. Haksar (New York: Penguin Books, 2012), 105.
32. Ibid, 107.
33. Beal, *Romantic Legend,* 101.
34. Rockhill, *Life of the Buddha,* 21–22
35. Jones, *Mahāvastu,* 2:129.
36. Nanamoli, *Life of the Buddha,* 9.
37. Alabaster, *Wheel of the Law,* 123.
38. Hardy, *Manual of Budhism,* 157.
39. Jones, *Mahāvastu,* 2:153.
40. Beal, *Romantic Legend,* 97.
41. Ibid., 97–98.
42. Ibid., 98.
43. Ibid., 98.
44. Ibid., 99.
45. Ibid., 99–100
46. Horner, *Women Under Primitive Buddhism,* 308; Thomas, *The Life of Buddha,* 110. See also *Buddhist Dictionary of Pali Proper Names* (http://www.palikanon.com/english/pali_names/dic_idx.html).
47. Jones, *Mahāvastu,* 2:152.
48. Beal, *Romantic Legend,* 379.
49. Hardy, *Manual of Budhism,* 521.
50. *Buddhist Dictionary of Pali Proper Names.*
51. Hallisey, *Therigatha,* 111, 113.

Chapter 4. The Great Departure: A Family Affair

1. DTC, *Lalitavistara,* chap. 13.
2. Stephen Batchelor, *Confession of a Buddhist Atheist* (New York: Spiegel & Grau Trade Paperbacks, 2011), 116–18.
3. Jones, *Mahāvastu,* 2:164.
4. Ibid., 2:140.
5. Ibid., 2:135.
6. Johnston, *Buddhacarita,* 68.
7. Jones, *Mahāvastu,* 2:137n1.
8. Ibid., 2:142
9. Ibid., 2:142–143.
10. Ibid., 2:143.
11. Ibid., 2:147.

12. Johnston, *Buddhacarita*, 34–36.

13. DTC, *Lalitavistara*, chap. 14.

14. Ibid.

15. Ibid.

16. Ibid.

17. Ibid.

18. Beal, *Romantic Legend*, 105.

19. Ibid., 115.

20. Ibid., 121–22.

21. Ibid., 123.

22. DTC, *Lalitavistara*, chap. 15.

23. Jones, *Mahāvastu*, 2:130.

24. Beal, *Romantic Legend*, 126.

25. Ibid., 123.

26. Ibid., 125.

27. Ibid., 126.

28. Johnston, *Buddhacarita*, 44.

29. Ibid., 52.

30. Ibid., 48–49.

31. Ibid., 57.

32. Ibid., 72–73.

33. Beal, *Romantic Legend,* 130.

34. DTC, *Lalitavistara*, chap. 15.

35. Ibid., chap. 13.

36. Ibid., chap. 13.

37. Ibid., chap. 14.

38. Rockhill, *Life of the Buddha*, 24.

39. Beal, *Romantic Legend*, 127.

40. Ibid., 128.

41. DTC, *Lalitavistara*, chap. 14.

42. Ibid.

43. Ibid.

44. Jones, *Mahāvastu*, 2:131.

45. Ibid., 2:133.

46. Beal, *Romantic Legend*, 142.

47. Alabaster, *Wheel of the Law*, 127.

48. Hardy, *Manual of Budhism,* 158.

49. Alabaster, *Wheel of the Law*, 128.

50. DTC, *Lalitavistara*, chap. 15.

51. Ibid.

52. Rockhill, *Life of the Buddha,* 25.

53. John S. Strong, *The Experience of Buddhism, Sources and Interpretations* (Belmont, CA: Wadsworth, 1995), 12.

54. DTC, *Lalitavistara,* chap. 15.

55. Strong, *Experience of Buddhism,* 12.

56. Jones, *Mahāvastu,* 2:159.

57. Ibid.

58. DTC, *Lalitavistara,* chap. 15.

59. Jones, *Mahāvastu,* 2:155.

60. Beal, *Romantic Legend,* 134.

61. Johnston, *Buddhacarita,* 85.

62. Ibid., 86.

63. Beal, *Romantic Legend,* 141.

64. Strong, *Experience of Buddhism,* 12–13; Rockhill, *Life of the Buddha,* 26.

65. Jones, *Mahāvastu,* 2:114.

66. DTC, *Lalitavistara,* chap. 16.

67. Beal, *Romantic Legend,* 139; DTC, *Lalitavistara,* chap. 15.

68. DTC, *Lalitavistara,* chap. 15.

69. Johnston, *Buddhacarita,* 105.

70. Beal, *Romantic Legend,* 148.

71. DTC, *Lalitavistara,* chap. 15.

72. Beal, *Romantic Legend,* 147.

73. DTC, *Lalitavistara,* chap. 15.

74. Ibid.

75. Beal, *Romantic Legend,* 148.

76. Johnston, *Buddhacarita,* 115–16.

77. Beal, *Romantic Legend,* 149.

78. Johnston, *Buddhacarita,* 109.

79. Jones, *Mahāvastu,* 2:183.

80. DTC, *Lalitavistara,* chap. 15.

81. Jones, *Mahāvastu,* 2:182.

82. Johnston, *Buddhacarita,* 111–12.

83. Beal, *Romantic Legend,* 149–50.

84. Johnston, *Buddhacarita,* 116–17.

85. DTC, *Lalitavistara,* chap. 15.

86. Ibid.

87. Ibid.

88. Beal, *Romantic Legend,* 147.

89. Johnston, *Buddhacarita,* 121.

90. Ibid., 122.

91. Ibid., 139–40.

Chapter 5. En Route to the Bodhi Tree

1. Beal, *Romantic Legend,* 153.
2. Ibid., 162.
3. Ibid., 169.
4. Ibid., 177–78.
5. Ibid., 154.
6. DTC, *Lalitavistara,* chap. 16.
7. Beal, *Romantic Legend,* 182.
8. Ibid., 184.
9. Bigandet, *Legend of Gaudama,* 1:68.
10. Hardy, *Manual of Budhism,* 163–64.
11. Jones, *Mahāvastu,* 2:119.
12. Alabaster, *Wheel of the Law,* 138.
13. Hardy, *Manual of Budhism,* 165.
14. Hardy, *Manual of Budhism,* 149; Alabaster, *Wheel of the Law,* 138; Rhys Davids, *Nidānakathā,* 182.
15. Rockhill, *Life of the Buddha,* 28.
16. Jones, *Mahāvastu,* 2:193–94.
17. Ibid., 2:119.
18. DTC, *Lalitavistara,* chap. 17.
19. Ibid.
20. Ibid.
21. Ibid.
22. Jones, *Mahāvastu,* 2:198.
23. Beal, *Romantic Legend,* 189.
24. Ibid.
25. Bigandet, *Legend of Gaudama,* 1:76.
26. DTC, *Lalitavistara,* chap. 17.
27. Ibid.
28. DTC, *Lalitavistara,* chap. 18.
29. Johnston, *Buddhacarita,* 184.
30. Jones, *Mahāvastu,* 2:125. See also Bhikkhu Bodhi, *In the Buddha's Words,* 64–65.
31. Beal, *Romantic Legend,* 190.
32. Alabaster, *Wheel of the Law,* 141.
33. Rhys Davids, *Nidānakathā,* 183.
34. Jones, *Mahāvastu,* 2:126–27.
35. Rhys Davids, *Nidānakathā,* 185.
36. Hardy, *Manual of Budhism,* 168.
37. Alabaster, *Wheel of the Law,* 146.

38. Bigandet, *Legend of Gaudama*, 1:82.

39. Rhys Davids, *Nidānakathā*, 187.

40. Alabaster, *Wheel of the Law*, 146.

41. DTC, *Lalitavistara,* chap. 18.

42. Beal, *Romantic Legend,* 186.

43. Ibid.

44. Beal, *Romantic Legend,* 195.

45. Bhikkhu Bodhi, e-mail message to the author, November 10, 2014.

46. Jones, *Mahāvastu*, 2:195n2.

47. In an e-mail message to the author on December 3, 2015, Bhikkhu Bodhi supplied this interpretation as a correction to the Jones translation.

48. Jones, *Mahāvastu*, 2:192.

49. Ibid., 2:192–93.

50. Ibid., 2:195–96.

51. Ibid., 2:196.

52. Ibid., 2:280–81.

53. Beal, *Romantic Legend*, 191–92.

54. Jones, *Mahāvastu,* 3:300.

55. Ibid.

56. Rockhill, *Life of the Buddha*, 29n2.

57. DTC, *Lalitavistara,* chap. 18.

58. DTC, *Lalitavistara,* chap. 18; Beal, *Romantic Legend,* 195.

59. Johnston, *Buddhacarita*, 185.

60. Jones, *Mahāvastu*, 2:281, 354

61. Alabaster, *Wheel of the Law,* 146.

62. Jones, *Mahāvastu*, 2:354–55.

63. Beal, *Romantic Legend,* 199.

64. DTC, *Lalitavistara,* chap. 19.

65. Ibid.

66. Shaw, *Buddhist Goddesses,* 22.

67. Johnston, *Buddhacarita*, 201.

68. Jones, *Mahāvastu*, 2:360.

69. Ibid., 2:285.

70. Beal, *Romantic Legend,* 207; Rockhill, *Life of the Buddha,* 31.

71. Ranjni Obeyesekere, *Yasodharā, The Wife of the Bodhisattva, the Sinhala* Yasodharāvata *and the Sinhala* Yasodharāpadānaya (Albany, NY: State University of New York Press, 2009), 84.

72. Hardy, *Manual of Budhism,* 173.

73. Alabaster, *Wheel of the Law*, 154.

74. Ibid., 153.

75. DTC, *Lalitavistara,* chap. 21.

76. Beal, *Romantic Legend,* 226.
77. DTC, *Lalitavistara,* chap. 21.
78. Ibid.
79. Alabaster, *Wheel of the Law,* 155.
80. Ibid.
81. Jones, *Mahāvastu,* 2:334.
82. Beal, *Romantic Legend,* 225.
83. Ibid., 226.

Chapter 6. Return to Kapilavastu

1. Alabaster, *Wheel of the Law,* 161–62.
2. Beal, *Romantic Legend,* 237.
3. Strong, *Experience of Buddhism,* 46.
4. DTC, *Lalitavistara,* chap. 24.
5. Beal, *Romantic Legend,* 241.
6. Rockhill, *Life of the Buddha,* 34.
7. Rockhill, *Life of the Buddha,* 34. See also DTC, *Lalitavistara,* chap. 24.
8. Hardy, *Manual of Budhism,* 186.
9. Beal, *Romantic Legend,* 249.
10. Rockhill, *Life of the Buddha,* 38–39; Beal, *Romantic Legend,* 266.
11. Strong, *Experience of Buddhism,* 49.
12. Bodhi, *Connected Discourses,* 2:1800.
13. Rockhill, *Life of the Buddha,* 40.
14. Bigandet, *Legend of Gaudama,* 1:58.
15. Strong, *Experience of Buddhism,* 10.
16. John S. Strong, "A Family Quest: The Buddha, Yaśodharā, and Rāhula in the Mūlasarvāstivāda Vinaya," in *Sacred Biography in the Buddhist Traditions of South and Southeast Asia,* ed. Juliane Schober (Honolulu: University of Hawaii Press, 1997), 113–24; Etienne Lamotte, *History of Indian Buddhism: From the Origins to the Saka Era,* trans. Sara Webb-Boin (Louvain-la-Neuve: Institut Orientaliste de L'Université Catholique de Louvain, 1988), 662–65; Reiko Ohnuma, *Ties That Bind: Maternal Imagery and Discourse in Indian Buddhism* (Oxford: Oxford University Press, 2012), 139–46; Beal, *Romantic Legend,* 126, 365–66; Jones, *Mahāvastu,* 2:154; Hardy, *Manual of Budhism,* 156.
17. Beal, *Romantic Legend,* 346.
18. Ibid. See also Jones, *Mahāvastu,* 2:220.
19. Strong, "Family Quest," 117–19; Ohnuma, *Ties That Bind,* 139–41.
20. Rockhill, *Life of the Buddha,* 32.
21. Ibid., 33.
22. Strong, "Family Quest," 119.

23. Ohnuma, *Ties That Bind,* 142; Lamotte, *History of Indian Buddhism,* 664.

24. Beal, *Romantic Legend,* 348.

25. Ibid.

26. Beal, *Romantic Legend,* 346–48. See also Jones, *Mahāvastu,* 2:222–24.

27. Beal, *Romantic Legend,* 349.

28. Ibid., 363.

29. Beal, *Romantic Legend,* 360–63; Jones, *Mahāvastu,* 3:167–70.

30. Jones, *Mahāvastu,* 2:161–70.

31. Ibid., 1:104.

32. Ibid., 3:155.

33. Ibid., 3:161.

34. Obeyesekere, *Yasodharā,* 8.

35. Rockhill, *Life of the Buddha,* 84.

36. Ibid., 107.

37. Jones, *Mahāvastu,* 1:102.

38. Ibid., 1:103.

39. Hardy, *Manual of Budhism,* 199.

40. Jones, *Mahāvastu,* 3:101.

41. Ibid., 3:105.

42. Ibid., 3:103.

43. Ibid., 3:108.

44. Beal, *Romantic Legend,* 352.

45. Ibid.

46. Bigandet, *Legend of Gaudama,* 1:175–76.

47. Ibid., 1:176.

48. Jones, *Mahāvastu,* 3:116.

49. Ibid., 3:127.

50. Ibid., 3:131.

51. Jones, *Mahāvastu,* 3:126–33; Beal, *Romantic Legend,* 366–68.

52. Jones, *Mahāvastu,* 3:245.

53. Ibid., 3:245–46.

54. Ibid., 3:246.

55. Rhys Davids, *Nidānakathā,* 224.

56. Hardy, *Manual of Budhism,* 203.

57. Ibid., 204.

58. Rhys Davids, *Nidānakathā,* 224–25; Bigandet, *Legend of Gaudama,* 178.

59. Beal, *Romantic Legend,* 360.

60. Ibid., 364.

61. Jones, *Mahāvastu,* 3:246.

62. Ibid., 3:247.

63. Ibid., 3:247–48.

64. Ibid., 3:250.

65. Ibid., 3:251.

66. Rockhill, *Life of the Buddha,* 56.

67. Rhys Davids, *Nidānakathā,* 226.

68. Hardy, *Manual of Budhism,* 206; Bigandet, *Life of Gaudama,* 181; Rhys Davids, *Nidānakathā,* 227.

69. Nanamoli, *Life of the Buddha,* 78.

70. Jones, *Mahāvastu,* 3:251.

71. Ibid., 3:252.

72. Ibid., 3:252–53.

73. Ibid., 3:254.

Chapter 7. Women during the Buddha's Ministry

1. E. B. Cowell, trans., "The Buddha-karita of Asvaghosha," in *Buddhist Mahāyāna Texts,* vol. 49 of *The Sacred Books of the East,* ed. Max Müller (Oxford: Clarendon Press, 1894), 198.

2. Bigandet, *Legend of Gaudama,* 1:207.

3. Ibid.

4. Hardy, *Manual of Budhism,* 312.

5. Ibid., 206.

6. Bigandet, *Legend of Gaudama,* 1:163.

7. Hardy, *Manual of Budhism,* 308.

8. Ibid.

9. Eugene Watson Burlingame, trans., vol. 29 of *Buddhist Legends: Translated from the Original Pali Text of the Dhammapada,* Harvard Oriental Series, vols. 28–30, ed. Charles Rockwell Lanman (Cambridge, MA: Harvard University Press, 1921), 336.

10. Rockhill, *Life of the Buddha,* 57.

11. Hardy, *Manual of Budhism,* 341.

12. Ibid.

13. Horner, *Women under Primitive Buddhism,* 102.

14. Cowell, "Buddha-karita of Ashvaghosa," 199–200.

15. Rockhill, *Life of the Buddha,* 58.

16. Hardy, *Manual of Budhism,* 310.

17. Ibid., 311.

18. I. B. Horner, trans., *The Book of the Discipline (Vinaya Pitaka)* (London: Luzac, 1963), 5:353.

19. Hardy, *Manual of Buddhism,* 311.

20. Ibid., 311.

21. Horner, *Book of the Discipline,* 5:354.

22. Ibid., 5:352–56; Hardy, *Manual of Budhism,* 312.

23. Hardy, *Manual of Budhism,* 311.

24. Rockhill, *Life of the Buddha,* 60.

25. Hardy, *Manual of Budhism,* 309–10.

26. Burlingame, *Buddhist Legends,* 59–60.

27. Hardy, *Manual of Budhism,* 220.

28. Burlingame, *Buddhist Legends,* 63.

29. Ibid., 65.

30. Ibid., 59–69; Hardy, *Manual of Budhism,* 220–24.

31. Burlingame, *Buddhist Legends,* 70.

32. Ibid., 71.

33. Ibid., 74.

34. Ibid., 74.

35. Ibid., 75.

36. Ibid., 81.

37. Horner, *Women under Primitive Buddhism,* 349.

38. Burlingame, *Buddhist Legends,* 80.

39. Ibid., 84.

40. Horner, *Women under Primitive Buddhism,* 338.

41. Ibid., 156.

42. Ibid., 338–39.

43. Nanamoli, *Life of the Buddha,* 153–55.

44. Ibid., 155.

45. Horner, *Women under Primitive Buddhism,* 358; Burlingame, *Buddhist Legends,* 356–57.

46. Nanamoli, *Life of the Buddha,* 156.

47. Bodhi, *In the Buddha's Words,* 128–30.

48. Horner, *Women under Primitive Buddhism,* 357.

49. Ibid.

50. Ibid.

51. Jonathan Walters, "Gotamī's Story," in *Buddhism in Practice,* ed. Donald S. Lopez, Jr. (Princeton, NJ: Princeton University Press, 1995), 114; Jonathan Walters, "Apadāna: Therī-apadāna: Wives of the Saints: Marriage and *Kamma* in the Path to Enlightenment," in *Women in Early Indian Buddhism: Comparative Textual Studies,* ed. Alice Collett (Oxford: Oxford University Press, 2013), 164n5.

52. Walters, "Apadāna," 162.

53. Hardy, *Manual of Budhism,* 313–15, 342; Obeyesekere, *Yasodharā,* 63–80. Walters, "Apadāna," 182–91; Walters, "Gotamī's Story," 111–38; Jonathan Walters, "A Voice from the Silence: The Buddha's Mother's Story," *History of Religions* 33, no. 4 (1994): 358–79.

54. Hardy, *Manual of Budhism,* 313.

55. Walters, "Gotamī's Story," 121.

56. Ibid.

57. Hardy, *Manual of Budhism*, 313.

58. Ibid.

59. Ibid.

60. Walters, "Gotamī's Story," 126.

61. Hardy, *Manual of Budhism*, 312.

62. Walters, "Gotamī's Story," 137.

63. Ibid., 117.

64. Walters, "Voice from the Silence," 373.

65. Walters, "Gotamī's Story," 117.

66. Walters, "Voice from the Silence," 375.

67. Ibid., 376.

68. Hardy, *Manual of Budhism*, 341–42.

69. Walters, "Apadāna," 186.

70. Ibid.

71. Ibid., 172.

72. Obeyesekere, *Yasodharā*, 73.

73. Ibid., 79.

74. Ibid., 65.

75. Ibid., 75.

76. Ibid., 79.

77. Walters, "Apadāna," 190.

78. Bigandet, *Legend of Gaudama*, 1:219.

79. Rockhill, *Life of the Buddha*, 80–81.

80. Hardy, *Manual of Budhism*, 298.

81. Bigandet, *Legend of Gaudama*, 1:223.

82. Hardy, *Manual of Budhism*, 300.

83. Hubert Durt, "The Meeting of the Buddha with Māyā in the Trāyastrimśa Heaven: Examination of the *Mahāmāyā Sūtra* and Its Quotations in the *Shijiapu*, Part 1," *Journal of the International College for Postgraduate Buddhist Studies* 11 (2007): 44–66.

84. Rockhill, *Life of the Buddha*, 117.

85. Ibid., 121.

86. I. B. Horner, trans., *The Book of the Discipline (Vinaya Pitaka)* (London: Luzac, 1962), 4:379.

87. Ibid.

88. Nanamoli, *Life of the Buddha*, 298.

89. Hallisey, *Therigatha*, 129.

90. Rockhill, *Life of the Buddha*, 130.

91. Hardy, *Manual of Budhism*, 345.

92. Ibid., 343.

93. Bigandet, *Legend of Gaudama,* 2:46.

94. Ibid., 2:48.

95. Strong, *Experience of Buddhism,* 37.

96. Hardy, *Manual of Budhism,* 346.

97. Bigandet, *Legend of Gaudama,* 2:48–49.

98. Rockhill, *Life of the Buddha,* 141, 154; Strong, *The Buddha,* 142–43.

99. Rockhill, *Life of the Buddha,* 143.

100. Bigandet, *Legend of Gaudama,* 2:80–81.

101. Hubert Durt, "The Post-Nirvana Meeting of the Buddha with Maya: Examination of the *Mahāmāyā Sūtra* and Its Quotations in the *Shijiapu,* Part 2." *Journal of the International College for Postgraduate Buddhist Studies* 12 (2008): 1–26; Strong, *The Buddha,* 144.

Annotated Bibliography of the Ten Principal Primary Sources

Alabaster, Henry, trans. *The Wheel of the Law: Buddhism Illustrated from Siamese Sources*. London: Trübner, 1871.
This biography of the Buddha from the Pali tradition was translated from the Thai *Pathomma Somphothiyan* (*Pathamasambodhi*), meaning "the recent perfect enlightenment." There are many versions of this text in Southeast Asia, appearing in at least four languages and numerous vernaculars. Alabaster was a British diplomat to the court of Siam and a member of the Royal Asiatic Society.

Beal, Samuel, trans. *Romantic Legend of Sakya Buddha: From the Chinese-Sanscrit*. London: Trübner, 1875.
This abridged version of the Chinese *Abhinishkramanasutra,* or "Great Departure Sutra," was translated from Sanskrit to Chinese circa 280 C.E. and is said to be the biography of the Buddha for the Dharmagupta sect. The Sanskrit original has been lost, although a Tibetan variant survives. Beal was an Asian scholar and the first Englishman to translate Buddhist texts from the Chinese.

Bigandet, Paul, trans. *The Life or Legend of Gaudama, the Buddha of the Burmese*. London: Kegan Paul, Trench, Trübner, 1911–12.
From the Pali tradition, this biography was translated from the Burmese *Mālāmkāravatthu*. It shares many details with the *Nidanakatha* and *Buddhavamsa* and appears to draw from the same or similar early Sinhalese sources. Paul Bigandet was a French Roman Catholic missionary who served as the vicar apostolic of Burma from 1870 to 1894.

Dharmachakra Translation Committee. *The Play in Full* [*Lalitavistara*]. New York: 84000, 2013 (online at http://read.84000. co/browser/released/UT22084/046/UT22084-046-001.pdf).
Originally composed in Buddhist Hybrid Sanskrit prose and verse, the *Lalitavistara* is an anonymous compilation from early sources that was elaborated according to the Mahayana view. It appeared in its present form around the third century C.E. and was translated into Tibetan in the ninth century C.E. Many verses are in close agreement with the Pali accounts, some appearing to be even older, suggesting that the two traditions reach back to a common earlier tradition.

Hardy, R. Spence, trans. *A Manual of Budhism in Its Modern Development.* **London: Partridge and Oakley, 1853.**
Providing many unique story elements, this biography draws from more than 460 Sanskrit, Pali, and Sinhalese sources, with particular use of the *Pujawaliya* (Sinhalese). Hardy was a British Wesleyan missionary based in Sri Lanka and a member of the Royal Asiatic Society.

Johnston, E. H., trans. *The Buddhacarita; or, Acts of the Buddha,* **by Aśvaghoṣa. 1935. Reprint, new enl. ed., Delhi: Motilal Banarsidas, 1977.**
Composed in ornate, classical Sanskrit verse in the second century C.E. and originally recited or sung as an epic ballad, the *Buddhacarita* is considered the first connected biography of the Buddha. It draws material from early Buddhist sources and reflects knowledge of Indian mythology and pre-Buddhist philosophies. Only fourteen chapters survive in Sanskrit, but twenty-eight original chapters are preserved in Chinese and Tibetan. Johnston was a Sanskrit scholar at Oxford.

Jones, J. J., trans. *The Mahāvastu.* **3 vols. London: Pali Text Society, 1949–56.**
Containing some of the earliest narrative material, the *Mahavastu* ("Great Story") describes itself as an introduction to the Vinaya Pitaka of the Lokottaravadin, a branch of the Mahasanghika school. Recorded in mixed Sanskrit and vernaculars, it is a loosely arranged, thousand-page tome that is less a coherent account of the Buddha's life than a treasure trove of Buddhism's early stories, traditions, and textual passages, including many *Jatakas* without analogues in the Pali literature. The core of the text is datable to approximately 200 B.C.E., with additions and interpolations made probably through the fourth century C.E.

The Pali Canon.
A vast body of literature known as the *Tipitaka* ("Three Baskets"), the Pali canon comprises the standard collection of Pali language scriptures in the Theravada Buddhist tradition. Composed in North India, the canon was preserved orally until it was written down in Sri Lanka beginning in the first century B.C.E. Several sources have been used for research purposes here, primarily the following:

Bodhi, Bhikkhu, trans. *The Connected Discourses of the Buddha: A New Translation of the Samyutta Nikaya.* Vol. 2. Boston, MA: Wisdom Publications, 2000.

Bodhi, Bhikkhu, ed. and trans. *In the Buddha's Words: An Anthology of Discourses from the Pali Canon.* Boston, MA: Wisdom Publications, 2005.

Horner, I. B., trans. *The Book of the Discipline (Vinaya Pitaka).* Vol. 4, *Mahāvagga.* London: Luzac, 1962.

Horner, I. B., trans. *The Book of the Discipline (Vinaya Pitaka).* Vol. 5, *Cullavagga.* London: Luzac, 1963.

Nanamoli, Bhikkhu, ed. and trans. *The Life of the Buddha According to the Pali Canon.* Onalaska, WA: BPS Pariyatti Editions, 1992.

Rhys Davids, T. W., trans. *Buddhist Birth-Stories (Jataka Tales): The Commentarial Introduction Entitled "Nidānakathā: The Story of the Lineage."* Rev. ed. by Mrs. [Caroline A. F.] Rhys Davids. London: George Routledge & Sons, 1908.

Known as the *Nidanakatha,* this connected biography of the Buddha was recorded in Sri Lanka in the fifth century C.E. as a commentary to the *Jatakas,* which were among the latest entries to the Pali canon. It shares many narrative elements with Sanskrit sources and thus is thought to have been based on the same early Indian tradition. Rhys Davids was a noted Pali scholar and founder of the Pali Text Society in London.

Rockhill, W. Woodville, trans. *The Life of the Buddha and the Early History of His Order.* London: Trübner Oriental Series, 1884.

From the Sanskrit tradition, this biography is an anthology compiled from selections appearing in the Vinaya Pitaka of the Kangyur (*Dege* version), one of two divisions of the Tibetan canon. Among the first American Tibetologists, Rockhill was a career diplomat who traveled extensively in Tibet and is remembered as the author of the U.S. Open Door Policy with China.

General Bibliography

Anandajoti, Bhikkhu, ed. and trans. *Jinacaritam* ("The Life of the Victorious Buddha," original Pali poem), by Venerable Medhankara Thera. 2006. http://www.ancient-buddhist-texts.net/Buddhist-Texts/X3-Jinacaritam/Jinacaritam.pdf.

Appleton, Naomi. "Multi-Life Stories in the Mahāvastu," 2010. http://www.cardiff.ac.uk/share/resources/Mah%C4%81vastu.pdf.

Ashvaghosha. *Life of the Buddha*. Translated by Patrick Olivelle. New York: New York University Press, 2008.

Batchelor, Stephen. *Confession of a Buddhist Atheist*. New York: Spiegel & Grau, 2011.

Bays, Gwendolyn, trans. *The Voice of the Buddha: The Beauty of Compassion*. 2 vols. Berkeley, CA: Dharma Publishing, 1983.

Beal, Samuel, trans. *The Fo-Sho-Hing-Tsan-King: Life of Buddha by Aśvaghosha Bodhisattva*. Vol. 19 of *The Sacred Books of the East*. Oxford: Clarendon Press, 1883.

———. *Si Yu Ki: Buddhist Records of the Western World, Translated from the Chinese of Hiuen Tsiang*. Delhi: Oriental Books Reprint Corporation, 1969.

Blackstone, Kathryn R. *Women in the Footsteps of the Buddha: Struggle for Liberation in the Therīgāthā*. Delhi: Motilal Banarsidass, 2000.

Bode, Mabel. "Women Leaders of the Buddhist Reformation, from the Manoratha Purani, Buddhaghosa's Commentary on the Anguttara Nikaya." *Journal of the Royal Asiatic Society* 25, no. 3 (1893): 517–56.

Brewster, E. H. *The Life of Gotama the Buddha (Compiled Exclusively from the Pali Canon)*. London: Kegan, Paul, Trench, Trübner, 1926.

Buddhist Dictionary of Pali Proper Names. http://www.palikanon.com/english/pali_names/dic_idx.html. (Website note: Most of the entries have been taken from the *Dictionary of Pali Names* by G. P. Malalasekera [1899–1973], which is available as printed version from the Pali Text Society, London.)

Burlingame, Eugene Watson, trans. Vol. 29 of *Buddhist Legends: Translated from the Original Pali Text of the Dhammapada Commentary*. Harvard Oriental Series vols. 28–30, edited by Charles Rockwell Lanman. Cambridge, MA: Harvard University Press, 1921.

Burnhouf, Eugene. *Introduction to the History of Indian Buddhism.* Translated by Katia Buffetrille and Donald S. Lopez Jr. Chicago: University of Chicago Press, 2010.

Buswell, Robert E., and Donald Lopez, eds. *The Princeton Dictionary of Buddhism.* Princeton, NJ: Princeton University Press, 2014.

Cleary, Thomas, trans. *Entry into the Realm of Reality.* Boston, MA: Shambhala Publications, 1989.

Collett, Alice, ed. *Women in Early Indian Buddhism: Comparative Textual Studies.* Oxford: Oxford University Press, 2014.

Cowell, E. B., trans. "The Buddha-karita of Asvaghosha." In *Buddhist Mahāyāna Texts.* Vol. 49 of *The Sacred Books of the East,* edited by Max Müller. Oxford: Clarendon Press, 1894.

———, ed. *The Jātaka, or Stories of the Buddha's Former Births.* 6 vols. Cambridge, UK: Cambridge University Press, 1895–1907.

Csoma Körösi, Alexander. "Analysis of the Dulva: A Portion of the Tibetan Work Entitled the Kah-Gyur" *Asiatic Researches* 20 (1836): 41–93.

———. "Notices of the Life of Shakya, Extracted from the Tibetan Authorities." *Asiatic Researches* 20 (1836): 285–317.

Cueppers, Christoph, Max Deeg, and Herbert Durt, eds. *The Birth of the Buddha: Proceedings of the Seminar Held in Lumbini, Nepal, October 2004.* Lumbini, Nepal: Lumbini International Research Institute, 2010.

Derris, Karen. "When the Buddha Was a Woman: Reimagining Tradition in the *Theravāda.*" *Journal of Feminist Studies in Religion* 24, no. 2 (2008): 29–44.

Durt, Hubert. "The Meeting of the Buddha with Māyā in the Trāyastriṃśa Heaven: Examination of the Sūtra of Mahāmāyā and Its Quotations in the Shijiapu, Part 1." *Journal of the International College for Postgraduate Buddhist Studies* 11 (2007): 245–66.

———. "The Post-Nirvana Meeting of the Buddha with Māyā: Examination of the Sūtra of Mahāmāyā and Its Quotations in the Shijiapu, Part 2." *Journal of the International College for Postgraduate Buddhist Studies* 12 (2008): 158–92.

Edgerton, Franklin. *Buddhist Hybrid Sanskrit Grammar and Dictionary.* 2 vols. Delhi: Motilal Banarsidass, 1972.

Foucher, A. *The Life of the Buddha, According to the Ancient Texts and Monuments of India.* Abridged translation from the French by Simone Brangier Boas. Middletown, CT: Wesleyan University Press, 1963.

Gethin, Rupert. *The Foundations of Buddhism.* Oxford: Oxford University Press, 1998.

Goswami, Bijoya, trans. *Lalitavistara.* Kolkata, India: Asiatic Society, 2001.

Griffith, Ralph T. H., trans. *The Hymns of the Atharva Veda, Translated with a Popular Commentary.* Vol. 2. Benares, India: E. J. Lazarus, 1917.

————. *The Hymns of the Rg Veda*. Delhi: Motilal Banarsidass, 1976.

Gross, Rita. *Buddhism after Patriarchy: A Feminist History, Analysis, and Reconstruction of Buddhism*. Albany, NY: State University of New York Press, 1993.

Hallisey, Charles. "Roads Not Taken in the Study of Theravāda Buddhism." In *Curators of the Buddha: The Study of Buddhism under Colonialism*, edited by Donald S. Lopez Jr. Chicago: University of Chicago Press, 1995.

————, trans. *Therigatha: Poems of the First Buddhist Women*. Murty Classical Library of India Volume 3. Cambridge, MA: Harvard University Press, 2015.

Hecker, Helmuth. "Buddhist Women at the Time of the Buddha." Translated by Sister Khema. Access to Insight (Legacy Edition). Kandy, Sri Lanka: Buddhist Publication Society. Last revised November 30, 2013. http://www.accesstoinsight.org/lib/authors/hecker/wheel292.html.

Horner, I. B. "Women in Early Buddhist Literature: A Talk to the All-Ceylon Buddhist Women's Association." Access to Insight (Legacy Edition). Kandy, Sri Lanka: Buddhist Publication Society. Last revised November 30, 2013. http://www.accesstoinsight.org/lib/authors/horner/wheel030.html.

————. *Women under Primitive Buddhism: Laywomen and Almswomen*. New York: E. P. Dutton, 1930. Facsimile reprint, New York: Gutenberg, 2011.

Kabilsingh, Chatsumarn. *Thai Women in Buddhism*. Berkeley, CA: Parallax Press, 1991.

Karetzky, Patricia Eichenbaum. *The Life of the Buddha: Ancient Scriptural and Pictorial Traditions*. Lanham, MD: University Press of America, 1992.

Kern, H. *Manual of Buddhism*. Delhi: Motilal Banarsidass, 1989.

Khosla, Sarla. *The Historical Evolution of the Buddha Legend*. New Delhi: Intellectual Publishing House, 1989.

Klein, Anne Carolyn. *Meeting the Great Bliss Queen: Buddhists, Feminists, and the Art of the Self*. Boston: Beacon Press, 1995.

Kosambi, D. D. *Myth and Reality: Studies in the Formation of Indian Culture*. Bombay: Popular Prakashan, 2013.

LaMotte, Etienne. *History of Indian Buddhism: From the Origins to the Saka Era*. Translated by Sara Webb-Boin under the supervision of Jean Dantinne. Louvain-la-Neuve, France: Institut Orientaliste de L'Université Catholique de Louvain, 1988.

Law, Bimala Churn. "Buddhist Women." Pts. 1–3. *Indian Antiquary* no. 3 (1928): 49–54; no. 4 (1928): 65–68; no. 5 (1928): 86–89.

————. *The Life and Work of Buddhaghosa*. Calcutta: Thacker, Spink, 1923.

————. *Some Ksatriya Tribes of Ancient India*. Calcutta: University of Calcutta, 1924.

————. *A Study of the Mahavastu*. Delhi: Bharatiya, 1978.

Li Rongxi, trans. *The Biographical Scripture of King Aśoka.* Berkeley, CA: Numata Center for Buddhist Translation and Research, 1993.

——. *The Great Tang Dynasty Record of the Western Regions.* Berkeley, CA: Numata Center for Buddhist Translation and Research, 1996.

Lurie, S. "The Changing Motives of Caesarean Section: From the Ancient World to the Twenty-First Century." *Archives of Gynaecology and Obstetrics* 271 no. 4 (2005): 281–85.

Mitra, R. L. *The Lalita-Vistara: Memoirs of the Early Life of Sakya Sinha (Chs. 1–15).* 1877. Reprint, Delhi: Sri Satguru, 1998.

——. *The Sanskrit Buddhist Literature of Nepal.* Calcutta: Asiatic Society of Bengal, 1882.

Mohr, Thea, and Jampa Tsedroen. *Dignity and Discipline: Reviving Full Ordination for Buddhist Nuns.* Boston, MA: Wisdom Publications, 2010.

Monier-Williams, Monier. *A Sanskrit-English Dictionary.* Delhi: Motilal Banarsidass, 1974.

Müller, E., ed. *Paramatthadīpanī: Dhammapāla's Commentary on the Therīgāthā.* London: Oxford University Press Warehouse, 1893.

Murcott, Susan, trans. *The First Buddhist Women: Translations and Commentary on the Therigatha.* Berkeley, CA: Parallax Press, 1991.

Nariman, J. K. *Literary History of Sanskrit Buddhism.* Delhi: Motilal Banarsidass, 1992.

Nhat Hanh, Thich. *Old Path, White Clouds.* Berkeley, CA: Parallax Press, 1991.

Norman, K. R. *A Philological Approach to Buddhism: The Bukkyb Dendo Kybkai Lectures 1994.* London: School of Oriental and African Studies, University of London, 1997.

Obeyesekere, Ranjini. "Yasodharā in the Buddhist Imagination, Three Portraits Spanning the Centuries." In *Family in Buddhism,* edited by Liz Wilson. Albany, NY: State University of New York Press, 2013.

——, trans. *Yasodharā, the Wife of the Bodhisattva: The Sinhala "Yasodharāvata" and the Sinhala "Yasodharāpadānaya."* Albany, NY: State University of New York Press, 2009.

Ohnuma, Reiko. *Ties That Bind: Maternal Imagery and Discourse in Indian Buddhism.* Oxford: Oxford University Press, 2012.

Oldenberg, Hermann. *Buddha: His Life, His Doctrine, His Order.* Translated by William Hoey. London: Williams and Norgate, 1882. Reprint, London: Forgotten Books, 2012.

Paul, Diana. *Women in Buddhism: Images of the Feminine in the Mahayana Tradition.* Berkeley, CA: University of California Press, 1985.

Penner, Hans H. *Rediscovering the Buddha: Legends of the Buddha and Their Interpretation.* Oxford: Oxford University Press, 2009.

Peoples, James, and Garrick Bailey. *Humanity: An Introduction to Cultural Anthropology.* 9th ed. South Melbourne, Australia: Wadsworth, 2012.

Pradhan, Bhuwan Lal. *Lumbini-Kapilavastu-Dewadaha.* Kathmandu: Tribhuvan University, 1979.

Purna Chandra Mukherji. "A Report on a Tour of Exploration of the Antiquities in the Tarai, Nepal, the Region of Kapilavastu," *Archaeological Survey of India* (1899).

Rhys Davids, C. A. F., and K. R. Norman, trans. *Poems of Early Buddhist Nuns (Therīgāthā).* Oxford: Pali Text Society, 1989.

Rhys Davids, T. W. *Buddhism: Being a Sketch of the Life and Teachings of the Gautama the Buddha.* London: Society for Promoting Christian Knowledge, 1894.

Rogers, H. T., trans. *Buddhaghosa's Parables.* London: Trübner, 1870.

Sasson, Vanessa R. "Māyā's Disappearing Act." In *Family in Buddhism,* edited by Liz Wilson. Albany, NY: State University of New York Press, 2013.

———. "A Womb with a View." In *Imagining the Fetus: The Unborn in Myth, Religion, and Culture,* edited by Vanessa R. Sasson and Jane Marie Law. Oxford: Oxford University Press, 2009.

Seth, Ved. *Study of Biographies of the Buddha.* Delhi: Akay, 1992.

Shaw, Miranda. *Buddhist Goddesses of India.* Princeton, NJ: Princeton University Press, 2006.

Strong, John S. *The Buddha: A Short Biography.* Oxford: Oneworld, 2002.

———. *The Experience of Buddhism, Sources and Interpretations.* Belmont, CA: Wadsworth, 1995.

———. "A Family Quest: The Buddha, Yaśodharā, and Rāhula in the Mūlasarvāstivāda Vinaya." In *Sacred Biography in the Buddhist Traditions of South and Southeast Asia,* edited by Juliane Schober. Honolulu: University of Hawaii Press, 1997.

———. *The Legend of King Aśoka: A Study and Translation of the* Aśokāvadāna. Princeton, NJ: Princeton University Press, 1983.

Srinivasachariar, M. *History of Classical Sanskrit Literature: Being an Elaborate Account of All Branches of Classical Sanskrit Literature, with Full Epigraphical and Archaeological Notes and References, an Introduction Dealing with Language, Philology, and Chronology, and Index of Authors & Works.* Delhi: Motilal Barnarsidass, 1974.

Swearer, Donald K. "Bimba's Lament." In *Buddhism in Practice,* edited by Donald S. Lopez Jr. Princeton, NJ: Princeton University Press, 1995.

Thomas, Edward J. *The Life of Buddha as Legend and History.* 1927. Reprint, Delhi: Motilal Banarsidass, 1997.

Vatsyayana. *Kama Sutra: A Guide to the Art of Pleasure.* Translated by A. N. D. Haksar. New York: Penguin Books, 2011.

Vergano, Dan. "Oldest Buddhist Shrine Uncovered in Nepal May Push Back Buddha's Birth Date." *National Geographic,* November 26, 2013. http://news .nationalgeographic.com/news/2013/11/131125-buddha-birth-nepal-archaeology -science-lumbini-religion-history.

Von Schiefner, F. Anton, trans. *Tibetan Tales, Derived from Indian Sources.* Translated by W. R. S. Ralston. London: Kegan, Paul, Trench, Trübner, 1906.

Walters, Jonathan S. "Apadāna: Therī-apadāna, Wives of the Saints: Marriage and *Kamma* in the Path to Arhantship." In *Women in Early Indian Buddhism: Comparative Textual Studies,* edited by Alice Collett. Oxford: Oxford University Press, 2013.

———. "Gotamī's Story." In *Buddhism in Practice,* edited by Donald S. Lopez Jr. Princeton, NJ: Princeton University Press, 1995.

———. "Stupa, Story, and Empire: Constructions of the Buddha Biography in Early Post-Aśokan India." In *Sacred Biography in the Buddhist Traditions of South and Southeast Asia,* edited by Juliane Schober. Honolulu: University of Hawaii Press, 1997.

———. "A Voice from the Silence: The Buddha's Mother's Story." *History of Religions* 33, no. 4 (May 1994): 358–79.

Warder, A. K. *Indian Buddhism.* 2nd rev. ed. Delhi: Motilal Banarsidass, 1980.

Wickeremesinghe, K. D. P. *The Biography of the Buddha.* Colombo, Sri Lanka: published by the author, 1972.

Willemen, Charles, trans. *Buddhacarita: In Praise of Buddha's Acts.* Berkeley, CA: Numata Center for Buddhist Translation and Research, 2009. http://www.bdk .or.jp/pdf/bdk/digitaldl/dBET_T0192_Buddhacarita_2009.pdf

Wilson, Liz. *Charming Cadavers: Horrific Figurations of the Feminine in Indian Buddhist Hagiographic Literature.* Chicago: University of Chicago Press, 1996.

Winternitz, Maurice. *A History of Indian Literature.* Vol. 2, *Buddhist Literature and Jaina Literature.* 1927. Translated by S. Ketkar and H. Kohn. Reprint, New Delhi: Oriental Books Reprint Corporation, 1977.

Young, Serinity, ed. *Encyclopedia of Women and World Religion.* New York: Macmillan Reference USA, 1999.

About the Author

Wendy Garling is a writer, mother, Buddhist practitioner, and independent scholar with a BA from Wellesley College and MA in Sanskrit language and literature from the University of California, Berkeley. She is an authorized dharma teacher and has taught women's spirituality with a focus on the sacred feminine and women's stories for many years.

INDEX